The Tyndale New Testament Commentaries

General Editor:
THE REV. CANON LEON MORRIS, M.Sc., M.Th., Ph.D.

1   CORINTHIANS

THE FIRST EPISTLE OF PAUL TO THE CORINTHIANS

AN INTRODUCTION AND COMMENTARY

by

THE REV. CANON LEON MORRIS
M.Sc., M.Th., Ph.D.

Inter-Varsity Press
Leicester, England

William B. Eerdmans Publishing Company
Grand Rapids, Michigan

Inter-Varsity Press
38 De Montfort Street, Leicester LE1 7GP, England
Wm. B. Eerdmans Publishing Company
255 Jefferson S.E., Grand Rapids, MI 49503

© Leon Morris 1985

First Edition 1958
Second Edition 1985

Reprinted, June 1989

Unless otherwise stated, quotations from the Bible are taken from the HOLY BIBLE: NEW INTERNATIONAL VERSION. Copyright © 1978 by the International Bible Society, New York. Published in Great Britain by Hodder and Stoughton Limited, and used by permission of Zondervan Bible Publishers, Grand Rapids, Michigan.

The diagrams on pp. 126, 127 and 242 are © by the American School of Classical Studies, Athens, and are used by permission.

Published and sold in the USA and Canada only by
Wm. B. Eerdmans Publishing Company

British Library Cataloguing in Publishing Data

Morris, Leon
  The first epistle of Paul to the Corinthians: an
  introduction and commentary.——2nd ed. ——(The
  Tyndale New Testament commentaries)
  1. Bible. N.T. Corinthians, 1st——Commentaries
  I. Title   II. Series
  227′.207   BS2675.3
British ISBN 0–85111–876–3

Library of Congress Cataloging in Publication Data

Morris, Leon, 1914-
  The First epistle of Paul to the Corinthians.

  (The Tyndale New Testament commentaries)
  Ser. t.p.: 1 Corinthians.
  1. Bible. N.T. Corinthians, 1st — Commentaries.
I. Title. II. Title: 1 Corinthians. III. Title:
One Corinthians. IV. Series.
BS2675.3.M67 1985   227′.207   85-4587
ISBN 0-8028-0064-5 (Eerdmans : pbk.)

Inter-Varsity Press is the publishing division of the Universities and Colleges Christian Fellowship (formerly the Inter-Varsity Fellowship), a student movement linking Christian Unions in universities and colleges throughout the United Kingdom and the Republic of Ireland, and a member movement of the International Fellowship of Evangelical Students. For information about local and national activities write to UCCF, 38 De Montfort Street, Leicester LE1 7GP.

GENERAL PREFACE

The original *Tyndale Commentaries* aimed at providing help for the general reader of the Bible. They concentrated on the meaning of the text without going into scholarly technicalities. They sought to avoid 'the extremes of being unduly technical or unhelpfully brief'. Most who have used the books agree that there has been a fair measure of success in reaching that aim.

Times, however, change. A series that has served so well for so long is perhaps not quite as relevant as it was when it was first launched. New knowledge has come to light. The discussion of critical questions has moved on. Bible-reading habits have changed. When the original series was commenced it could be presumed that most readers used the Authorized Version and comments were made accordingly, but this situation no longer obtains.

The decision to revise and up-date the whole series was not reached lightly, but in the end it was thought that this is what is required in the present situation. There are new needs, and they will be better served by new books or by a thorough up-dating of the old books. The aims of the original series remain. The new commentaries are neither minuscule nor unduly long. They are exegetical rather than homiletic. They do not discuss all the critical questions, but none is written without an awareness of the problems that engage the attention of New Testament scholars. Where it is felt that formal consideration should be given to such questions, they are discussed in the Introduction and sometimes in Additional Notes.

But the main thrust of these commentaries is not critical. These books are written to help the non-technical reader understand his Bible better. They do not presume a knowledge of Greek, and all Greek words discussed are transliterated; but the authors have the Greek text before them and their comments are made on the basis of what the originals say. The authors are free to choose their own modern translation, but are asked to bear in mind the variety of translations in current use.

The new series of *Tyndale Commentaries* goes forth, as the former series did, in the hope that God will graciously use these books to help the general reader to understand as fully and clearly as possible the meaning of the New Testament.

LEON MORRIS

CONTENTS

AUTHOR'S PREFACE TO THE FIRST EDITION

It is no new observation that the letters of St Paul are not easy reading (2 Pet. 3:15f.), but for him who is prepared to take time and trouble their study is immensely rewarding. Not least is this the case with 1 Corinthians, a letter arising out of the practical difficulties besetting a far-from-ideal first-century Greek church. Here we have a typical Pauline letter. The apostle praises his correspondents for their Christian virtues, and rebukes them roundly for their many failings. He adds to their knowledge with some great passages, notably his discussion of love in chapter 13 and of the resurrection in chapter 15. Whatever he touches he deals with in the light of great Christian principles. He sees things temporal always in the light of things eternal. What he writes has relevance to our own, in many ways very different, needs. He shows us how to take our problems back to the light shed upon them by the great Christian verities. We cannot fail to profit as we ponder his words.

In writing this commentary I have been greatly indebted to very many. Notably is this the case with regard to the commentaries to which I have referred in the notes. I have endeavoured to indicate my many indebtednesses in specific matters, but I have learned more from my predecessors than I can sufficiently acknowledge. I have also found some modern translations very helpful, for what are translations but compressed commentaries?

Finally I would like to express my gratitude to Miss G. Mahar and Miss M. McGregor who very kindly typed the manuscript for me.

LEON MORRIS

PREFACE TO THE SECOND EDITION

The call for a new edition of this commentary has given me the opportunity of working through the material again, with the help of much that has been written in the years since the first edition appeared. I have been grateful for the commentaries to which I have referred, and especially to those by Barrett and Conzelmann.

The change from the Authorized Version to the New International Version as the base has meant many small alterations, and I have gone further and re-written the whole. It is essentially the same commentary, though here and there the reader may notice a change of emphasis and even sometimes of opinion.

It may help the general reader if I point out that all cross-references have been checked against the Greek text; a reference to the English translation will not always make this clear. For example, I speak of Paul's calling himself a 'slave of Christ' and refer to Romans 1:1. Now NIV has there 'a servant of Christ' and the English reader may wonder a little about the accuracy of the reference. But 'servant' translates *doulos*, which means 'slave'. Despite NIV, Paul really did call himself 'a slave of Christ'. It would have taken up a lot of space to make this sort of thing clear on every occasion, so I have often simply given the reference. But, as I have said, on every occasion the reference has been checked against the Greek.

It remains only for me to express the hope that in its new format this commentary will meet a continuing need. And to express my appreciation to Mrs D. Wellington, my former secretary, for her kindness in typing the manuscript so expertly.

LEON MORRIS

CHIEF ABBREVIATIONS

AS	G. Abbott-Smith, *A Manual Greek Lexicon of the New Testament* (T. & T. Clark, 1937).
AV	The Authorized (or King James') Version.
BAGD	*A Greek-English Lexicon of the New Testament and Other Early Christian Literature* (trans. of W. Bauer, *Griechisch-Deutsches Wörterbuch*), ed. by William F. Arndt and F. Wilbur Gingrich; second ed. rev. and augmented by F. Wilbur Gingrich and F. W. Danker (University of Chicago Press, 1979).
Barclay	William Barclay, *The Letters to the Corinthians* (Saint Andrew Press, 1956; *Daily Study Bible*).
Barrett	C. K. Barrett, *A Commentary on the First Epistle to the Corinthians* (Black, 1971; *Black's New Testament Commentary*).
BDF	F. Blass and A. Debrunner, *A Greek Grammar of the New Testament and Other Early Christian Literature*, trans. and rev. by Robert W. Funk (Cambridge University Press, 1961).
Beet	J. Agar Beet, *A Commentary on St. Paul's Epistles to the Corinthians* (Hodder & Stoughton, 1889).
Bengel	J. A. Bengel, *Gnomon of the New Testament* (T. & T. Clark, 1873).
BJRL	*The Bulletin of the John Rylands Library.*
Bruce	F. F. Bruce, *1 and 2 Corinthians* (Marshall, Morgan & Scott, 1982; *New Century Bible*).
Calvin	John Calvin, *The First Epistle of Paul the Apostle to the Corinthians*, trans. by J. Pringle (Calvin Translation Society, 1848).

CBQ	*The Catholic Biblical Quarterly.*
Conzelmann	Hans Conzelmann, *1 Corinthians* (SCM Press, 1975).
Craig	Clarence T. Craig, *The First Epistle to the Corinthians* (Abingdon, 1978; *The Interpreter's Bible*, vol. 10).
Deluz	Gaston Deluz, *A Companion to 1 Corinthians* (Darton, Longman & Todd, 1963).
Edwards	Thomas Charles Edwards, *A Commentary on the First Epistle to the Corinthians* (Hodder & Stoughton, 1885).
Ellicott	Charles J. Ellicott, *St Paul's First Epistle to the Corinthians* (Longmans, Green & Co., 1887).
Erdman	Charles R. Erdman, *The First Epistle of Paul to the Corinthians* (Westminster, 1966).
EVV	English Versions (the Authorized Version and the Revised Version).
Findlay	G. G. Findlay, *St. Paul's First Epistle to the Corinthians* (1901; Eerdmans reprint 1979; *The Expositor's Greek Testament*).
GNB	Good News Bible: Today's English Version, 1976.
Godet	F. L. Godet, *Commentary on First Corinthians* (1893; Kregel reprint 1979).
Goudge	H. L. Goudge, *The First Epistle to the Corinthians* (Methuen, 1915).
Grammar	A. T. Robertson, *A Grammar of the Greek New Testament in the Light of Historical Research* (Hodder & Stoughton, n.d.).
Green	Michael Green, *To Corinth with Love* (Hodder & Stoughton, 1982).
Grosheide	F. W. Grosheide, *Commentary on the First Epistle to the Corinthians* (Marshall, Morgan & Scott, 1954; *New London Commentary*).
Grudem	Wayne A. Grudem, *The Gift of Prophecy in 1 Corinthians* (University Press of America, 1982).
HDB	James Hastings (ed.), *A Dictionary of the Bible*, 5 vols. (T. & T. Clark, 1898–1904).
Héring	Jean Héring, *The First Epistle of Saint Paul to the Corinthians* (Epworth Press, 1962).

Hillyer	N. Hillyer, '1 and 2 Corinthians' in the *New Bible Commentary, Third Edition* (IVP, 1970).
Hodge	Charles Hodge, *An Exposition of the First Epistle to the Corinthians* (Nisbet, 1873).
Hurd	John Coolidge Hurd, Jr., *The Origin of 1 Corinthians* (SPCK, 1965).
IBNTG	C. F. D. Moule, *An Idiom Book of New Testament Greek* (Cambridge University Press, 1953).
IDB	*The Interpreter's Dictionary of the Bible*, 4 vols. (Abingdon, 1962); supplementary vol. (1976).
ISBE	*The International Standard Bible Encyclopaedia*, 5 vols. (Howard Severance, 1929; rev. ed., 4 vols, Eerdmans, 1979–).
JB	The Jerusalem Bible, 1966.
JBL	*Journal of Biblical Literature.*
Jones	J. D. Jones, *An Exposition of First Corinthians 13* (Klock & Klock reprint, 1982).
JTS	*The Journal of Theological Studies.*
Kay	W. Kay, *A Commentary on the Two Epistles of St. Paul to the Corinthians* (Macmillan, 1887).
LAE	Adolf Deissmann, *Light from the Ancient East*, trans. by L. R. M. Strachan (Hodder & Stoughton, 1927).
LB	The Living Bible, 1972.
Lenski	R. C. H. Lenski, *The Interpretation of St. Paul's First and Second Epistles to the Corinthians* (Augsburg, 1963).
Lightfoot	J. B. Lightfoot, *Notes on Epistles of St. Paul* (Macmillan, ²1904).
LSJ	*A Greek-English Lexicon*, compiled by H. G. Liddell and R. Scott, rev. and augmented by H. S. Jones and R. McKenzie, 2 vols. (Oxford University Press, 1940).
LXX	The Septuagint Version.
Mare	W. H. Mare, *1 Corinthians* (Zondervan, 1976; *The Expositor's Bible Commentary*, vol. 10).
Metzger	Bruce M. Metzger, *A Textual Commentary on the Greek New Testament* (United Bible Societies, 1971).

MM	J. H. Moulton and G. Milligan, *The Vocabulary of the Greek Testament* (Hodder & Stoughton, 1914–29).
Moffatt	James Moffatt, *The First Epistle of Paul to the Corinthians* (Hodder & Stoughton, 1943; *Moffatt New Testament Commentary*).
NASB	The New American Standard Bible, 1963.
NEB	The New English Bible, Old Testament, 1970; New Testament, ²1970.
NIV	The Holy Bible: New International Version, Old Testament, 1978; New Testament, ²1978.
NTS	*New Testament Studies*.
Orr and Walther	William F. Orr and James Arthur Walther, *1 Corinthians* (Doubleday, 1976).
Parry	R. St John Parry, *The First Epistle of Paul the Apostle to the Corinthians* (Cambridge University Press, 1926; *The Cambridge Greek Testament*).
Proctor	W. C. G. Proctor, '1 Corinthians' in *The New Bible Commentary* (Inter-Varsity Fellowship, 1953).
Prolegomena	J. H. Moulton, *A Grammar of New Testament Greek*, vol. i, *Prolegomena* (T. & T. Clark, 1906).
Redpath	Alan Redpath, *The Royal Route to Heaven* (Revell, 1960).
Robertson	F. W. Robertson, *Expository Lectures on St. Paul's Epistles to the Corinthians* (King, 1876).
Robertson and Plummer	Archibald Robertson and Alfred Plummer, *A Critical and Exegetical Commentary on the First Epistle of St Paul to the Corinthians* (T. & T. Clark, 1929; *International Critical Commentary*).
RSV	The Holy Bible, Revised Standard Version, Old Testament, 1952; New Testament, ²1971.
Ruef	J. Ruef, *Paul's First Letter to Corinth* (SCM Press, 1977; *Pelican New Testament Commentary*).
RV	The Revised Version, 1881.
Smedes	Lewis B. Smedes, *Love within Limits* (Eerdmans, 1978).
SPC	Jerome Murphy-O'Connor, *St. Paul's Corinth* (Glazier, 1983).

TDNT	*Theological Dictionary of the New Testament*, trans. by G. W. Bromiley of *Theologisches Wörterbuch zum neuen Testament*, 10 vols. (Eerdmans, 1964–76).
Theissen	Gerd Theissen, *The Social Setting of Pauline Christianity* (T. & T. Clark, 1982).
Thrall	Margaret E. Thrall, *The First and Second Letters of Paul to the Corinthians* (Cambridge University .Press, 1965; *Cambridge Bible Commentary*).
TNTC	*Tyndale New Testament Commentary.*
TOTC	*Tyndale Old Testament Commentary.*
Williams	C. S. C. Williams, 'I and II Corinthians' in *Peake's Commentary on the Bible*, ed. by M. Black and H. H. Rowley (Nelson, 1980).
Wilson	Geoffrey B. Wilson, *1 Corinthians* (Banner of Truth, 1978).

The translations by E. J. Goodspeed, R. Knox, J. B. Phillips, H. J. Schonfield, A. S. Way and R. F. Weymouth are cited by the translator's surname.

INTRODUCTION

I. BACKGROUND

The geographical position of Corinth, on the narrow neck of land between the Corinthian Gulf (where its port was Lechaeum) and the Saronic Gulf (and the port of Cenchrea) guaranteed its commercial prosperity. Merchants and sailors sent goods across the isthmus rather than risk the long voyage round the rocky, storm-tossed capes at the south of the Peloponnesus.[1] Trade routes from east to west intersected those from north to south at this city. Corinth was totally destroyed by the Roman, L. Mummius Achaicus, in 146 BC, but when it was re-founded a century later as a Roman colony it speedily regained much of its former greatness.

As the new city was a Roman colony, its inhabitants were at first Romans. Eventually Greeks came back in numbers and the city also attracted people from other races. Included among them was a Jewish population large enough to have a synagogue (Acts 18:4).[2] The Roman element[3] is illustrated by the number of Latin names associated with Corinth in the New

[1] See G. E. Wright and F. V. Filson, *The Westminster Historical Atlas to the Bible* (SCM Press, 1946), pp. 80,88f. This meant transhipping cargoes, but small vessels were hauled across the isthmus 'by means of a ship tramway with wooden rails' according to J. E. Harry (*ISBE*, ii, p. 710). Strabo calls it the *diolkos* (*Geography* 8.2.1). Nero tried to cut a canal, but without success. The modern canal follows the route planned by Nero.

[2] An inscription on part of the lintel of a synagogue has been found. It is agreed that this is later than the time of Paul, but it may show the site (*LAE*, p. 16, n. 7; G. E. Wright, *An Introduction to Biblical Archaeology* (Duckworth, 1960), p. 177).

[3] Parry sees evidence of the Roman character of the city in that it was the first city of Greece to admit the gladiatorial games (p. ix). Robertson and Plummer maintain that by New Testament times the descendants of the original Italian colonists 'had become to a large extent Hellenized' (p. xi). Corinth's population was a medley of races which had apparently retained most of the worst features of the original stocks.

Testament, such as Lucius, Tertius, Gaius, Erastus, Quartus (Rom. 16:21–23), Titius Justus, Crispus (Acts 18:7–8), Fortunatus and Achaicus (1 Cor. 16:17). But Greek ways of thought lie behind some of the questions raised in Paul's letters to Corinth and the manner in which they are treated. Edwards says of Corinth: 'Of Greek cities the least Greek, it was at this time the least Roman of Roman colonies.'[1] It was a city where 'Greeks, Latins, Syrians, Asiatics, Egyptians, and Jews, bought and sold, laboured and revelled, quarrelled and hob-nobbed, in the city and its ports, as nowhere else in Greece'.[2]

Old Corinth had been a by-word for licentiousness,[3] and this hotch-potch of races would have hastened the process by which the new Corinth acquired an equally unsavoury reputation. A. M. Hunter says that in the popular mind Corinth suggested 'culture and courtesans. . . "Corinthian words" implied pretensions to philosophy and letters, and to "Corinthianize" was popular Greek for "go to the devil".'[4]

Yet for all that the city was one of the most important in Greece. It was populous[5] and wealthy.[6] It was the capital of the

[1] Edwards, p. xii.

[2] Moffatt, p. xvii.

[3] There were more than a thousand prostitutes connected with the temple of Aphrodite in old Corinth (Strabo, 8.6.20). This goddess could be styled Aphrodite Kallipygos, 'Aphrodite of the Beautiful Buttocks' (Athenaeus, 12.554c). Shrines were 'everywhere' erected to 'Aphrodite the *hetaira* ('courtesan')' 'as patroness of harlots' (*ibid.*, 13.559a and note, Loeb ed.); this was presumably the reason for the 'ancient custom in Corinth . . . whenever the city prays to Aphrodite in matters of grave importance, to invite as many prostitutes as possible to join in their petitions' (*ibid.*, 13.573c). Murphy-O'Connor doubts whether Corinth was worse than other ports in the Eastern Mediterranean. He thinks both Strabo and Athenaeus were in error (*SPC*, pp. 55–57, 127f.), and ascribes much to Athenian propaganda. But even he admits that Corinth had 'a certain reputation in sexual matters' (*SPC*, p. 56), and the ancient writers account for it better than he does. Dio Chrysostom speaks of Diogenes observing large numbers gathering at Corinth because of its harbours and its prostitutes (*Discourses*, 8.5). Murphy-O'Connor quotes from Plutarch a reference to 'the great army of prostitutes' at Corinth, and explains them as 'city prostitutes' rather than the servants of Aphrodite (*SPC*, p. 106). But they were still prostitutes and there was an army of them, even if Murphy-O'Connor is right.

[4] A. M. Hunter, *Introducing the New Testament* (SCM Press, 1945), p. 76.

[5] Hunter puts the population at half a million (*ibid.*), while Godet (p. 5) and *ISBE* (ii, p. 713) say it was between 600,000 and 700,000. J. Cambier gives this figure with some precision, speaking of 200,000 free men and 400,000 slaves (A. Robert and A. Feuillet, *Introduction to the New Testament* (Desclee, 1965), p. 413). Ellicott, however, thinks of 100,000. Murphy-O'Connor, discussing archaeological work at Corinth, says no hypothesis about the population has been put forward (*SPC*, p. 32). It is clear that the population was large, but just how large it is impossible to say with our present knowledge.

[6] Strabo calls Corinth 'wealthy' and gives three reasons: its position, so advantageous for trade; the Isthmian Games; and the thousand prostitutes (8.6.20). He refers to the city's

Roman province of Achaia. And the finest athletes were attracted to the Isthmian Games celebrated near the city, games so important that they continued to be celebrated even when the city was destroyed (*SPC*, p. 14). There was fertile soil nearby, and grapes flourished (our word 'currant' derives from 'Corinth' and is a reminder of the success of the city's horticulture).

The city to which Paul came preaching the gospel was, then, a very cosmopolitan place. It was an important city. It was intellectually alert, materially prosperous, but morally corrupt. There was a pronounced tendency for its inhabitants to indulge their desires of whatever sort. In the words of von Dobschütz:

> The ideal of the Corinthian was the reckless development of the individual. The merchant who made his gain by all and every means, the man of pleasure surrendering himself to every lust, the athlete steeled to every bodily exercise and proud in his physical strength, are the true Corinthian types: in a word the man who recognised no superior and no law but his own desires.[1]

Corinth was a prestigious centre from which the gospel could radiate out to the surrounding districts. There was a large floating population, with merchants and travellers staying a few days and then going their way. Anything preached in Corinth would be sure of a wide dissemination.

II. PAUL AT CORINTH

When Paul first reached Corinth he had experienced a great deal of discouragement. At Philippi he had had a promising beginning smashed by the opposition of fanatical Jews. The same thing had happened at Thessalonica and Beroea. In Athens he had had little success. Small wonder that he came to busy, proud, intellectual Corinth 'in weakness and fear, and with much trembling' (1 Cor. 2:3). His companions on this

---

statesmen, its painters and craftsmen, but does not speak of philosophers. He also refers to its great paintings and works in bronze (8.6.23). Pausanius has a detailed description of the city (*Description of Greece*, 2:1–5). Horace quotes a proverb, 'It is not every man's lot to get to Corinth' (*Epistles*, I.17.36); the Loeb editor explains that this 'originally referred to the great expense of a self-indulgent life at Corinth'.

[1] Cited in Parry, p. x.

missionary journey, Silas and Timothy, were occupied in Macedonia, so that Paul was probably alone, which would not have
made things any easier. In Corinth he lodged with Aquila and
Priscilla, Jews who had been expelled from Rome by a decree
of the Emperor Claudius (which most date in AD 49). Like
Paul, they were tentmakers (=leatherworkers?) by trade. In due
course Silas and Timothy rejoined him and brought news that,
despite all opposition, Paul's converts at Thessalonica were
standing firm. Paul saw that, despite the difficulties and
discouragements he had met, the blessing of God was upon
the work that he had done. The news put new heart into him
and he gave himself over to the proclamation of the gospel with
renewed energy. He 'devoted himself exclusively to preaching,
testifying to the Jews that Jesus was the Christ' (Acts 18:5).

But his preaching did not prove acceptable to the Jews and
he had to leave the synagogue. Not very tactfully he went to
the house of Justus, right next door,[1] and this apparently
became his new preaching base.[2] Crispus, the 'synagogue
ruler', believed, together with his household (Acts 18:8).[3] But
these are the only Jewish converts in Corinth of whom we read
in Acts (unless Aquila and Priscilla were converted there). It is
in harmony with this that Jewish names do not figure largely
in the Corinthian Epistles. But many of the Corinthians believed
and were baptized. Paul was encouraged by a vision, perhaps
at the time of his expulsion from the synagogue, assuring him
that God had 'many people in this city' (Acts 18:10). He
remained in Corinth for eighteen months and evidently made
many converts. We are not told expressly, but it seems likely

[1] *Cf.* K. Lake, 'It must be admitted that he chose a position which was not likely to avoid
trouble, though it had the advantage of being easily found by the God-fearer who had
previously frequented the synagogue' (*The Earlier Epistles of St. Paul* (Rivingtons, 1911),
p. 104).

[2] This appears to be the meaning of Acts 18:7, rather than that he ceased living with
Aquila and Priscilla and came to live with Justus.

[3] It is possible that there is another Jew. The Sosthenes who is joined with Paul and
Timothy in the salutation (1 Cor. 1:1) may be the synagogue ruler of Acts 18:17. But this
is far from certain. J. Massingberd Ford emphasizes the Jewish element in the Corinthian
church in an article entitled, 'The First Epistle to the Corinthians or the First Epistle to the
Hebrews?' (*CBQ*, xxviii, 1966, pp. 402–416). But others, *e.g.* T. W. Manson, see the Corinthian church as largely Gentile (*Studies in the Gospels and Epistles* (Manchester University
Press, 1962), pp. 190–209). This seems indicated by Acts 18:6; 1 Cor. 12:2 (though there
were some Jewish Christians, 1 Cor. 7:18).

that here, as elsewhere, the bulk of the believers came from the group of devout pagans who attached themselves loosely to the synagogue. They were dissatisfied with paganism and found themselves attracted by Judaism's lofty morals and pure monotheism, but repelled by its narrow nationalism and by ritual practices like circumcision. Such people found in Christianity a faith that satisfied and was free from what they found objectionable in Judaism.

Some of the converts were people of substance. Gaius gave hospitality to Paul and to the whole church (Rom. 16:23, almost certainly written from Corinth). Erastus was 'the city's director of public works' (Rom. 16:23; an inscription in Corinth speaks of an Erastus who laid down a pavement at his own expense[1] and this might be the same man). Some see Chloe as another wealthy Corinthian Christian, but we do not know whether she was a believer or not, nor whether she came from this city or elsewhere. But Paul's references to believers engaging in litigation and attending private banquets point to men of means. It seems, however, that these were exceptions, and that most of the believers came from the lower social strata (1 Cor. 1:26–29).[2]

Throughout Greece the Jews tended to stir up opposition whenever Paul's missions looked like being successful.[3] The Thessalonian Epistles, almost certainly written from Corinth, show us something of the determined opposition he was experiencing (1 Thes. 2:15; 2 Thes. 3:1f.). He was compelled to cease preaching in the synagogue and was even brought before the proconsul Gallio and accused of 'persuading the people to worship God in ways contrary to the law' (Acts 18:13). But he had broken no Roman law and Gallio refused to hear the charge.

[1] Wright, *Biblical Archaeology*, p. 177; Murphy O'Connor, *SPC*, p. 37.

[2] Theissen, while agreeing that most of the Corinthians were lower class, points to evidence that some were not. Thus nine out of seventeen persons (or circles of people) linked with Corinth engaged in travel (pp. 91f.), not normally an occupation of the poor. Some reproached Paul 'repeatedly' for not accepting hospitality (p. 97; he cites 9:1ff.; 2 Cor. 10–13), which argues the means for providing it; the eating of meat (chs. 8–10) concerned the wealthy rather than the poor (pp. 125f., 128). He finds all this important, for 'associations of the ancient world were, to a great extent, socially homogeneous. Religious associations give evidence of expressing class-specific forms of sociability to an even greater degree than do professional groups . . .' (p. 146). The Christians differed in including people of various social classes and treating them all as 'brothers'.

[3] 'He was not merely a renegade Pharisee who believed in messiah, but a successful one' (Moffatt, p. xiii). That is what they found impossible to forgive.

He saw it as merely a dispute among Jews (which incidentally gave Christianity protection for the time being; Gallio had classed it as part of Judaism; *cf*. Bruce, p. 20). Paul was free to continue his work unhindered. From the length of his stay we gather that he regarded his mission at Corinth as possibly the most important he had undertaken up to this point.

III. PAUL'S SUBSEQUENT RELATIONS WITH THE CHURCH AT CORINTH

Some time after Paul left Corinth Apollos, a learned man from Alexandria, arrived there. He had been in Ephesus teaching Christianity, though he knew only John's baptism. There Aquila and Priscilla 'explained to him the way of God more adequately' (Acts 18:26). Armed with this new knowledge, Apollos went to Achaia, of which province Corinth was the capital. Here his eloquence was employed in 'proving from the Scriptures that Jesus was the Christ' (Acts 18:28). This implies that preacher and hearers alike looked for the coming of the Messiah (the Christ). Apollos was able to say, 'The Messiah you expect is Jesus and Scripture makes this clear.'[1]

His method of preaching probably differed from that of Paul. Paul's preaching had a studied simplicity (1 Cor. 2:2–4), that of Apollos was probably highly rhetorical (Acts 18:24, 27–28). There was no fundamental difference in the message preached, for Paul speaks of Apollos as continuing the work that he had begun (1 Cor. 3:6, 8). But the difference in presentation was enough to cause a certain partisanship with some of the Corinthians.[2]

Some time after this Paul wrote a letter to the Corinthian church, a letter that has perished. The evidence for its existence

[1] *Cf*. K. Lake, *op. cit.*, p. 110.

[2] 'In these cities, with their mobile, eager, and excitable populations, crazes of some kind are not only a common feature, but almost a social necessity. . . . As Renan says . . . let there be two preachers, or two doctors, in one of the small towns in Southern Europe, and at once the inhabitants take sides as to which is the better of the two. The two preachers, or the two doctors, may be on the best of terms: that in no way hinders their names from being made a party-cry and the signal for vehement dissensions' (Robertson and Plummer, p. xx). Proctor remarks that the process would have been helped by the multiplicity of races at Corinth (p. 969).

is Paul's statement that he had previously written a letter telling the Corinthian believers 'not to associate with sexually immoral people' (1 Cor. 5:9). We know nothing more about this letter or how Paul came to write it. Some scholars think that part of it is preserved in 2 Corinthians 6:14–7:1. If, as is probable, this hypothesis is to be rejected, the letter has entirely disappeared.[1] This need cause no surprise. The letter had been misunderstood (1 Cor. 5:9–10) and Paul mentioned it only to clear up a misconception. The newer letter superseded the older, and thus there was no point in preserving it.[2]

Next came some contacts with the Corinthians. The household of Chloe brought him news of cliques in the church (1 Cor. 1:11). The church wrote him a letter (1 Cor. 7:1), presumably brought by Stephanas, Fortunatus and Achaicus (1 Cor. 16:17), who would have added their own comments. Paul answered with the letter we know as 1 Corinthians. From it we learn that all was not well in the Corinthian church. There is some very plain speaking.

The situation was serious and Paul determined to send Timothy to Corinth; indeed, he had sent him before he despatched 1 Corinthians (1 Cor. 4:17; 16:10–11). Timothy is joined with Paul in the salutation in 2 Corinthians, so his visit was short (if indeed he ever reached Corinth). Clearly he was not able to do much.

The situation worsened. It is curious that we do not know the nature of what was plainly a very serious dispute. It may have been one of the matters mentioned in 1 Corinthians, but if so we have no way of knowing which. But clearly it involved a denial of Paul's authority. Paul felt it necessary to leave his work in Ephesus and pay a hurried visit in the attempt to set things right. This visit is implied in passages in 2 Corinthians which speak of Paul as being ready to pay a third visit to Corinth (2 Cor. 12:14; 13:1; his second visit is past in 2 Cor. 13:2). When Paul wrote this letter he had clearly made a visit additional to the one when the church was founded. The words

---

[1] See the Introduction to R. V. G. Tasker's Commentary on 2 Corinthians (*TNTC*).

[2] Hurd thinks that the letter the Corinthians wrote to Paul (1 Cor. 7:1) was in reply to the misunderstood letter. He holds that an examination of what Paul says about the Corinthians' letter enables us to reconstruct something of Paul's lost letter (pp. 213–239).

will not refer, as some have maintained, to Paul's intentions and not to an actual visit. As Moffatt cogently argues, 'Against people who suspected his consistency and goodwill, it would have been of little use to plead that he had honestly intended to come, that he had been quite ready to visit them.'[1] His references to coming again in sorrow (*e.g.* 2 Cor. 2:1) show that that visit had been an unpleasant one.

Some scholars place this visit before the writing of 1 Corinthians,[2] but no good reason has been shown for this. That Epistle seems to imply one previous visit only, the one when the church was founded (*e.g.* 2:1; 3:2; 11:2). Another visit is foreshadowed (4:19), but is not yet an accomplished fact. Paul's knowledge of recent affairs at Corinth is not personal, but derived from Chloe's people (1:11; *cf.* 5:1; 11:18), and from a letter from the Corinthian church (7:1). The second visit was clearly a very painful one and the general tone of 1 Corinthians is inexplicable after such a visit. It is much more likely that the situation implied in 1 Corinthians deteriorated after the receipt of that letter. Thus the 'painful' visit became necessary. But, despite some plain speaking, it failed to clear up the situation, and Paul went away profoundly disturbed.[3]

The apostle determined to write another letter. This obviously had a very severe tone and cost him much to write (2 Cor. 2:4; 7:8). Had it not been successful it might conceivably have meant a final rupture between Paul and this church he had founded. Like his first letter, this 'severe' letter has been lost, unless, as some scholars think, part of it is preserved in 2 Corinthians 10–13[4] The letter was apparently taken by Titus, who was to

[1] J. Moffatt, *An Introduction to the Literature of the New Testament* (T. & T. Clark, 1927), p. 117.

[2] See the list in Robertson and Plummer, p. xxiv.

[3] T. W. Manson denies that Paul visited Corinth from Ephesus. He holds that Paul completed his work in Ephesus, then paid the 'painful' visit to Corinth, after which he went on to Macedonia (2 Cor. 1:15ff.). But Paul speaks of that plan as though it was not carried out, and a further disadvantage is that Manson has to postulate a special missionary expedition in the neighbourhood of Troas, for Paul was certainly there (2 Cor. 2:12; see *Studies*, pp. 211–217). It is better to see the 'painful' visit as an interruption of the Ephesian ministry.

[4] The view is held strongly by some. Thus K. and S. Lake maintain that 'there is overwhelming reason for believing that II Cor. x–xiii is part of the severe letter and that II Cor. i–ix is a later letter' (*An Introduction to the New Testament* (Christophers, 1938), p. 122). So also Willi Marxsen, *Introduction to the New Testament* (Fortress Press, 1980), pp. 79ff. On

return via Macedonia and Troas. Paul was impatient to know how it had been received. He went to Troas but Titus was not there. Unable to rest, he crossed to Macedonia (2 Cor. 2:12–13). Here Titus met him with the news that all was well (2 Cor. 2:12–17; 7:6–7). Out of his great relief and joy Paul wrote the letter we call 2 Corinthians. Almost certainly he visited the church soon afterwards.

Thus we have knowledge of three visits Paul paid to Corinth:
1. When the church was founded.
2. The 'painful' visit.
3. A visit after 2 Corinthians had been sent.

There were four letters:
1. The 'previous' letter.
2. 1 Corinthians.
3. The 'severe' letter.
4. 2 Corinthians.

A more detailed discussion of this framework more properly belongs to the introduction to 2 Corinthians. Here it is sufficient to notice enough of the evidence for us to place 1 Corinthians in its proper place in the sequence of Paul's dealings with the church at Corinth.

IV. THE OCCASION AND PURPOSE OF 1 CORINTHIANS

The immediate occasion of the Epistle was the letter Paul had received from the Corinthian church, for which a reply was necessary. But what mattered much more to Paul was clearly the news that had come to him independently of the letter. There were disquieting irregularities in the conduct of the

---

the other hand, M. Dibelius says, 'ancient letters had a fairly certain protection against such accidental interweavings, in the fact that the address of the letter stood on the reverse of the papyrus. This would make it difficult accidentally to take part of one letter for another letter, and an editor who without visible grounds made two letters out of four would be a strange figure, especially if he deleted from the intermediate letter the essential matter referred to in 2 Cor. ii and vii, and yet used a fragment of that letter in 2 Cor. x–xiii. Hence we shall have to content ourselves with the loss of these two letters, viz. the original first and the intermediate third' (*A Fresh Approach to the New Testament and Early Christian Literature* (Ivor Nicholson and Watson, 1936), p. 154). See also Orr and Walther, pp. 21–24. R. Batey rejects the idea that 2 Cor. 10–13 is part of the 'severe' letter, and sees it as later than the others, part of a fifth letter to the Corinthians (*JBL*, lxxxiv, 1965, pp. 139–146).

believers at Corinth. Paul was troubled by the 'tendency on the part of some members to make the break with pagan society as indefinite as possible. . . . The Church was in the world, as it had to be, but the world was in the Church, as it ought not to be'.[1] So much did this matter to Paul that he spent six chapters dealing with it before he so much as touched on the matters about which they had written to him.

Paul was troubled about the divisions within the church. Parties had been formed attaching themselves to the names of Paul, Apollos and Peter, and even that of Christ. Paul spent a lot of time dealing with this and clearly he regarded it as very serious. Then there was a case of incest, but the church had not censured the offender. 'They found it hard to hate the sensuality which in their earlier days they had regarded as divine.'[2] There was also a quarrelsome spirit. Some church members had actually gone to law with others, and Paul felt that this had to be put right. He speaks also of sexual impurity; gross sins like this must not continue. First and foremost 1 Corinthians is a letter directed at the reformation of conduct.

Having dealt with these grave evils Paul turns to the matters mentioned in the letter written to him, questions about marriage and celibacy, about food offered to idols, probably also about public worship and spiritual gifts. Paul wrote to help his friends in their difficulties. This part of his letter contains a wonderful treatment of love (1 Cor. 13) and a magnificent passage on the resurrection, this latter elicited, it would seem, by the fact that some of the Corinthians denied that the dead would rise (1 Cor. 15:12). The result of all this is ' "an inexhaustible mine of Christian thought and life." Nowhere else in the NT is there a more many-sided embodiment of the imperishable principles and instincts which should inspire each member of the body of Christ for all time'.[3]

Paul's purpose then is principally to set right disorders which the Corinthians took lightly, but which he saw as grave sins. Secondly, he wrote to answer some questions put to him. Thirdly, he wrote to give doctrinal teaching, particularly on the

[1] Moffatt, p. xv.

[2] L. Pullan, *The Books of the New Testament* (Rivingtons, 1926), p. 135.

[3] A. Robertson, in *HDB*, i, pp. 489–490.

resurrection.[1]

Some recent scholars, notably W. Schmithals, have argued that the Epistle must be seen against a background of Gnosticism at Corinth. Gnosticism (from the Greek *gnōsis*, 'knowledge') appeared in a variety of forms, all stressing the importance of knowledge. Usually there was the idea of a high good God, infinitely removed from this evil world. From this God there were 'emanations' until a spirit appeared who was powerful enough to create but foolish enough not to see that matter is evil. A right 'knowledge' enables spiritual people to escape the bondage of evil matter and in due course to gain heavenly bliss. But Gnosticism, as a system, does not seem to be attested until well into the second century AD. It was eclectic, picking up ideas from many places, and some of these ideas existed in the first century. It may well be that the Corinthians held to some such ideas, but this does not make them Gnostics. The most we can say is that in Corinth there were some ideas which later were taken up and systematized by the Gnostics. But we do not need a knowledge of Gnosticism to make sense of the Corinthian correspondence.[2]

1 Corinthians is very much an occasional letter, directed to the immediate local needs of Paul's converts.[3] But it would be

[1] Manson sees the Epistle as probably written against the background of Paul's 'struggle with agents of Palestinian Jewish Christianity either under the direct leadership or acting in the name of Peter' (*Studies*, p. 207). However, though Manson's treatment is very stimulating, he does not seem to have established this point.

[2] Schmithals has set out his ideas in books like *Gnosticism in Corinth* (Abingdon, 1971) and *Paul and the Gnostics* (Abingdon, 1972). W. G. Kümmel holds that 'the entire epistle shows a front against a new Gnostic interpretation of the Christian message', though he does not accept all of Schmithal's position (*Introduction to the New Testament* (SCM Press, 1966), p. 202). Willi Marxsen regards 1 Corinthians as 'a polemic against Gnosticism' (*Introduction*, p. 72). But Conzelmann denies that there are 'any traces of such a myth (*i.e.* a Gnostic myth) in Corinth'; he finds only 'isolated traces of the beginnings of the formation of what later presented itself as "Gnosticism"' (p. 15). Bruce sees it as 'anachronistic' to call the Corinthians 'Gnostics' (p. 21), and R. P. Martin accepts Bruce's view of 'incipient gnosticism' (*New Testament Foundations*, 2 (Paternoster Press, 1978), p. 173). R. McL. Wilson has a helpful article entitled 'How Gnostic were the Corinthians?' (*NTS*, 19, 1972–73, pp. 65–74). He concludes that at Corinth we have 'at most only the first tentative beginnings of what was later to develop into full-scale Gnosticism', and warns that 'careless and indiscriminate use of terms like gnostic and gnosticism in this connection is dangerous and misleading' (*ibid.*, p. 74).

[3] *Cf.* A. H. McNeile, this is 'the most intensely practical of all St. Paul's letters. The whole of it was written to meet immediate needs of his converts' (*An Introduction to the Study of the New Testament* (Oxford University Press, 1927), p. 122).

a mistake to regard it as on that account irrelevant to our needs. The heart of man does not change, and the principles on which Paul works are just as important to us as to the Corinthians of the first century. As Godet puts it,

the tendency to make religious truths the subjects of intellectual study rather than a work of conscience and of heart-acceptance, the disposition resulting therefrom, not always to place the moral conduct under the influence of religious conviction, and to give scope to the latter rather in oratorical discourse than in vigour of holiness, – these are defects which more than one modern nation shares in common with the Greek people.[1]

Not only does Paul deal with problems which have a way of recurring in other ages and regions; he gives us the principles on which to act. He deals with everyday problems 'from a central point of view, and places everyday troubles in the light of eternity'.[2]

V. THE AUTHENTICITY OF THE EPISTLE

There seem no solid grounds for doubting the authenticity of 1 Corinthians. Robertson and Plummer can say, 'Both the external and the internal evidence for the Pauline authorship are so strong that those who attempt to show that the Apostle was not the writer succeed chiefly in proving their own incompetence as critics.'[3] There is accordingly no need to do more than indicate briefly where the strength of this evidence lies.

The external attestation is all that we could wish. It is cited in 1 Clement 47:1, a first-century letter; 1 Corinthians is the first New Testament document to be cited with the name of its author. It is freely quoted by Ignatius and Polycarp and from then on is often referred to, with no doubts expressed about its authorship. None of Paul's other letters was quoted as widely and as early as this. In the Muratorian Fragment (a list of books

---

[1] Godet, p. 2.

[2] M. Dibelius, A Fresh Approach, p. 155. Cf. Conzelmann, 'here Paul is practicing applied theology, so to speak' (p. 9).

[3] Robertson and Plummer, p. xvi.

accepted as canonical, probably at Rome, and dating from some time after the middle of the second century) and in some other lists it is the first of Paul's letters. No satisfactory reason has been suggested for this, but at the least it shows that 1 Corinthians was regarded as very important.

Internal evidence likewise points to Paul. The style and language are those of the universally accepted Pauline writings. The letter fits in with what we know of the situation in Corinth. It reads naturally as Paul's attempt to deal with a difficult situation. It contains forthright condemnations of the Corinthians and the very preservation of a letter like this when others of Paul's letters have been lost is strong evidence of authenticity.[1]

There is little that need be said about the integrity of the Epistle. Some critics have suspected interpolations, but the reasons they put forward have not commended themselves. In earlier years J. Weiss held that a number of writings have been put together to form this letter and in recent years others (*e.g.* Héring and Hurd) have argued that the work is composite. But we must not expect the same orderly classification of topics in a letter as in a theological treatise. 1 Corinthians reads very much like an original letter. As Moffatt says, 'if some editor really put together fragments from two or three letters, he has done his work so well that it is beyond our powers to recover their original shape and sequence.'[2] It seems reasonably clear then that this is a genuine writing of Paul and that it is free from any substantial interpolation.[3]

[1] Beet points out that no church would accept 'without careful scrutiny, so public a monument of its degradation' (p. 5).

[2] Moffatt, p. xxvi. Conzelmann finds 'no conclusive proof of different situations within 1 Corinthians. The existing breaks can be explained from the circumstances of its composition. Even the complex that gives the strongest offense, chaps. 8–10, can be understood as a unity' (p. 4).

[3] Robertson and Plummer say there may occasionally be doubt about a word, 'but there is probably no verse or whole clause that is an interpolation' (p. xviii). Moffatt is of opinion that 'its unity hardly requires detailed proof' (*An Introduction to the Literature of the New Testament*, p. 113).

VI. THE DATE AND PLACE OF ORIGIN

The place of origin is indicated by Paul's statement, 'I will stay on at Ephesus until Pentecost' (16:8). But just when he wrote it is not immediately obvious.

Paul paid a brief visit to Ephesus immediately after he had established the church at Corinth (Acts 18:18–21), but it seems impossible to hold that our Epistle was written during this stay. There is no indication that anything was seriously amiss in the church when Paul left it, but by the time 1 Corinthians was penned much had happened. We must allow time for this. Even when trouble began it was the 'previous' letter that was sent off, not 1 Corinthians. Our letter must date from Paul's later stay in Ephesus, a period of three years (Acts 19; 20:31). If the apostle's determination to stay till Pentecost means that he left Ephesus then, we must place 1 Corinthians during the last of the three years in that city. It will be towards the beginning rather than at the end of that year, for we must allow time for the events leading up to the writing of 2 Corinthians before the year was up.

One of the important points for the chronology of the New Testament is afforded by the statement in Acts 18:12 that Gallio was proconsul of Achaia while Paul was in Corinth. The meaning appears to be that Gallio came to Corinth during Paul's time there. An inscription at Delphi gives the decision of the Emperor on a question referred to him by Gallio, and from the date of the inscription it seems that Gallio entered on his office during the early summer of AD 51.[1] The impression left by the story in Acts is that Paul left Corinth not long after Gallio's arrival, though not immediately after it (cf. 'for some time', Acts 18:18).

There does not seem to be anything that enables us to date the Epistle with precision. The Gallio date is the last fixed point before its composition. When we allow time for the events in Acts 18:18–19:1 between Paul's departure from Corinth and his

---

[1] I have discussed this inscription in my *TNTC* on 1 and 2 Thessalonians (p. 21). The inscription is quoted and discussed by K. Lake, *The Beginnings of Christianity*, v (Baker reprint, 1966), pp. 460ff. A more recent discussion, with additional data, is that by J. Murphy-O'Connor (*SPC*, pp. 141–152).

arrival at Ephesus on his third missionary journey, we see that
1 Corinthians would have been written somewhere about the
mid fifties.[1]

---

[1] J. A. T. Robinson points to wide agreement on AD 55 (*Redating the New Testament* (SCM
Press, 1976), p. 54). S. M. Gilmour also opts for AD 55 'on the basis of the chronology most
commonly assumed' (*IDB*, i, p. 692). Others prefer a date a year or two later.

ANALYSIS

COMMENTARY

I. INTRODUCTION (1:1–9)

A. SALUTATION (1:1–3)

1. Paul's opening is the usual one in a first-century letter: first the name of the writer(s), then that of the addressee(s), and a prayer. But to each part Paul gives a characteristically Christian twist. Thus his name is followed by *called to be an apostle*, very appropriate in this letter where his apostolic authority is used so freely to put wrong matters right. *Called* (*cf*. Rom. 1:1) points to the divine origin of his apostolate (*cf*. Gal. 1:1), as does the insistence that it is *by the will of God* (*cf*. 2 Cor. 1:1). *Our brother Sosthenes* may be the Jewish 'synagogue ruler' (Acts 18:17), in which case he was subsequently converted. But the name is not uncommon and it may not be the same man.

2. The letter is addressed to *the church of God in Corinth*, 'a great and joyful paradox' (Bengel). *Church* (*ekklēsia*) is a term which in ordinary Greek could apply to any secular assembly (it is used of the rioting Ephesians in Acts 19:32,41; *cf*. v. 39). The Christians by-passed the regular words for religious brotherhoods, and made this their usual self-designation. They were probably influenced by the fact that it is used in LXX of the people of Israel. The usage reflects their deep conviction that the church is not merely one religious group among many. It is unique. Ordinary religious words will not do. And it is not any 'assembly': it is the *ekklēsia of God*. This is further defined as *those sanctified in Christ Jesus and called to be holy*. *Holy* is from

35

the same root as *sanctified*, where the basic idea is not that of high moral character as with us, but of being set apart for God (though, of course, the character implied in such separation is not out of mind).

It is possible that *together with all those everywhere* widens the salutation to include all Christians (Conzelmann sees a reference to 'the idea of the universal church'), and this is the most natural interpretation of the Greek. T. W. Manson takes 'every place' (*topos*) to mean 'every place of worship', as in some Jewish synagogue inscriptions.[1] But a strong objection to both is that the Epistle gives no sign of being a circular or a general manifesto. It sticks stubbornly to local issues. It is thus better to take the phrase closely with the preceding. The Corinthians are called to be holy, not as an isolated unit, but along with other people. It is unusual to have Christians described as *those who call on the name* of Christ (though it is readily intelligible). In the Old Testament people call on the name of Yahweh (Joel 2:32, *etc.*), so that in using the expression Paul is assigning the highest possible place to Christ.

3. *Grace* is one of the great Christian words. It resembles the usual Greek greeting, but there is a world of difference between 'greeting' (*chairein*) and 'grace' (*charis*). *Grace* speaks of God's free gift to us, and more especially of his free gift in Christ. *Peace* is the usual Hebrew greeting. But the Hebrew *šālôm* means more than 'peace' does in English. It means not the absence of strife, but the presence of positive blessings. It is the prosperity of the whole person, especially his spiritual prosperity.

This is the typical greeting, found in almost every letter in the New Testament (sometimes with 'mercy' added). And not only are these two qualities mentioned, but God the Father and the Lord Jesus Christ are linked as joint-authors. No higher place could be given to Christ.

[1] *Studies*, pp. 192, 208–209.

B. THANKSGIVING (1:4–9)

Paul usually has a thanksgiving at the beginning of his letters. In view of his trenchant criticisms of the Corinthians some feel that this particular thanksgiving is ironical. There seems no real basis for this. Paul does not give thanks for qualities in the Corinthians like faith and love (contrast 1 Thes. 1:2–3), but for what God's grace has in fact done in them. With all its faults, 'the Christian community at Corinth must have presented as a whole a marvellous contrast to their heathen fellow-citizens' (Lightfoot on v. 5).

4–5. Merely human achievement means little to Paul; in the flesh 'nothing good lives' (Rom. 7:18). He gives thanks, not for what the Corinthians have done of themselves, but for what God's *grace given . . . in Christ Jesus* has accomplished in them. He singles out two points, *speaking*, the telling forth of the truth, and *knowledge*, the grasp of the truth (Robertson points out that it is important to have something worth saying and not mere fluency). 'He selects the gifts of which the Corinthians were especially proud' (Parry). He later combines the two in 'the word of knowledge' (12:8).

6. *Our testimony about Christ* points to the derivative nature of the gospel. The gospel is the good news of what God has done; all that the preachers do is pass it on, bear their witness to it. This witness *was confirmed* in the Corinthians. The verb is often used in the papyri in the legal sense of guaranteeing.[1] Paul is saying that the changed lives of the Corinthians, specifically their 'speaking' and their 'knowledge' (v. 5), demonstrated the validity of the message preached to them. The effects of the preaching were the guarantee of its truth.

7. The result (*Therefore*) of all this is that the Corinthians lack no *spiritual gift* (*charisma*). This word is used (*a*) of salvation (Rom. 5:15), (*b*) of God's good gifts in general (Rom. 11:29), and (*c*) of special endowments of the Spirit (12:4ff.). Here the

[1] See A. Deissmann, *Bible Studies* (T. & T. Clark, 1901), pp. 104–109; H. Schlier, *TDNT*, i, pp. 602–603; MM.

thought is the wider one (*b*). God has enriched their lives so that they lack no spiritual gift. The reference to the Lord's second coming is unexpected. But the present foretaste of the Spirit may well turn our thoughts to the fuller experience that awaits us at the last great day (*cf.* Rom. 8:23; Eph. 1:13–14). The word *revealed* (actually the noun 'revelation') points to the fuller knowledge that the coming of the Lord will bring (*cf.* 2 Thes. 1:7). We shall see him as he is (1 Jn. 3:2). Believers wait, not in apathy, but in positive hope (*cf.* Conzelmann).

8. The verb *keep you strong* is that translated 'was confirmed' in v. 6. Christ, who has enriched the Corinthians and given them grace and every good gift, is their guarantee that right through until the last time nothing will be lacking to them. The enriching with the Spirit's gifts is itself an assurance, a foretaste of the good things to come. Just as the end of time may be referred to as the 'revelation' of Christ (v. 7), so it may be spoken of as *the day of our Lord Jesus Christ*. The Old Testament looks for the coming of 'the day of the LORD' (Am. 5:18); the New sees this as the day of Christ. Here the thought is that because it is his day and because it is he who will 'guarantee' the Corinthians, they may be assured that they will be *blameless* in that day. No charge can be laid against those whom Christ guarantees (*cf.* Rom. 8:33).

9. This is not a vain boast. It is a sure confidence grounded in the fact that *God . . . is faithful*. The Corinthians may confidently look for the continuance of his blessing, for his character is at stake. Paul goes back to beginnings. The faithful God *has called* the Corinthian Christians *into fellowship with his Son Jesus Christ our Lord*. Paul has said that he is an apostle because of the divine call (v. 1). Now we see that there is a call to every believer. It is because God has called us and not on account of some initiative of our own that we have become Christians. NIV takes the genitive after *koinōnia* as subjective, 'fellowship with' (as fellowship with the Spirit, Phil. 2:1). But such a genitive may be objective, 'fellowship in' (as 'fellowship in his sufferings', Phil. 3:10). Here it is possible that Paul means that the fellowship is a common partaking of Christ (*cf.* NEB, 'called you to share in the life of his Son'). But the genitive of a person is more likely to be subjective and we should accept *fellowship with his Son* as the meaning (Ellicott thinks it is both, fellowship 'in Him and with Him'). The word is the direct opposite of 'divisions' in v. 10. It is fellowship with (and in) Christ to which we are called, not divisions from one another.

We should notice the way Paul dwells on the name of his Saviour. Nine times in these nine verses he makes use of this name, and he will do it again in the next verse. Christ is absolutely central. Paul lingers lovingly over the name.

II. DIVISION IN THE CHURCH (1:10 – 4:21)

A. THE FACT OF DIVISION (1:10–17)

1. The parties (1:10–12)

10. The adversative conjunction *de*, 'but' (which NIV omits) sets what follows in contrast to the preceding. So far from fellowship being realized there is division. Paul leads into the subject with a tender appeal. He uses the verb *appeal*, and the affectionate address, *brothers*, a word he will use thirty-nine times in this letter, far and away the most frequent use in any of his letters (next are Romans and 1 Thessalonians, each with nineteen). Further, he implores them *in the name of our Lord Jesus Christ*. The full title heightens the solemnity of his appeal and the one name stands over against all party names.

That all of you agree (more literally, 'speak the same thing') makes use of a classical expression for being united. The use of party cries always tends to deepen and perpetuate division and Paul calls for their abandonment. To 'speak the same thing' can be a first step to real unity, whereas catch cries promote division. *Divisions* (*schismata*) are not 'schisms', but 'dissensions' ('cliques', Moffatt). The divisions were internal, and the groups were still one church and, for example, still met for Holy Communion (11:17ff.). Paul looks for them to *be perfectly united*, where his verb is used of restoring anything to its right condition. It is used of mending nets (Mt. 4:21), and of supplying what is lacking in the faith of the Thessalonians

(1 Thes. 3:10). The condition of the Corinthian church was far from what it should have been. Restorative action was demanded. Paul looks to them to come to be perfectly *united in mind and thought*. The two words do not differ greatly, but *mind* may mean 'frame of mind' and *thought* 'opinion'.

11. Chloe is not otherwise known. As Paul mentions her name it is perhaps more likely that she was an Ephesian than a Corinthian, but we do not know. Nor do we know whether she was a Christian, though this may be judged probable. She was evidently well to do, with interests in both Ephesus and Corinth, and some of her people had *informed* Paul of the situation. The verb means 'made clear'. Paul was not left in any doubt. Possibly also the word 'implies that the Apostle was reluctant to believe the reports which had come to his ears' (Edwards). *Quarrels* are one of the 'acts of the sinful nature' (Gal. 5:19–21, there translated 'discord'). They do not belong among God's people.

12. Paul's charge becomes precise. Clearly the trouble was widespread, and cliques had appeared, each attaching itself to a favourite teacher. Many try to outline the teachings of the various factions, but this is all guesswork. We have no information. From the general tone of Paul's references to Apollos and from what we know of this disciple from other passages it is clear that there was no great difference in their teaching. Paul makes not one criticism of him, and he had urged him to return to Corinth (16:12). The choice would perhaps have been made on the basis of their methods of preaching (see Introduction, p. 22).

The *Cephas* party (Cephas is the Aramaic form of the name 'Peter') raises difficulties of another sort. We do not know whether Peter had ever been in Corinth or not. If he had been, the basis of attachment may have been personal. But there were other considerations. Peter had been a Christian longer than Paul. He had been the leader of the Twelve. He seems to have been more ready to conform to the Jewish Law than was Paul (*cf.* Gal. 2:11ff.). There may have been some different emphasis in his preaching from that of Paul, though if so it must have been slight. For whatever reason, a section of the Corinthians felt that there was something about Peter that made him the man to appeal to.

Some have thought that there was no *Christ* party, understanding *I follow Christ* as Paul's own interjection. The construction of the sentence makes this most unlikely; the Greek seems to point to a fourth party, as does the question 'Is Christ divided?' (v. 13; is 2 Cor. 10:7 relevant?). Whether these people were simply tired of the other three, and so said 'We belong to Christ, not any human leader', or whether they had some distinctive teachings we have no way of knowing. Either way they had absorbed the spirit of partisanship. It is this that bothers Paul. He does not attack the teaching of any of the parties, but the fact that there were parties. He does not exempt those who clung to his own name. The whole thing was wrong. He would have none of it.

2. *Not due to Paul* (1:13–17)

13. The apostle's indignation explodes in a series of questions. *Is Christ divided?* has been understood as an exasperated exclamation rather than a question (so GNB, NEB). Others take the verb as middle (as it is in Lk. 12:13), which would give the sense, 'Has Christ shared (you) with others?' and indicate that part only of them had been devoted to Christ. But the passive seems much more likely. This could mean 'Has Christ been apportioned?' (*i.e.* to one of the conflicting groups; *cf.* Moffatt, JB, 'Has Christ been parcelled out?'), or, 'Has Christ been divided up?' This last is the most likely meaning, but whichever we adopt Paul is envisaging an utter impossibility. Christ is one, and the Church, which is his body, must be one.

Was Paul crucified for you? also points to the unthinkable, and goes to the heart of the Christian way. The Corinthians, with their emphasis on wisdom, seem to have overlooked the truth that Christ's cross is absolutely central. No other than he could accomplish the crucial work of redemption. The third question shows that they had not realized the significance of their baptism (baptism and the cross are connected again in Rom. 6:3ff.). They had been baptized into Christ, not into any man. Their allegiance was to Christ alone.

14–16. Paul had baptized very few of the Corinthian converts, and he regards this as providential. He thanks God for it. Some think that baptism established a 'mystic relationship' (Héring) between baptizer and baptized, but it is not easy to establish this in the New Testament. Christ himself delegated baptism to his followers (Jn. 4:1–2). Peter seems to have done this too (Acts 10:48). Paul had made exceptions in the cases of Crispus ('the synagogue ruler', Acts 18:8), Gaius (his host, Rom. 16:23), and the household of Stephanas (the mention of the latter after a little interval is a natural touch in a dictated letter). It is unlikely that this was done on account of the importance of these people, for 'this idea would contradict the very drift of the whole passage' (Godet). Paul does not disclose his reasons. There may have been a few others (v. 16), but clearly it was well known that it had not been Paul's practice to baptize.

This fact makes it clear that he had made no attempt to bind converts to himself personally (*cf.* v. 15). The 'name' in antiquity meant far more than it does with us. It stood for the whole personality; it summed up the whole person. The preposition *eis* is literally 'into', and ' *"Into* the name" implies entrance into fellowship and allegiance, such as exists between the Redeemer and the redeemed' (Robertson and Plummer). There could be no suggestion that Paul had said or done anything to bring his converts into such a relation to him personally. He had pointed people to Christ.

17. The essence of Paul's commission was *to preach the gospel*, not to perform liturgical functions, even important ones like baptism. Preaching is primary in the original commission Christ gave the Twelve (Mk. 3:14) and throughout the New Testament it is this that is primary in the work of the apostles. They had a unique place as the witnesses of God's saving act in Christ. Their main business was to proclaim it.

Some at least of the Corinthians were setting too high a value on human wisdom and human eloquence in line with the typical Greek admiration for rhetoric and philosophical studies. In the face of this Paul insists that preaching *with words of human wisdom* ('cleverness in speaking', BAGD) was no part of his commission. That kind of preaching would draw people to the preacher. It would nullify the cross of Christ. The faithful preaching of the cross leads people to put their trust, not in any human device, but in what God has done in Christ. A reliance on rhetoric would cause trust in men, the very opposite of what the preaching of the cross is meant to effect.

B. THE 'FOOLISHNESS' OF THE GOSPEL (1:18 – 2:5)

1. The message was 'foolish' (1:18–25)
The Corinthians had clearly emphasized the importance of wisdom. In bold and forceful language Paul contrasts the wisdom of God, which seems folly to the sophisticated Corinthians, with the worldly wisdom that they so admired and that was so ineffective. Williams remarks that 'the world has had enough teachers, it needs a Redeemer' and it is something like this that Paul is saying. Notice that he is in opposition to all the groups, not any one of them in particular.

18. *The message* (NEB, 'the doctrine') is literally 'the word'; it contrasts with 'words of human wisdom' in v. 17 (where 'words' is really singular). It includes both the manner and the matter of the apostolic preaching. The message does not please the perishing, any more than the simplicity with which it is presented. In their 'wisdom' they see in it nothing but *foolishness* ('nonsense', Phillips). A well-known graffito in Rome depicts a worshipper standing before a crucified figure with the body of a man and the head of an ass and the inscription 'Alexamenos worships his god'.[1] That was the way the worldly-wise regarded the message of the cross. There is a contrast between *those who are perishing* and *us who are being saved* (cf. Lk. 13:23; 2 Cor. 2:15). Ultimately all must fall into one of these two classes; there is no other. Those *being saved* have not yet all the wisdom of heaven, but their newness of life enables them to weigh spiritual things. They perceive the greatness of the gospel, whereas *those who are perishing* are blind to it. The opposite of *foolishness* is 'wisdom' and we expect Paul to speak of the gospel as 'the

[1] Jack Finegan, *Light from the Ancient Past* (Princeton, 1946), p. 292, and fig. 124.

wisdom of God'. Instead he says it is *power* (*cf.* Rom. 1:16). It is not simply good advice, telling us what we should do. Nor is it information about God's power. It *is* God's power.

19. Paul clinches his argument with a quotation from Isaiah 29:14 (with a slight variation from LXX). Paul is not saying something new. From of old God's way had stood in contrast with that suggested by human wisdom (*cf.* Ps. 33:10). People always think their way is right (*cf.* Pr. 14:12; 16:25). But God confutes their 'wisdom'; he reduces their systems to nothing. In this context there is not much difference between *wisdom* and *intelligence*. Properly the former denotes mental excellence in general, the latter the intelligent critical understanding of 'the bearings of things' (Lightfoot on Col. 1:9). Neither can stand before God.

20. Paul hammers home the point with a series of rhetorical questions (*cf.* Jb. 28:12; Is. 19:12; 33:18). Some have thought that *the wise man* means the Greek sophist, *the scholar* the Jewish scribe, while *the philosopher of this age* means both. Others reverse the significance of the first and the last. But it is unlikely that Paul had such distinctions in mind. His point is that no human wisdom can avail before God, and he uses three typical terms for the learned and acute of this world. There is a glance at the transitory nature of human wisdom in the use of *this age* (*aiōn*; *cf.* NEB, 'limited, all of them, to this passing age'). This world is but a passing show and its wisdom passes with it. God has not simply disregarded this wisdom or shown it to be foolish; he has *made* it *foolish*. Paul leaves not the slightest doubt that God has rejected all that rests on merely human wisdom.

21. It is unlikely that *the wisdom of God* here refers to the revelation in nature as some hold (*cf.* Rom. 1:19–20). They think Paul means that when people failed to hear God speaking through the world of nature he spoke to them in another way. But the thrust of the passage is against all such views. Paul is saying that God in his wisdom chose to save people by the way of the cross and by no other way. *Pleased* fixes attention on God's free and sovereign choice. It was never his plan that people should come to know him by their exercise of wisdom. He *was pleased* to reveal himself in quite a different way. Paul brings out the total unexpectedness of this way with the bold assertion that it is *foolishness*. People never have acclaimed the gospel as a masterpiece of wisdom. To the natural man it does not make sense. Paul was not unaware of what he was up against as he preached the gospel. *What was preached* (the *kērygma*) is the content of the proclamation. It is not merely the fact that men preach the gospel that is 'foolish'; it is the gospel itself, the message that God saves us through a crucified Saviour. People do not receive salvation by exercising wisdom. Salvation comes to *those who believe* (the present tense points to a continuing faith).

22. In setting the Jews' demand for *miraculous signs* over against the Greeks' quest for *wisdom* Paul brings out the characteristics of two nations. The matter-of-fact Jews showed little interest in speculative thought. Their demand was for evidence and their interest was in the practical. They thought of God as active in performing mighty wonders, and in this vein they had demanded a sign from Jesus (Mt. 12:38; 16:1,4; Mk. 8:11-12; Jn. 6:30). They thought the Messiah would be attested by striking manifestations of power and majesty. A crucified Messiah was a contradiction in terms.

The Greeks were absorbed in speculative philosophy. No names were more honoured among them than the names of their outstanding thinkers. From the lofty heights of their culture they looked down on and despised as barbarians all who failed to appreciate their *wisdom*. They took no notice of the fact that this *wisdom* often degenerated into meaningless sophistries (*cf.* Acts 17:21). They were proud of their intellectual acuteness and found no place for the gospel. Proctor refers to 'the high intellectual perception of the Greek philosophers' and to 'the nobility of much of their writing'. But he adds, 'Yet all this has no saving power for mankind.'

23. In contrast with this (*but*, *de*, is adversative, and *we*, *hēmeis*, is emphatic), Paul sets the preaching of *Christ crucified*. The verb *preach* (*kēryssō*) is that appropriate to the action of a

45

herald. The message came from God, not the preacher. In this sense it is a peculiarly Christian term. It is used little, if at all, in this way in the classics, in LXX, or in current religious systems like the mystery religions (see *TDNT*, iii, pp. 697–700). *Crucified* is a perfect participle; not only was Christ once crucified, but he continues in the character of the crucified one. The crucifixion is permanent in its efficacy.

But the Jews will have none of it. To them a crucified Messiah was a complete impossibility, *a stumbling block* (Lenski thinks this too weak for *skandalon* and translates 'deathtrap'). It was an occasion of offence (those hanged bore the curse of God, Dt. 21:23). It was no better with the Gentiles who saw it as *foolishness*, sheer unmitigated folly. God would never act like that! The crucifixion is the heart of the Christian faith, but it was acceptable neither to Jew nor to Gentile. Paul includes all mankind in the rejection of the crucified Messiah.

24. But the rejection is not the whole story. Those who are called, Jew or Greek, welcome the message. There is emphasis on 'the called themselves' (RV mg.); 'themselves' is in an emphatic position. The important thing is the divine initiative, the call of God. Here, as usually in Paul's writings, *called* implies that the call has been heeded; it is an effectual call. Those *called* know that the crucified Christ means power. Before the call they were defeated by sin; now there is a new power at work in them, *the power of God*.

Christ is also *the wisdom of God*. The idea of wisdom runs through this passage; clearly the Corinthians had emphasized it. But to Greek intellectuals the cross was utter folly; it made no sense; there was no wisdom in it. Paul's conjunction of *power* and *wisdom* is important. Had the way to God been through 'wisdom', Christianity would have opened the way to salvation only to the intellectually gifted. The power in the cross opens the way for the humblest to know God and to overcome evil, and that is a wisdom superior by far to anything the philosophers could produce. On the level of the search for wisdom the 'foolishness' of God proved to be the true wisdom.

25. So Paul rounds off this section with the conclusion that what in God proud man is wont to dub *foolishness* is *wiser than man's wisdom*. Paul does not use the word 'foolishness' (*mōria*) as in vv. 18,21,23, but says 'the foolish thing' (*mōron*), *i.e.* the cross. So with *the weakness*; the cross is 'the weak thing' of God that is stronger than anything man can produce.

The sign-seeking Jews were blind to the significance of the greatest sign of all when it was before them. The wisdom-loving Greeks could not discern the most profound wisdom of all when they were confronted with it.

2. The believers are insignificant (1:26–31)

The contradiction God's method offers to worldly wisdom is illustrated by the kind of people he has called. He might have concentrated on the intelligentsia or other outstanding people, but in fact he has chosen people with little to commend them from the worldly standpoint. His power works miracles in the most hopeless material and thus his wisdom excels the best that men can produce. Paul works this out, incidentally, in a way that has called forth tributes to his style (BDF 490 has comments on his 'artistry').

26. Paul directs his readers to reflect on the kind of person whom God has in fact *called* (the word points us to the divine initiative). The large number of unimportant people in the church did not come about because the only people who would become Christians were from the depressed classes. It came about because God chose to work his marvels through people who were, from the human point of view, the most unprom-ising. It is probably for the same reason that Paul begins with *Not many of you were wise by human standards*. Wisdom has been prominent in the discussion and clearly the Corinthians revered it in the typical Greek fashion. But Paul decisively rejects this as God's criterion for calling people. That is not to say that there were none from the classes Paul mentions. *Not many* implies that there were some, though not a large number (*cf.* Introduction, p. 21; as Deluz remarks, God *a priori* 'excludes no one from his Church'). That there were no wise people among the Christians is an accusation as old as Celsus and refuted by Origen (*Contra Celsum* III. 48; Celsus's attack on Christianity is dated *c*. AD 180, while Origen lived *c*. 185–254). The *influential* and those *of noble birth* are the leading figures in the community. But 'the things which elevate man in the world, knowledge, influence, rank, are not the things which lead to God and salvation' (Hodge).

27. The repetition of *chose* underlines the purpose of God. The change from the masculine (*wise, influential* and *of noble birth* are all masculine in the Greek) to the neuter, *the foolish things*, may concentrate on the quality of foolishness seen in these people, but it is probably also intended to include a reference to salvation by the cross (*cf.* v. 23). There is another change of gender to the masculine *wise*, *i.e.* 'wise men'; such men are shamed by the contrast between their estimate of themselves and what God's choice reveals. The Greek construction (*hina*) indicates purpose ('in order to shame'); Paul makes sure we do not overlook God's plan in all this. Some commentators take *of the world* to mean 'in the world's opinion', but this is to miss the sting in Paul's words. God has not chosen only those whom the world counts *foolish* and *weak*: he has chosen those who really are *foolish* and *weak* in this world.

28. *Lowly* means 'of lowly birth', though often with the added notion of morally worthless (*cf.* 6:11). It is the direct opposite of 'of noble birth' in v. 26. *The despised* is a strong word, meaning 'treated as of no account' (Knox, 'contemptible'). But the following expression is even stronger, *the things that are not*, 'the "nothings" ' (Orr and Walther), 'those who in the eyes of the world did not exist' (Erdman). God's activity is creative. He makes out of what does not exist what is in accordance with his will. The verb rendered *to nullify* (*katargeō*) is not easy to translate. It occurs twenty-seven times in the New Testament and is translated in seventeen different ways in AV. RV does away with seven of these, but brings in another three, and the process is repeated in subsequent translations (I have a list of eighty renderings from reputable translations). Basically it means something like 'to render idle' or 'inoperative'. Here the meaning is that God has chosen *the things that are not* to render completely ineffective *the things that are*.

29. God does all this with a view to (*hopōs* indicates purpose) taking away from everyone every occasion of boasting. Whatever we may do before one another, we have nothing to boast of before God.

30. From the negative Paul turns to the positive. The saved are 'of him' (*ex autou*), where the preposition gives the idea of source. Their new life derives from God (*cf.* Rom. 9:11; 2 Cor. 5:17–18; Eph. 2:8). They are *in Christ Jesus*. Whole books have been written about this enigmatic phrase which Paul habitually uses to indicate the relationship between believers and Christ. Briefly, it shows that the believer is connected to his Lord in the closest possible fashion. Christ is the very atmosphere in which he lives. But we must not interpret this mechanically. Christ is a person. The phrase describes personal attachment to a personal Saviour. E. Best has shown that the expression has a corporate aspect. To be 'in Christ' is to be closely related to all those others who are also 'in Christ'.[1] It is to be part of the body of Christ. The adversative conjunction 'but' (*de*; see AV; NIV omits) and the emphatic *you* set believers in strong contrast to the worldly-wise of the preceding verses. The contrast with worldly wisdom comes out in another way when Christ is said to have *become for us wisdom*. Paul has already argued forcibly that the apparent 'foolishness' of the gospel is the true wisdom, and this is his thought here, too. The wisdom of God is embodied in Christ (*cf.* Col. 2:3), who offered himself that people might be saved. This is real wisdom, let the philosophers argue as they will.

Some see *righteousness* and the rest as co-ordinate with *wisdom* (*e.g.* AV), but NIV seems correct in taking them as explaining *wisdom*. *Righteousness* (there is no *our* in the Greek) in this context means the right standing Christ makes available for his own, 'the state of having been justified' (Edwards). Christ is our righteousness (*cf.* 2 Cor. 5:21). We know no other. We could never attain *holiness* in our own strength, but Christ is holiness, too (*cf.* Rom. 6:19; 1 Thes. 4:3–7). And he is *redemption* (last with a certain emphasis, perhaps as pointing to the last great day,

[1] E. Best, *One Body in Christ* (SPCK, 1955), ch. 1. This chapter gives an excellent summary of several views of the meaning of the phrase.

the consummation of redemption). He has paid the ransom price (*cf*. Mk. 10:45) in his own body on Calvary.

31. There is nothing to justify boasting before God (v. 29), but we may boast in what Christ has done (*cf*. Gal. 6:14). Characteristically Paul proves his point from Scripture (Je. 9:23–24). In the Old Testament the words refer to Yahweh; no higher view could be taken of the Person of Christ.

3. *Paul's preaching was in divine power* (2:1–5)
Paul reminds his hearers that when he was in their city his own preaching had conformed to what he has been saying about the 'foolishness' of the gospel. It had been a plain, unvarnished setting forth of the simple gospel. There had been nothing attractive about it. But precisely because it was so simple and unpretentious its results convincingly demonstrated the power of God.

1. The emphatic *kagō*, 'and I', stresses that Paul was not making an exception of himself. His preaching in Corinth had conformed to what he has just said. There seems no reason for NIV's taking *superior* with *wisdom* only; in the Greek it seems to apply to *eloquence* as well (*cf*. RSV). Paul is making no claims of superiority either for his speech, the way he presented his facts, or his *wisdom*, the way his mind marshalled his facts (Héring sees a reference to 'the arts of the rhetorician and philosopher'). *As I proclaimed* means 'in order to proclaim' (Conzelmann; *cf*. BDF 339 (2) (c)). There is the thought of purpose. Some MSS read 'the mystery of God' (the word occurs again in v. 7, there translated 'secret'), but we should accept *testimony* (as in 1:6). Preaching the gospel is not delivering edifying discourses, beautifully put together. It is bearing witness to what God has done in Christ for our salvation.

2. As was his custom (*cf*. Gal. 3:1), Paul excluded not only from his preaching, but even from his knowledge, everything but that great central truth. He *resolved to know* among them *nothing . . . except Jesus Christ* (the power and the wisdom of God, 1:24) *and him crucified*. The crucifixion is at the heart of the

gospel (for the force of the perfect participle *crucified* see on
1:23). On that Paul concentrated.

3. From the message Paul turns to the manner of the
preaching. He had had much to discourage him just before he
came to Corinth (see Introduction, pp. 19f.). He must have been
somewhat down-hearted, and this was reflected in his general
manner. In any case the Corinthians were not very impressed
by his personal presence (2 Cor. 10:10; in the second-century
Acts of Paul and Thecla Paul is said to be 'a man small of stature,
with a bald head and crooked legs, in a good state of body,
with eyebrows meeting and nose somewhat hooked'[1]). Paul
says that he had been without strength and afraid, even to the
point of trembling (Phillips, 'I was feeling far from strong, I was
nervous and rather shaky'). He did not, of course, fear men;
he feared God in the light of the task committed to him – it was
what Kay calls 'anxious desire to fulfil his duty'.

4. It is not easy to see the difference between *my message* and
my preaching. *Message* is literally 'word' and probably includes
both the manner and the matter of the preaching (as in 1:18).
Preaching means the content of the message (as in 1:21). Probably Paul is not differentiating between the two with any exact-
ness (Conzelmann speaks of 'rhetorical duplication'), but simply
uses two terms to bring out both the way he preached and the
content of his sermons. *Persuasive* translates a very unusual
word (not found anywhere before this passage). Paul is denying
that he used the methods of human wisdom when he preached.
Rather, his preaching had been a clear demonstration of the
power of *the Spirit*. The word translated *demonstration* (*apodeixis*)
means the most rigorous proof. Some proofs indicate no more
than that the conclusion follows from the premises, but with
apodeixis 'the premises are known to be true, and therefore the
conclusion is not only logical, but certainly true' (Robertson and
Plummer). Paul's very defects had afforded the most convincing
demonstration of the power of the Spirit. Though there was
nothing impressive about his preaching from a human stand-

[1] Cited from E. Hennecke, *New Testament Apocrypha*, ed. W. Schneemelcher, vol. 2
(Lutterworth, 1965), p. 354.

point, it had carried conviction. It was not human excellence that accomplished this, but *the Spirit's power* (*cf.* 2 Cor. 12:9; for the linking of power with the Spirit, *cf.* Rom. 15:13; 1 Thes. 1:5; with the gospel, Rom. 1:16).

5. *So that* (*hina*) indicates purpose. Paul's intention had been to ground his converts in the divine power and to make them independent of human wisdom. Wilson points out that 'a faith that depends upon clever reasoning may be demolished by a more acute argument, but the faith which is produced by the power of God can never be overthrown'. So Paul had refused to employ rhetorical arts and had concentrated on the message that was so unpalatable to natural men, the message of the cross.

C. A REVEALED MESSAGE (2:6–16)

1. The gospel is not human wisdom (2:6–9)
Up to this point Paul has been insisting that the gospel owes nothing to human wisdom. Both the message and the messengers were despised by this world's 'wise' and 'great' ones. Now he emphasizes the truth that the gospel embodies true wisdom, the wisdom of God. Héring and others think that Paul is here contrasting simple Christians, who know the story of the cross, with the more 'mature' who go on to profound wisdom. But his words do not bear this out. He is developing the thought that the divine wisdom which brought about Christ's saving act in the cross is the real wisdom, and further, that this wisdom is in total opposition to the worldly wisdom so beloved in Corinth.

6. *However* (*de*) introduces a contrast. Paul is rejecting 'men's wisdom', but not all wisdom. Actually *wisdom* comes first in the Greek with emphasis: *'Wisdom* we speak' – even if the world does not recognize it! (The Greek has nothing corresponding to NIV's *a message of*.) The plural *we*, coming after two emphatic 'I's' as it does (vv. 1, 3), is significant. It is not to be taken as equivalent to 'I' (as NEB), but it links Paul with other Christian teachers in a common understanding and proclamation of wisdom. They speak this wisdom *among the mature* (*teleioi*, which means those who have reached their end or aim, *telos*). Paul is possibly indulging in a little gentle irony at the expense of the Corinthians with their exalted estimate of their own spiritual state. More probably he is perfectly serious. Those who have welcomed the message of the cross are *mature*, whereas the worldly-minded who reject it are not. Conzelmann holds that Paul has in mind 'a higher class of believer' and that he is referring to a superior wisdom which only the more mature can receive. But Paul's contrast is rather between those who receive God's wisdom (the message of the cross) and those who do not (*cf.* Bornkamm, *TDNT*, iv, p. 819). Later Paul will face the fact that there are 'mere infants in Christ' (3:1), but that is not his concern at this point. And when he comes to it he will criticize the 'infants' for being deficient in love, not knowledge (*cf.* Bruce). The fact is that the New Testament writers do not envisage 'grades' of Christians. All believers should go on to maturity (Heb. 6:1). Some of the later Gnostics classified people into permanent groups according to their spiritual potential. They held that some were 'perfect', while others could never attain that standing. Paul is not making this kind of distinction. He is contrasting Christians (who have accepted the wisdom of the cross) with outsiders (who have not). It is *mature* to accept God's wise provision, even if the world sees it as folly.

With unwearied persistence the apostle points out that the *wisdom* of which he speaks is not *the wisdom of this age*. He has been stressing this for some time and he now adds *or of the rulers of this age*. In antiquity Origen took this to refer to the demonic powers behind world rulers, an interpretation which Chrysostom rejected, and this difference of opinion has persisted through the centuries. Among modern commentators Conzelmann, for example, sees a reference to the demons, while Orr and Walther think of earthly rulers. The 'demonic' view sees Christ as engaged in a gigantic struggle with evil forces of the unseen world, a view which is undoubtedly to be found in Paul's writings (*e.g.* Rom. 8:38–39; Col. 2:15; *cf.* 2 Cor. 4:4). But it may be doubted whether this is his meaning here. Three points are especially important. One is that throughout this whole passage the contrast is between the wisdom of God shown in the gospel and the wisdom of this world. To introduce now the thought of the wisdom of demonic powers is to bring in an extraneous concept, and one that is out of harmony with v. 9, which clearly refers to humans. Paul could scarcely have expected his readers to grasp this without one word of explanation. A second is that it was *the rulers of this age* who are said to have crucified Christ and this same word *rulers, archontes,* is repeatedly used of the Jewish and Roman leaders (Acts 3:17; 4:5,8,26; Rom. 13:3, *etc.*). The third is that it is explicitly said that they carried out the crucifixion in ignorance (Acts 3:17; 13:27; *cf.* Jn. 16:3), but, by contrast, the demons are often said to have known who Jesus was when people did not (Mk. 1:24,34, *etc.*). Paul habitually ascribes power to the demonic forces, but not ignorance. The very concept of a struggle between demonic forces and the power of God implies that the demons knew what they were up against. Paul's use of *this age* probably points to the transitory nature of the office of *rulers*, over against the truth of the gospel, which is permanent. This transitoriness is also in mind in the concluding *who are coming to nothing* (the verb is *katargeō*; see on 1:28). The *rulers* are being rendered completely ineffective; their vaunted power and wisdom are made null and void.

7. *No* is the strong adversative *alla*. The *wisdom* we speak is certainly not 'the wisdom of this age'; it is God's wisdom, and the word *God* is in an emphatic position. *Secret* translates *en mystēriō*, 'in a mystery', where 'mystery' does not mean a puzzle we find difficult to solve. It means a secret we are wholly unable to penetrate, but which God has now revealed: 'God's pre-temporal counsel which is hidden from the world but revealed to the spiritual' (Bornkamm, *TDNT,* iv, p. 820). At one and the same time it points to the impossibility of our knowing God's secret, and to the love of God which makes that secret known to us. The wisdom *has been hidden* (the perfect participle denotes a continuing state). Where unbelievers are concerned it remains hidden; they are still in the dark about it. It is revealed to believers, but it is not a matter of common knowledge among members of the human family.

Paul proceeds to stress the truth that the gospel is no afterthought. It was planned in the mind of God *before time began* (*cf.* Eph. 3:2–12). *Destined* translates the verb *proorizō*, which means 'to foreordain'. It stresses the plan of God and the sovereignty of God. *For our glory* adds the thoughts of the tenderness of God and of our supernatural destiny (*cf.* Rom. 8:18). Before time began God was concerned for our well-being; he planned the gospel that would bring us into *glory*.

8. God's secret was not known by any way other than revelation. For all their eminence *the rulers of this age* did not know it, as is shown by the fact that they crucified Jesus (*cf.* Acts 3:17; 4:25–28, and Jesus' words, 'they do not know what they are doing', Lk. 23:34). Had they really understood who Jesus was and the consequent enormity of rejecting him, they would never have done what they did. *The Lord of glory* ('the Lord whose essential attribute is glory', Ellicott) is an outstanding and unusual title, applied to Christ only here (though Jas. 2:1 is similar). The epithet *of glory* is applied to the Father (Acts 7:2; Eph. 1:17), and in the apocryphal *Book of Enoch* the expression *the Lord of glory* is used of God several times (22:14; 25:3; 27:3–4; 63:2; 75:3). More than one scholar has thought that this is the loftiest title Paul ever applied to Christ. It stands fitly alongside the application to him of words originally referring to Yahweh (1:31). Both show that Paul habitually assigned to Christ the highest place of all.

9. It is difficult to know the source of this quotation. The formula *as it is written* (*kathōs gegraptai*) is one Paul uses when citing Scripture, but there is no passage in the Old Testament that runs exactly like this. Perhaps the nearest is Isaiah 64:4, though some see parts of Psalm 31:20; Isaiah 52:15; 65:17 (note that 'mind' here is 'heart' in LXX). From the time of Origen some have thought that Paul was quoting from *The Apocalypse of Elias*, an apocryphal book now lost, or from *The Ascension of Isaiah*, but it is far from certain that either was in existence at the time (*cf. TDNT*, iii, pp. 988–989; v, p. 557). Another view is that it is a saying of Jesus not recorded in our Gospels. That there were such sayings is indisputable (*cf.* Acts 20:35), but whether Paul would cite them in this way is another matter. Where was this one written? On the whole it seems best to think of this as a rather free citation of Isaiah 64:4, with reminiscences of other scriptural passages.

Mind translates *kardia*, 'heart' (so AV). But 'heart' does not stand for the emotions as with us; among the Greeks the seat of the emotions was rather the intestines (*cf.* 'bowels of compassion'), while thought was located in the midriff, the diaphragm. 'Heart' stood for the whole of the inner life, including thought and will as well as the emotions, though sometimes it leans to one or another of these. Here the mind is perhaps most in view (*TDNT*, iii, p. 612 classes this passage under 'the seat of understanding, the source of thought and reflection'). Paul is saying that there is no method of apprehension open to us (eyes, ears, or understanding) which can give any idea of the wonderful things that God has made ready for *those who love him* (*cf.* Rom. 8:28). 'Not *gnōsis* but love is the touchstone of Christian maturity and spirituality' (Barrett). The verb *has prepared* reinforces the earlier thought that God is working out his plan (v. 7). The glories that come to believers are not haphazard, but are in accordance with God's plan from of old.

2. Words 'taught by the Spirit' (2:10–13)

Paul brings out the divine origin of the message by stressing the role of the Holy Spirit.

10. *To us* comes first in the Greek with emphasis; it is not the learned philosophers but the humble Christians to whom God's truth has been *revealed*. That it is *revealed* takes away all suggestion of superiority. There can be no feeling of pride when it is clear that all is of God. Believers can claim no special skill or insight, only that God has revealed truth to them.

Paul proceeds to emphasize the activity of the Spirit. He has mentioned him only once up till now, but in vv. 10–14 he speaks of him six times. It is the Spirit who made the revelation. And the Spirit *searches all things*, which means, not that he conducts searches with a view to obtaining information, but that he penetrates *all things*. There is nothing beyond his knowledge. In particular Paul specifies *the deep things of God*. *Deep* is often used of the mighty depths of the sea, and thus comes to mean the 'unfathomable'. It is impossible for any creature to know the innermost depths of the divine counsel, 'the depths of God'. But they are known to the Spirit, the Spirit who has revealed the truths of which Paul speaks.

11. The Spirit's insight into the mind of God is brought out by an analogy from the nature of man. Nobody can really know what is going on in a man's mind, nobody but the man's own spirit. From outside we can but guess. But the spirit of the man does not guess. He knows. In the same way, reasons Paul, no-one outside God can know what takes place within God, nobody but the Spirit of God. The Spirit knows God from the inside. This ascribes full deity to the Spirit. And it shows that the revelation of which Paul has been speaking is authentic. Because the Spirit who reveals is truly God, what he reveals is the truth of God.

12. Once again an emphatic *we* contrasts Christians with 'wise' heathen. Whatever be the case with others, *we* are led by God's Spirit. Some understand *the spirit of the world* to mean Satan, and this would give an excellent sense. However, Satan does not seem to be referred to in just this way (though 'the prince of this world', Jn. 12:31, comes near to it, and *cf.* Eph. 2:2). Further, it goes beyond what is required by the context. Throughout this passage Paul is opposing a 'wisdom' that is not satanic but human. It seems that we should accept some such meaning as 'the spirit of human wisdom', 'the temper of this world' (Lenski, 'It is what makes the world "world" '). Believers have not received the spirit of worldly wisdom. In passing we notice that the word for *world* here is *kosmos*, 'the ordered universe', not *aiōn*, 'age' (as in vv. 7–8), which means the world in its temporal aspect.

We who are Christ's have received *the Spirit who is from God* (*cf.* Gal. 3:2), and this brings the assurance that we have real knowledge. The Christian's certainty is a certainty of faith, but that does not make it any the less a certainty. He has under-standing of *what God has freely given us*.

13. And what we receive we pass on; the revealed truths are spoken by believers to others. This is not done *in words taught us by human wisdom*; the worldly-wise way is not the way to commend the truth of God. Rather, we teach *in words taught by the Spirit*. The Spirit's activity extends to providing the actual words used, and is not confined to the supplying of general ideas (*cf.* Mk. 13:11). As Moule says, the expression 'is a very bold but quite unambiguous use of the Subjective Genitive' (*IBNTG*, p. 40); the Spirit teaches the words.

This probably gives us the clue to the difficult expression that follows. It is fairly clear that the participle *synkrinontes* should be rendered 'combining'. It can mean 'comparing' (2 Cor. 10:12), but this is not usual and should be adopted only if the context plainly indicates it, which is not the case here. A surprising number prefer 'interpreting' or the like (*e.g.* RSV, NEB, Moffatt), but it would seem without sufficient reason. This meaning is found only in LXX, and there only of interpreting dreams. In each case the context makes this plain. It cannot be said to be a common meaning of the verb. We should retain the usual meaning, 'combining'.

We are to combine 'spiritual things with spiritual (*pneumatikois pneumatika*)'. There is no question about 'spiritual things' (NIV, *spiritual truths*), for *pneumatika* is neuter. But *pneumatikois* might be neuter or masculine. If neuter it means 'combining spiritual things with spiritual things', which probably signifies linking spiritual truths to spiritual words. If it is masculine we get combining spiritual truths with either 'spiritual men' or 'spiritual words' (since 'word' is masculine in the Greek). There seems no good reason for accepting a reference to men, so in one way or another Paul is saying that Christians combine 'spiritual things' with 'spiritual words'. They use words taught by the Spirit.

3. *Spiritual discernment* (2:14–16)

The presence of the Spirit makes all the difference. Without that, people lack discernment; with it they have the root of the matter within them.

14. *The man without the Spirit* ('the natural man', AV) has his limitations. *Psychikos*, 'natural', refers to the animal life. There is nothing inherently evil about it; it does not mean 'sinful'. But it does point to an absence of spiritual discernment, to the man whose horizon is bounded by this life (BAGD, 'one who lives on the purely material plane, without being touched by the Spirit of God'). It is the worldly-wise man again, the one who has been so much in Paul's thoughts throughout this passage. This man *does not accept* the things of the Spirit. The verb (*dechomai*) has an air of welcome about it; it is the usual word for the reception of a guest. But 'the natural man' does not welcome the things of the Spirit; he refuses them, he rejects them. He is not equipped to discern the activities of God's Spirit; to him they are no more than *foolishness* (*cf.* 1:18,21,23). Paul goes so far as to say that it is quite impossible for him to *understand* them (*cf.* Jn. 8:47). The reason is that they are *spiritually discerned*. The verb, *anakrinō* (ten times in 1 Corinthians, nowhere else in Paul) 'is used of judicial investigation, especially prior to the hearing proper' (*TDNT*, iii, p. 943; the corresponding noun is used of such a preliminary hearing in Acts 25:26). It comes to mean 'to scrutinize', 'to examine', and so 'to judge of', 'to estimate'. It may be that the use of a verb proper to a preliminary examination is by way of reminding us that all human verdicts are no more than preliminary. It is God who gives the final verdict. Anyone whose equipment is only of this world, who has not received the Holy Spirit, has no ability to make an estimate of things spiritual. 'The unspiritual are out of court as religious critics; they are deaf men judging music' (Findlay).

15. By contrast the *spiritual man* can form a judgment on *all things*. Paul is not, of course, referring to someone with a different natural endowment from the one he has just been considering. It is not a question of natural endowment, but of the working of the Spirit of God within him. When the Spirit enters the life everything is changed and one new thing that appears is the ability to make a right judgment. This does not mean that the man has acquired greatness; it means that the Spirit of God is guiding him. He has the point of reference within himself and is thus able to make judgments *about all things*. The force of *all* should not be overlooked. The spiritual principle is the basis of judgment on what we call the secular as well as the sacred.

Not subject to any man's judgment is to be taken in the sense 'any natural man'. It is clear from the whole tenor of Paul's writings that he did not hold that men in whom was the Spirit of God could not be called upon to account for their actions (*cf.* 14:29). Much of this epistle is a criticism, if a loving and spiritual criticism, of *spiritual* men. His point is that the *spiritual* man cannot be judged by the natural man for precisely the same reason that he himself can judge all things. He has the Spirit of God within him and the natural man has not. This makes him an enigma to the natural man. What does the natural man know of spiritual things? Because he cannot know spiritual things (v. 14), he cannot judge spiritual people.

16. This impossibility is shown by a question quoted from Isaiah 40:13. Paul has already spoken of the impossibility of knowing 'the things of God' (v. 11). Then his concern was to show that the Spirit does indeed have complete knowledge of 'the depths of God', and that is relevant here. As none but the Spirit knows these depths it is clearly impossible for the natural man to have knowledge of the person in whom is the Spirit, and who therefore, in a sense, shares in the divine (*cf.* 2 Pet. 1:4). It is because of this that Paul can make the bold assertion that *we* (the pronoun is emphatic) *have the mind of Christ*. He does not mean that every Christian can understand all Christ's thoughts. He means that the indwelling Spirit reveals Christ. The spiritual person accordingly does not see things from the viewpoint of the worldly. He sees them from the viewpoint of Christ.

Notice that the question in Isaiah 40:13 refers to the mind of Yahweh. But Paul moves easily to *the mind of Christ*, so closely does he associate the two.

D. MISUNDERSTANDING OF LEADERSHIP (3:1–9)

1. *Baby Christians* (3:1–4)
The conduct of the Corinthians shows that they have not progressed in the faith, but are still 'infants'.

1. The affectionate address *Brothers* softens the rebuke Paul is about to make; he must make it, but he makes it in love. In the days of the mission in Corinth he had not been able to address them as *spiritual*; in those early days the kind of maturity he has just been speaking about had not been possible. The converts had been *worldly* (*sarkinos*, which means 'fleshy, (made) of flesh', BAGD), which Paul explains as *mere infants in Christ*. There was nothing wrong in this at that time. It is inevitable that those who have just been won for Christ should be *mere infants in Christ*. Maturity comes from growth and development. It takes time. Beginners in the faith cannot be mature.

2. Paul taught them then in accordance with their position as 'infants'. It is not possible to speak 'wisdom among the mature' (2:6) when addressing potential converts and new converts. Paul gave them then *milk, not solid food* (*cf.* Heb. 5:12; 1 Pet. 2:2). He did not push the infant believers beyond their capacity, but gave them the teaching that was suited to their state. There was nothing blameworthy in their being 'not yet ready for it'. But it is otherwise when he says *you are still not ready. Indeed* (*all' oude*) is a strong expression 'used to introduce an additional point in an emphatic way' (BDF 448(6)). The present situation is different. It was all very well for the Corinthians to have been in the position of 'infants' when they actually were 'infants'. But they should have outgrown that state long since.

3. Paul gets to the root of the matter with his accusation that they are *still worldly*. He has changed his word for *worldly* from *sarkinos* (v. 1) to *sarkikos*. The *-inos* termination means 'made of . . .'; thus tablets 'made of stone', *lithinos*, are contrasted with those 'made of flesh', *sarkinos* (2 Cor. 3:3). The *-ikos* ending rather means 'characterized by . . .'; we see it in *psychikos* of the 'natural' man and *pneumatikos* of the 'spiritual' man (2:14–15). The difference between *sarkinos* and *sarkikos* is like that between 'fleshy' and 'fleshly' (*cf.* Lenski, ' "fleshy," and you cannot help it; "fleshly," and you can but do not help it'). The more thoroughgoing word is *sarkinos*, but there is no blame attaching to it as applied to those who are young in the faith. But *sarkikos*, 'characterized by flesh', when used of those who have been Christians for years, is blameworthy. The mature believer is *pneumatikos*, 'characterized by spirit'. To be characterized instead by flesh, as the Corinthians were, is the very opposite of what Christians should be. 'Flesh', of course, as often in Paul, is used in an ethical and moral sense. It indicates the lower aspects of human nature (*cf.* Rom. 13:14; Gal. 5:13,19; Eph. 2:3, *etc.*).

The accusation is made specific: there is *jealousy* and *quarrelling*. The former word means basically something like 'zeal', 'ardour'. It is usually ranked as a virtue by classical writers, and sometimes also by New Testament writers (*e.g.* 2 Cor. 7:7; 11:2). But this temper all too easily leads to envy and the like, and characteristically the New Testament writers use the word for that evil thing that is one of 'the works of the flesh' (Gal. 5:20). For *quarrelling*, *cf.* 1:11. Both terms point to self-assertion and unhealthy rivalries. Whereas Christians should be considerate of others (*cf.* Rom. 12:10), the Corinthians were asserting themselves (*cf.* 4:8). Paul asks whether this is not *worldly* (*sarkikos*), and *acting like mere men*. This last expression means 'like natural men' (2:14).

4. *For* gives the reason for this. *When* is the indefinite *hotan*, 'whenever'; each time such an affirmation is made Paul's point is demonstrated over again. It is not clear why he repeats the catch-cries of only two of the parties, but it may be significant that he selects those of Apollos (who might be thought to be close to him, *cf.* 4:6), and himself. Again he asks, *are you not mere men?* (Moffatt, 'what are you but men of the world?'). Their outlook is that of worldly wisdom, not that of Spirit-filled men. Paul has been hammering away at this ever since he introduced the matter of the dissensions (1:10–12). The divisions were a standing witness to the worldly mentality of the Corinthians, not to their spiritual perception. Where they should have been 'spiritual' (2:15) or 'mature' (2:6), they were but 'fleshly'.

2. The true relation between Paul and Apollos (3:5–9)
Paul proceeds to develop the thought that people like himself and Apollos are no more than servants, depending on one

another and on God. It is God who brings about spiritual growth.

5. The neuter *What* (*cf.* 'anything', v. 7) where we expect 'Who' takes attention away from the persons of the preachers and concentrates it on their functions. *Servants* translates *diakonoi*, a term which originally meant a table waiter. It came to be used of lowly service generally, and in the New Testament it is often used of the service that any Christian should render to God. In time it was applied to one of the regular orders of the ministry, the deacon, but this is not an example of that use. The term stresses the lowly character of the service rendered and ridicules the tendency to make much of preachers. Who would set servants on pedestals? The real work is done by God; Paul and Apollos are no more than instruments *through whom* he does his work. These ministers could work only 'as the Lord gave' to them.

6–8. The process is likened to agriculture. Paul *planted* and Apollos *watered* (the same verb as that rendered 'gave' in v. 2), but neither made the plants grow. The comparative unimportance of their work is clear. It is only God who *made it grow*. This verb is imperfect, whereas those for planting and watering are aorist. The work of Paul and Apollos is viewed as completed, but God's activity in giving the increase goes on.

Having established this important point, Paul proceeds to draw conclusions. Neither the planter nor the waterer is important (Conzelmann says this breaks up the Paul and Apollos parties; 'Both lose their heads'!). The attention of the Corinthians should have been fastened on God, who alone effects all spiritual work, and not on his unimportant instruments. Further, there is an essential unity between planter and waterer. Obviously the work of neither can be successful without that of the other. So far from being rivals, Paul maintains that he and Apollos *have one purpose* (really, 'are one'). This does not minimize their distinctive contributions; Paul goes on to point out that each has his own responsibility. Each will receive his own 'wage' (so, rather than *be rewarded* for *misthos*; BAGD defines the word as 'pay, wages'; *cf.* Lk. 10:7), and that *according to his own labour*. Only God, of course, can determine what the 'wage' will be; it is not for us to try to work out who is deserving of more! Notice further that the criterion is not 'his success', nor 'how he compares with others', but *his own labour*.

9. Three times in this verse the word *God* comes first: 'God's fellow-workers are we; God's field, God's building are you.' This puts strong emphasis on the divine action. Ministers and those they serve are no more than God's instruments. All is of God and all belong to God. The Greek translated *we are God's fellow-workers* could be understood as 'we are partners working together for God' (GNB), which would suit the context very well. Despite its attractiveness, however, we should probably not accept it, for the more natural way to understand the Greek is *God's fellow-workers* (*cf.* Mk. 16:20). It is a startling expression, which sets forth in striking fashion the dignity of Christian service. As someone has said, 'Without God, we cannot; without us, he will not.'

The word for *field*, *geōrgion*, occurs only here in the New Testament. It can mean *field* ('farm', Orr and Walther; 'garden', NEB), or the process of cultivation. There is a similar ambiguity about *oikodomē*, *building*, which may signify the edifice or the process of erection. Either sense is suitable here. Paul may be saying that the Corinthians are the field, the building, in which God is at work, or that they are that work in cultivation and building. Incidentally, the metaphor of building is a favourite one with Paul, but it is not often found in the New Testament outside his writings.

E. THE FOUNDATION AND THE BUILDING (3:10–17)

1. *The test of good building* (3:10–15)

Paul develops the thought of building, his emphasis being on the quality of the materials used. With Christ as the foundation of the Christian life, it is important that the building be worthy.

10. Paul ascribes his work at Corinth to *the grace God has given*. *Grace* means more than 'commission' (Moffatt, Goodspeed), or 'gift' (GNB), or 'kindness' (LB). Such translations miss the thought of God's enabling power. Paul insists on the primacy of God and the insignificance of God's ministers. He speaks of himself as *an expert builder*, where *expert* translates *sophos*, 'wise' (which recalls the discussion of 'wisdom' in chs. 1,2). *Builder* is *architektōn*, the man who superintends the work of building. Plato differentiates him from the *ergastikos*, 'workman', as one who contributes knowledge rather than labour (Robertson and Plummer). Paul laid the foundation, but *someone else* was carrying on the work of building. Paul cautions every builder to be *careful*. *Each one* (*hekastos*, twice more in v. 13) points to individual responsibility. Many commentators restrict the application of this passage to the work of teachers, and it surely has special reference to their work. But the words seem capable of more general application and vv. 16–17 certainly refer to a wider circle. It is true of every believer that he is building on the one foundation. Let him be *careful* how he builds. Exactly what is being built? Some, impressed by the emphasis on right teaching, think it is sound doctrine. Others see a reference to building the church, or building up Christian character. Probably none is completely out of mind, and it is best to see the reference as quite general.

11. Paul does not leave the *foundation* open to choice, with the implication that he just happened to lay the foundation he did. There is only one possible foundation and that is *already laid*, namely *Jesus Christ*. That is basic. No-one can begin anywhere else, a truth still worthy of emphasis in the light of attempts to build 'Christianity' without Christ, on a foundation of good works, or humanism, or the like.

12. But if there can be only one foundation it is otherwise with the superstructure. It is all too possible for astonishing varieties to make their appearance. Paul lists several materials which may be used for building, and ingenuity has sometimes been exercised in trying to find edifying meanings for them all. Such labour is probably in vain, for Paul seems concerned simply with two classes, the valuable, typified by *gold, silver, costly stones*, and the worthless, the *wood, hay or straw*. The workman may try to make the building as worthy of the found-ation as possible. Or, in slovenly fashion, he may be content to put into it that which costs him little or nothing. *Costly stones* may be 'precious stones' used for ornamentation, or costly build-ing materials, like marble.

13. There will come a time of testing for all we build. *The Day* is not further defined, but clearly it is the day when Christ returns, the day of judgment (*cf.* 1 Thes. 5:4; Heb. 10:25). That day is often referred to in terms of the believer's joy at being united to the Lord. But it will also be a time when the work God's people have done will be judged. Here the thought is that of a searching test, one likened to *fire*. The picture is that of fire sweeping through a building. It consumes what is combustible, but leaves metal and stone. The quality of the work *will be shown*, for the Day will *bring it to light*, 'show it in its true character', 'reveal it for what it is'. The 'it' in *It will be revealed* may be the *work*, but is more probably the *Day*. The meaning is 'the Day reveals itself (or, is revealed) in fire' (*cf.* Mal. 4:1); the present tense perhaps gives a greater sense of certainty.

14–15. The test in fire will determine whether or not a man will receive a 'wage' (*misthos*, see on v. 8; here it is the wage of the building worker whose work is approved; *cf.* Lk. 19:16–19; Rev. 22:12). All those considered here are saved, for they have built on the one foundation, Jesus Christ. Even of the one whose work is burnt up it is said that *he himself will be saved*. The distinction is not between the lost and the saved, but among the saved between those who have built well and those who have built poorly. *He will suffer loss* means he will lose his wage, a workman fined for poor workmanship. Being saved 'as through fire' (RSV) may have been a proverbial expression to indicate one saved and no more (like the brand plucked from the burning, Am. 4:11; Zc. 3:2). The imagery is that of one who has to dash through the flames to escape to safety. The fire is, of course, a fire of testing, not one of purifying, and the passage lends no support to the doctrine of purgatory as some claim (see Godet for a refutation).

2. The temple of God (3:16–17)
Paul brings out the sacredness of the community of believers by likening the building to a temple in which God dwells.

16. *Don't you know* introduces a mild rebuke and is a device Paul uses ten times in this letter (and once only elsewhere). It introduces a question on a matter which ought to be common knowledge. Believers are *God's temple*, which makes it clear that Paul is addressing the whole church, not teachers only. There is no article with *temple* in the Greek, but this does not imply that there are several temples (though Godet renders 'a temple of God', saying 'The Church of Corinth is not the universal Church'). It simply puts a certain emphasis on their character as God's temple. There are two Greek words for 'temple', *hieron*, which includes all the temple precincts, and *naos* (used here) which denotes the shrine proper, the sanctuary. It points to the very presence of God. This is brought out explicitly with the assertion that *God's Spirit lives* in the Corinthian believers. The expression 'the Spirit of God' is not common. It emphasizes the connection of the Spirit with the Father and underlines the deity of the Spirit. The Spirit is God as he dwells in his church. The words are sometimes applied to the individual believer, but the thought is rather that the whole community of believers is God's shrine. *Temple* is singular, but *you* is plural; the reference is to the church (the individual is also God's temple, as we see from 6:19, but that is not the thought here).

17. The seriousness of the divisions at Corinth is seen in the light of this understanding of the church. Because it is *God's temple* anyone who fails to react rightly towards it is guilty of no light sin. The repetition of the verb *destroy* shows that the punishment is not arbitrary; it 'fits the crime'. To engage in making divisions is to *destroy* the divine society and thus to invite God to *destroy* the sinner. The word is not specific and cannot be pressed to mean either annihilation or eternal torment. It simply makes it clear that one who commits a grave sin lays himself open to a grave penalty. In v. 15 the bad workman is yet saved. Here a greater sin than inferior workmanship is in mind, and salvation is excluded. *Sacred* (*hagios*) means something like 'set apart for God'. In the plural it is the usual New Testament word for the 'saints', those who are God's people. The word draws attention to the character of the church as God's own possession, so that its 'destruction' is a very serious matter. The concluding words, 'such are you' may be understood as NIV, *you are that temple*, or 'of such kind are you' (Lenski). Either way, *you* is emphatic (both by the use of the pronoun and by coming last in the sentence); it brings home the character and hence the responsibility of the readers.

F. THE PREACHERS' LOWLY PLACE (3:18 – 4:13)

1. *Worldly wisdom is foolishness* (3:18–23)

Paul further rebukes the divisions in the Corinthian church by showing that the preachers, whom they have set up so high, are really very lowly. He leads up to this with a further treatment of the 'foolishness' of worldly 'wisdom', a subject which has occupied him already and which is important enough to be treated again. The things of God are not to be estimated in accordance with the rules of the philosophers.

18. Paul calls for realism: *Do not deceive yourselves* (this verb occurs in Paul six times and nowhere else in the New Testament). The present imperative suggests that some were in fact deceiving themselves; they should stop it. Clearly some of the Corinthians saw themselves as *wise* in attaching themselves to a particular teacher. But such 'wisdom' accords with the standards *of this age*, a transient affair as the word itself hints. In the Greek 'among you' immediately precedes 'in this age'; the two are set in contrast. The believer is both in the church and in the world, but his relationships to the two are different. Paul counsels the reader to *become a 'fool' so that he may become wise.* If anyone is to have genuine spiritual insight he must become what the world calls 'a fool'. True wisdom is found in renouncing 'the wisdom of this world' (*cf.* 2:14–15).

19. Paul had asked, 'Has not God made foolish the wisdom of the world?' (1:20). He returns to the thought with his assertion that the world's wisdom is *foolishness in God's sight*. He comes back to this again and again. The worldly-wise, whom the Corinthians held in such high esteem, are totally unable to understand 'the wisdom of God' (1:24), though the humblest believer can appreciate it. God's wisdom is for ever hidden from the wise of this world; their wisdom is but *foolishness* where it counts, *i.e. in God's sight*. Is this Paul's private opinion? Not at all. Scripture says so. Paul quotes Job 5:13 in a version differing from LXX and which may be his own translation from the Hebrew. *Panourgia, craftiness*, originally meant 'a readiness to do anything'. From this it developed a meaning rather like our 'cunning'; it might be used in a good sense, but the bad sense tended to predominate. Paul is not minimizing the capacity of the worldly-wise within their own field. But he stoutly denies that their *craftiness* is of any value when they stand before God. 'Though *craftiness* may deceive men, it cannot deceive God' (Hillyer).[1]

20. In the second quotation (Ps. 94:11) it is not certain whether Paul has substituted *the wise* for 'men' to bring out the best that the world can do, or whether he is quoting from a manuscript which no longer survives. His point is that God knows the thoughts of every one. Nothing can be hidden from him. Moreover he knows the emptiness of such thoughts; they are *futile* (*mataioi*; 'without result', 'fruitless'). The 'wise' are unable to effect any solid achievement. The end result of their vaunted wisdom is futility. It is all concerned with things that pass away.

21–22. Paul turns the thoughts of the Corinthians away from the wisdom of men that had meant so much to them; *no more boasting about men!* For Paul there was a legitimate place for boasting (1:31), but he does not find it in *men*. The Corinthians

---

[1] Orr and Walther illustrate the point from Edward Hall's Chronicle, which tells of Bishop Tonstall's purchase of Tyndale's translation of the Bible in order to burn the books. But Tyndale used the money to print an increased number of Bibles so that in the end the bishop aided the cause he sought to destroy. Hall comments that Tonstall thought 'that he had God by the toe, when indeed he had . . . the devil by the fist'. Orr and Walther go on, 'Paul's quotation from a Psalm is to the same intent: human reasoning in no way outwits God.'

were glorying in the creature; the Christian glories in the Creator.

Paul, however, does not develop his argument in that direction. Rather he reasons, 'Why do you limit yourselves by claiming that you belong to a particular teacher? Do you not realize that all teachers, indeed all things that are, belong to you in Christ?' So far from enriching themselves by staking their claim to exclusive rights in one teacher, the Corinthians were impoverishing themselves. They were cutting themselves off from greater treasures that were really theirs. Paul says *All things are yours*, not simply 'all Christian teachers'. He puts no limit to their possessions in Christ (*cf.* Rom. 8:32, 38–39). Diogenes Laertius could say, 'all things belong to the wise' (vii. 125), but Paul's horizon is broader. He is not confining himself to the things of this world (as Diogenes was), as his next words show.

The apostle particularizes by referring first to the three teachers to whom the Corinthians claimed to belong. So far from being outstanding people at the head of large and influential parties, the teachers *are yours*. They belong to those whose ministers they are ('minister'='servant'; see on v. 5). In a lyrical passage Paul goes on to assure his friends that they possess all things, present or to come. The *world* (*kosmos*) is the ordered physical universe (here the word is not used in the ethical sense). We find the clue to the references to *life* and *death* in Paul's saying, 'to me, to live is Christ and to die is gain' (Phil. 1:21). Life in Christ is the only real life. And Christ has overcome *death*, so that for the Christian it is not disaster but 'gain' (*cf.* 15:55–57), though to the unbeliever it is the end of everything. Thrall comments, 'Every possible experience in life, and even the experience of death itself, *belongs* to Christians, in the sense that in the end it will turn out to be for their good.' *The present* and *the future* add up to an impressive total. Paul does not mention the past, perhaps because we were not responsible for it and we can do nothing about it. But it is otherwise with the present and the future. These belong to the Christian; he rejoices to co-operate with the purpose of God in both. Paul rounds off his list of our possessions with the comprehensive *all are yours*.

23. But he does not stop there. Believers have great possessions, certainly. But only because they are Christ's. We should probably translate *de* by 'but' (JB) rather than *and*. Paul is not adding another to the list of possessions, but by contrast turning to responsibilities (*cf.* 6:19–20). Believers should live lives of service befitting those who 'are Christ's' (NIV has *you are of Christ*, but the possessive is like that in the previous verses); their lives should tell forth what they are. The self-assertiveness of the Corinthians was out of character for Christians. They were acting as though they were their own masters, whereas they really belonged to Christ.

The passage reaches its climax with 'Christ is God's'. We have noticed more than once how Paul sets Christ on a level with the Father. This passage does not contradict such teaching, for Paul is not speaking of Christ as he is in his essential nature, but with reference to his saving work. He does not lose sight of the deity of the Son. But he does not lose sight either of the truth that the Son became man, and took a lowly place that he might bring about our salvation. There is a strong statement of this subordination in 15:28. There, as here, the thought is that the Son did indeed take a place among men when he took upon him to deliver man. He, too, is God's.

2. God's commendation is what matters (4:1–5)

From the glorious possessions of the Corinthians Paul turns to the preachers. He shows that the judgment of men on ministers (and 'men' includes the partisan Corinthians) is of no importance. It is before God that they stand or fall, and only God is able to give a true and valid judgment on them.

1. *So then* roots the argument in what has just been said. Given these truths about Christian service, certain things follow about the apostles. People should see them as *servants of Christ*, where *servants* is not the word used in 3:5 (*diakonos*), but *hypēretēs* (which Paul uses only here). It meant originally an 'under-rower', *i.e.* one who rowed in the lower part of a large ship. From this it came to signify service in general, though generally service of a lowly kind ('subordinates', NEB), and subject to direction. The preachers are also *those entrusted with the secret* *things of God. Those entrusted with* translates *oikonomoi*, a term which refers to the person who supervised a large estate ('administrators', Héring; 'managers', Goodspeed). Unless he was to be a slave to his slaves, a rich landowner had to find someone to do the routine work of running the estate. This deputy was called an *oikonomos* (*cf.* Lk. 16:1). He held a responsible position; he was set over others and directed the day-to-day affairs. But he was subject to a master and was often a slave. Then in relation to the master he was a slave, but in relation to the slaves he was the master. For *secret things* (*mystērion*) see on 2:7. The sphere of the preachers' responsibility is God's revelation.

2. Paul appeals to contemporary practice with regard to *oikonomoi*. In the nature of the case the work of such a man was not closely supervised; if the master was to check up on everything he might as well do the job himself. The prime requirement in an *oikonomos* accordingly was that he be *faithful* ('trustworthy', NEB). This applies to all believers, not just apostles, as we see from the use of the word of Christians generally (1 Pet. 4:10).

3. 'To me' comes first in the Greek with emphasis; Paul contrasts his attitude to that of the Corinthians. They valued human judgments highly; Paul dismissed them. The preachers were indeed the servants of the Corinthians, but the Corinthians were not their masters. Their only Master is God. So it is a very small matter what the Corinthians think of them, or for that matter what anyone else thinks of them (*cf.* Rom. 14:4). *Am judged* renders the verb *anakrinō*, used in 2:14f. (where see notes). Strictly it means not final judgment, but the critical preliminary examination that leads up to that judgment (Moffatt, 'cross-question'). Paul is not interested in any preliminary human sifting; he prefers to await the Judge. *Human court* translates a curious expression meaning literally 'human day' (*cf.* Acts 28:23). It is found on an amulet of the second or third century (cited in BAGD), but as far as I know nowhere else. 'Day' seems to point us to a day of judgment (*cf.* 3:13; *cf.* also our 'day in court'). Paul is saying that it matters little to him whether people pass a judgment on him or not. 'This does not mean that he was not hurt by their criticism, but that he was not moved by it' (Wilson).

He takes this to its logical conclusion; his own judgment is irrelevant. It is, of course, very difficult to make an accurate assessment of one's own achievement, and Paul's point is that in any case it does not matter. His own views about himself are as irrelevant as are those of anyone else. The Christian is to be judged by his Master. Introspection is not the way forward. Often people think that they know exactly what their spiritual state is and just what their service for God has effected. The result may depress beyond reason or exalt beyond measure; neither is relevant. It is not the task of the servant to pass such judgments, but rather to get on with the job of serving the Lord. This does not, of course, mean that there is no place for times of heart-searching and self-scrutiny with a view to more whole-hearted and more efficient service. It is the attempt to anticipate the verdict of the Lord that Paul is condemning.

4. NIV omits 'for' (*gar*) which ties this in with the preceding argument. Paul is not aware of any great matter in which he has failed in his Christian service, but he does not rest his confidence in that. *Make me innocent* translates *dedikaiōmai*, a legal word which means 'acquitted' (JB), 'declared "not guilty" '. Paul delights to use it of the believer's standing in the sight of God; it is the ordinary word for 'justify'. Here it is probably not used in this technical sense; rather Paul is saying that the verdict on whether he had been faithful in his ministry was given by *the Lord*, not his own conscience. *Judges* is *anakrinō* once more. While there is no emphasis here on the preliminary character of the judging, it accords with the meaning of this verb that the final judgment does not appear until the next verse. *The Lord*, as commonly in Paul, denotes the Lord Jesus (*cf.* 2 Cor. 5:10).

5. Arising from all this is an exhortation not to *judge* (*krinō*) prematurely. The use of *mē* with the present imperative may imply that the Corinthians had been engaging in this activity. 'Stop judging' is then the force of it. *Till* renders *heōs an* with the subjunctive, a construction that means that the coming of the Lord is certain, but the time is unknown. The Lord's judgment will be perfect, for he will *bring to light what is hidden in darkness*. Quite often in the New Testament *darkness* has an ethical significance and Paul may thus be referring to evil deeds. But here it seems better to take it of all those deeds which in this present darkness are kept hidden. *The motives of men's hearts* ('the most inward intentions of the inner life', G. Schrenk, *TDNT*, i, p. 635) are the secret desires and drives, good and bad alike. Only the Lord's judgment can take account of these secret things (*cf.* Rom. 2:16), and this is the judgment that counts. Anyone who is praised then has *praise from God*, the only praise that matters. Conzelmann sees this *praise* as 'a question of reward, not of merit' and notes that the word is used by magistrates. *From* (*apo*) denotes the source and thus the finality of the judgment. It comes from God. There can be no appeal against it.

3. *Learn from Paul and Apollos* (4:6–7)

Paul has been speaking about the function of ministers, more particularly of himself and Apollos. It might be thought that he was addressing his remarks primarily to such preachers, laying down how they should think of themselves and their work. But this is not so. His concern has been to teach the Corinthians and he proceeds to make this clear.

6. This use of the verb translated *applied* (*meteschēmatisa*) is unique. The word means 'to change the form of', 'to transform' (Phil. 3:21); it may be used of disguising oneself (2 Cor. 11:13–15). Here the meaning appears to be that Paul has done something like use a figure of speech (the noun *schēma* is often used of a rhetorical figure): 'I have given this teaching of mine the form of an exposition concerning Apollos and myself' (BAGD; *cf.* Phillips, 'I have used myself and Apollos above as an illustration'). Paul's concern for the Corinthians comes out in the affectionate address, *brothers*, and the affirmation that what he has done is *for your benefit*.

Paul amplifies this with a statement of his purpose, though unfortunately what he says is not clear to us (Conzelmann says that the Greek is 'unintelligible' and Héring and others delete it). NIV reads smoothly, but it has inserted the verb *go* which is absent from the text. Paul is saying something like 'that you may learn in us the "not beyond what is written" '. The article points to the following words as a well-known saying, possibly one used by the Corinthians or by Paul when he was at Corinth. Either way, it was a catch-cry familiar to both Paul and his readers. 'What is written' employs the formula Paul generally uses when quoting holy Scripture. The problem is that there is no passage in the Old Testament that runs exactly like this. Accordingly some have suggested a reference to some other writing. On the basis of the papyri Parry argues for the sense, ' "not to go beyond the terms," i.e. of the commission as teacher'; cf. GNB, 'Observe the proper rules'. This is possible, but it is more likely that Paul is referring to Scripture, even though he does not cite a particular passage. M. D. Hooker thinks he is referring to the quotations he has just made (3:19–20); the Corinthians, by adding 'their philosophy and rhetoric' to the simple gospel, were going beyond 'what is written' (NTS, x, 1963–64, pp. 127–132). Paul is saying that, by considering what he has said about Apollos and himself, they will learn the scriptural idea of the subordination of man. Uniformly the Bible elevates God. The Corinthian emphasis on the teachers meant that they were thinking too highly of men. Paul does not want them to *take pride in one man over against another*. There is a sense in which Christians may legitimately rejoice in the leadership given by their spiritual men. But when they find themselves so much in favour of one leader that they are *against another* they have overstepped the bounds. This is the evil of partisanship. The verb *take pride* (*physioō*, 'to be puffed up') occurs six times in this letter (again in 4:18, 19; 5:2; 8:1; 13:4), once in Colossians, and nowhere else in the New Testament. Evidently Paul regarded it as particularly appropriate in the case of the Corinthians. They, more than others, were addicted to the sin of pride. What is party spirit other than oneself writ large?

7. Paul's *you* is in the singular; he is addressing his remarks to an imaginary Corinthian who has become 'puffed up'. The verb *makes . . . different* (*diakrinei*) means first, 'to put a difference between', and then, 'to regard as superior'. It is probably the latter use here (*cf.* Robertson and Plummer). The rhetorical

75

question is followed by a second which reminds them that they have no native endowment that they did not receive from God, and this by a third which points to the stupidity of boasting about what is, after all, a gift given by God and in no sense a personal achievement. It is the point made in the rejection of worldly wisdom all over again. By the standards of the world the Corinthians may have had something to boast about. But Christians do not accept the standards of the world. They realize that in themselves they are nothing. They owe everything to the grace of God. There is no place at all for such worldly activities as boasting.

4. *The trials endured by the apostles* (4:8–13)

Paul turns from his explanation of principles to show something of the lowliness of the apostles as seen in the many trials they had to endure. He does this in the form of a contrast between their wretched lot and the comparative ease of the Corinthians. The result is an impassioned and incisive piece of prose, with irony so biting that some have felt that Paul can scarcely be addressing the church as a whole. They point out that there is nothing like it elsewhere in the entire letter and suggest that here he has in mind the leaders only. But this is a precarious inference. There is no indication at all that Paul is addressing a different audience here. The whole church would hear the letter read, and, in the absence of some mark of a change of addressees, would take it as meant for them all.

8. *You have all you want* (*kekoresmenoi este*) translates a verb that is used properly of food (*e.g.* Acts 27:38). It denotes satiation (LB, 'you already have all the spiritual food you need'), a feeling of satisfaction. In contrast to those on whom Jesus pronounces a blessing ('Blessed are those who hunger and thirst for righteousness', Mt. 5:6), the Corinthians felt no lack. The next two verbs, *you have become rich* and *you have become kings* both indicate that the Corinthians felt themselves secure and in want of nothing, a dangerous state (*cf.* Rev. 3:17; contrast Rom. 8:17). Moffatt appositely cites the Stoic catch-cry (taught by Diogenes): 'I alone am rich, I alone reign as king'; *cf.* also Philo, 'the kingdom of the Sage comes by the gift of God' (*On Abraham*, 261). Far from

76

the Corinthians having progressed in the Christian faith, they were approximating to the Stoic ideal of self-sufficiency. Some take *without us* to mean 'without our help', but in view of the second part of the verse it means rather 'without our company'. The Corinthians thought that they had attained a position to which neither Paul nor the other apostles dared lay claim. Paul expresses the wish that they really were in the royal position they imagined. Then perhaps he and his associates might be linked with them in this splendour! The construction Paul employs implies that the wish has not been fulfilled: 'Would that you did reign (though in fact you do not)' is the sense of it.

9. This brings us to the actual plight of the apostles. Paul thinks of God as having set them where they were. He is not railing at some cross fate, but calmly accepting what God has done. The repeated references to the present (down to v. 13) shed light on the hardships Paul had to endure at Ephesus (*cf.* 16:8; Acts 19:23ff.). The verb *has put* (*apedeixen*) conveys the thought that it is owing to divine action that they are in the place where they are; God has appointed them to this position. The imagery is derived from the arena, as Moffatt's rendering brings out, 'God means us apostles to come in at the very end, like doomed gladiators in the arena!' *Epithanatious, condemned to die,* is a rare word, and apparently refers to condemned criminals who were often paraded before the public gaze as objects of derision. They are *a spectacle* (*theatron* means 'theatre', and thus 'what one sees at a theatre'). The apostles are exhibited on a vast stage, for they are a spectacle *to the whole universe* (*kosmos*), *to angels as well as to men* (for the angels as spectators of human happenings *cf.* 11:10; Jn. 1:51; 1 Tim. 3:16; 5:21; 1 Pet. 1:12, *etc.*). The combination *angels* and *men* embraces the totality of personal existence.

10. Paul steadily brings out what is involved in being made a public spectacle. His first point is that the apostles are *fools for Christ*. Once again he directs attention to the incompatibility between what the world counts as wisdom and what Christians esteem. Paul has referred to this more than once, but this time he introduces a startling contrast by asserting that the Corinthians are *so wise in Christ!* His word for *wise (phronimos)* is different from that used hitherto in this letter *(sophos)*. There is no great difference in meaning (Conzelmann speaks of 'rhetorical variation'), though it is possible that by using a different word he puts some difference between his readers and the worldly-wise he has castigated earlier. But it is also possible that he is hinting that 'this Church is on dangerously good terms with the world' (Findlay). He means not that the Corinthians were actually wise, but that they claimed treasures of wisdom which Paul could not claim for himself. Similarly they held themselves to be *strong* and *honoured (endoxoi,* 'eminent', 'glorious'), whereas Paul knew himself to be *weak* (2:3; *cf.* 2 Cor. 10:10; 12:10), and *dishonoured* (*cf.* 2 Cor. 11:24–25; his word is *atimos,* 'without honour', sometimes used of those deprived of citizenship).

11. Paul now drops comparisons and concentrates on the hardships suffered by the apostles. He is not thinking of the distant past, but of what happens *to this very hour*. The apostles lacked food (which is in sharp contrast to 'you have all you want' in v. 8), drink, and clothing. They were *brutally treated,* where Paul's word *(kolaphizō)* is that used of the ill-treatment accorded Jesus (Mt. 26:67). K. L. Schmidt sees it as indicating insult as well as maltreatment (*TDNT,* iii, p. 819, n. 5).

12. On several occasions Paul refers to the fact that he earned his own living (*e.g.* 1 Thes. 2:9; 2 Thes. 3:8; *cf.* 1 Thes. 4:11). This is all the more significant in that the Greeks despised all manual labour, thinking of it as fit only for slaves. He is referring to really hard work; his verb indicates labour to the point of weariness. In the middle of this verse Paul changes his construction and turns attention to the reaction of the apostles to the hardships they experienced. They *are cursed* (another word used about Christ, 1 Pet. 2:23), but their response is *we bless* (*cf.* Mt. 5:38–45; Lk. 6:27–36, especially v. 28). They *are persecuted,* but simply *endure it*.

13. When they *are slandered* they *answer kindly*. Such conduct did not commend itself to the Greeks, for whom it was evidence of pusillanimity, a lack of proper manliness. Throughout this whole passage Paul emphasizes the contradiction between the values of the Christian and the worldly-wise Greek. He reaches his climax with two very expressive terms, translated *scum* and *refuse*. The former, the plural *perikatharmata* means 'things removed as the result of cleaning all round'. It is the refuse after a thorough cleaning, the filth that is thrown out. It does not differ greatly from *refuse*, *peripsēma*, which is simply a little more precise. It is 'that which is wiped off by rubbing all round'. Because the removal of filth has the effect of cleansing, both words came to have the derived meaning of 'propitiatory offering', that offering that cleanses from sin. It was not used of sacrifices in general, but of human sacrifices which were offered in some places. We might think this would give the words a noble tinge, but not so. The people who were sacrificed were those who could most easily be spared, the meanest and most worthless in the community. On *perikatharma* F. Hauck says three strands meet, 'the expiatory offering, that which is contemptible, and that which is to be thrown out' (*TDNT*, iii, p. 431), while G. Stählin finds that *peripsēma* among other things suggests that they 'were poor and useless people . . . who threw away their own lives . . . in a ridiculous way' (*TDNT*, vi, p. 90). Paul's point then is that the apostles were regarded as the most contemptible of people (*cf*. La. 3:45). *Up to this moment* (which comes last in the Greek) once more brings out the point that his sufferings were not past history. He was describing the present position of the apostles. The Corinthians might claim a splendid place, but Paul was under no illusion about the place reserved for such as him in this world.

G. A PERSONAL APPEAL (4:14–21)

There is a marked change of mood at this point, but we should bear in mind that Paul's letters are real letters, not systematic theological treatises. Real letters not infrequently contain abrupt changes of tone and mood like this one.

14. Paul's sternness gives way to tenderness. What he has

79

said might be understood as an attempt to make the Corinthians feel shame. On occasion Paul can intend to do just that (6:5; 15:34), but not here. He has the warmest of feelings for his *dear children*, and his purpose is simply *to warn* them. His verb (*noutheteō*) does indeed convey the thought of blame for wrong-doing (it is often translated 'admonish'), but it is criticism in love that is meant as this verse shows plainly. The cognate noun is used of the duty of a father to his children (Eph. 6:4).

15. We see Paul's affection in his reference to the unique tie between him and the Corinthians. They may have *ten thousand guardians*, but not one of them is a *father* to them, and it is that that Paul became *through the gospel*. It is not easy to translate *paidagōgous* (NIV, *guardians*), for in our community we do not have the equivalent. The word referred to a slave who had special responsibility for a boy. 'The *paidagōgos* was the personal attendant who accompanied the boy, took him to school and home again, heard him recite his "lines", taught him good manners and generally looked after him; he was entitled to respect and normally received it' (Bruce). Clearly he was important, but Craig reminds us that he could be a quite worthless slave and that he could be replaced. There was a great difference between him and the father. By virtue of his activity in founding the church at Corinth Paul stood in the relation of a father in Christ to the believers (*cf.* 9:2; Phm. 10). This makes two things clear. The one is that his affection for them was, in the nature of things, great (*cf.* Chrysostom, 'He is not here setting forth his dignity, but the exceeding greatness of his love'). The other is that, no matter how much they had profited from the ministry of others, they owed most of all to Paul; they should therefore heed his injunctions.

16. Thus he can appeal to them *to imitate* him (*cf.* 11:1; Gal. 4:12; Phil. 3:17; 2 Thes. 3:7,9). He does not wish to attach his followers to himself personally; that would be in contradiction of the whole tenor of this passage. He wants them to imitate him only so that they may in this way learn to imitate Christ (*cf.* 11:1; 1 Thes. 1:6). While in the different circumstances of today preachers may well hesitate to call on others to imitate them, it still remains that if we are to commend our gospel it must be because our lives reveal its power.

17. Not much is known about Timothy's visit to Corinth (see Introduction, p. 23). Clearly Paul felt that trouble was beginning and he sent Timothy to clear it up. NIV takes the aorist as epistolary, *I am sending*, but most see it as the past tense; Paul had already sent him. This is supported by the fact that Timothy is not included in the greetings at the beginning of this letter (contrast 2 Cor. 1:1; *cf.* 1 Thes. 3:2). He was sent to *remind* the Corinthians of Paul's 'ways (NIV, *way of life*) in Christ Jesus'. Once more appeal is made to Paul's example; the term 'ways' probably reflects his Jewish background, for it 'seldom has a moral significance in Greek' (Barrett), whereas the Jews made much of it in the rabbinical concept of *halakah* (rule based on Scripture). Paul makes the further point that he was not making exceptional demands on the Corinthians, but that *which agrees with what I teach everywhere in every church* (*cf.* 7:17; 11:16; 14:33,36). He had said and done the same kind of thing at Corinth as elsewhere, and he looked for the same kind of behaviour there as elsewhere in the church.

18. Some had *become arrogant* (see note on 'puffed up', v. 6). They had evidently asserted confidently that Paul would not visit their city again. They would have pointed out that it was Timothy, not Paul, who was to visit them. They would say that Paul did not dare to face them; the Corinthians then had nothing to gain from adherence to Paul, and nothing to fear from opposing him.

19. Paul assures them that such assumptions are erroneous. He will come *very soon*, subject always to the proviso *if the Lord is willing* (*cf.* 16:7 and the note there). He is not a free agent. He is subject to the Lord's direction and recognizes that the Lord may not open up the way for him to go to Corinth at this time. But his point is that it is only divine restraint of this kind that will stop him. There is a characteristic Pauline differentiation between words and deeds (2:4,13; 1 Thes.1:5; *cf.* Rom. 1:16). His opponents at Corinth may be good talkers, but

can they show *power*? The gospel does not simply tell people
what they ought to do; in it God gives them power to do it. It
does not matter whether Paul's opponents can speak well, but
it does matter whether the power of God is manifest in them,
'that spiritual efficacy, with which those are endowed who
dispense the word of the Lord with earnestness' (Calvin).

20. *The kingdom of God* is the most frequent topic in the
teaching of Jesus. It is not so prominent in the rest of the New
Testament, but Paul speaks of it several times in this epistle
(6:9-10; 15:24,50). The kingdom involves divine power, as in
the casting out of devils (Lk. 11:20), and it is power that is
emphasized here. God's kingdom is not simply good advice; it
is more than *a matter of talk*, 'for how small an affair is it for any
one to have skill to prate eloquently, while he has nothing but
empty tinkling' (Calvin). People know what they ought to do.
The trouble is that, knowing the good, they do the evil. They
need God's power to enable them to live as befits his kingdom.
There is probably an intentional contrast with the claims of the
Corinthians (v. 8). Here is true royalty.

21. The question is not whether Paul will come, but how he
will come. He puts the issue squarely before them. He could
come *with a whip*, *i.e.* in sternness, ready to chastise and rebuke.
Or, he could come *in love and with a gentle spirit*. But this assumes
that they are ready to receive him as such. The choice rests
with the people of Corinth.

III. MORAL LAXITY IN THE CHURCH (5:1 – 6:20)

Paul turns from one manifestation of the pride of the Corinthians to another, this one an unsavoury sexual sin. In the
ancient world the Jews had high standards of sexual morality,
but laxity was rife elsewhere, specifically among the Greeks.
The Christian attitude to the prevailing practice was one of
uncompromising opposition. The Corinthians, however, proud
in their emancipation in Christ, seem to have felt that they
could take a line quite different from that of other believers,

even though this meant condoning serious sin. This brings forth Paul's stern rebuke.

A. A CASE OF INCEST (5:1-13)

1. The fact (5:1-2)

Paul draws attention to a case of incest at Corinth. He says more about the church's error in countenancing it than he does about the offender's guilt. He says nothing about the woman, which may mean that she was a pagan (v. 12).

1. The beginning is rather abrupt; Paul is not wasting time on niceties. The exact nature of the sin is not clear. *Sexual immorality* (*porneia*) strictly denotes the use of the harlot (*pornē*), but comes to signify any form of sexual sin. *Has* might mean 'has as wife' or 'has as concubine'. *His father's wife* probably does not mean 'his mother', else Paul would have said so. But whether it means that the offender had seduced his step-mother, or that the woman was divorced from his father, or that the father had died, leaving her a widow, is not clear. What is quite clear is that an illicit union of a particularly unsavoury kind had been contracted. That it *does not occur even among pagans* does not mean that it never occurred, but that it was infrequent and that it was condemned as evil. It was, for example, forbidden by Roman law, and, of course, by the Old Testament (Lv. 18:8; 20:11; Dt. 22:30; 27:20). Perhaps we should notice that Hurd tries to minimize the evil by seeing it as 'a real possibility' that Paul is referring to a 'spiritual marriage' (p. 278). But could a spiritual union be called *porneia*?

2. The attitude of church members to this happening had been all wrong. They were *proud* ('puffed up'; see on 4:6); their view of their superior standing, rather than a decent Christian humility, had governed their behaviour. Evidently they saw their Christian freedom as giving them licence for almost any kind of conduct (*cf.* 6:12; 10:23). Paul says that they should rather *have been filled with grief*. His verb (*epenthēsate*) is often, though not by any means exclusively, used of mourning for the dead. It may accordingly be a hint that the church has suffered a bereavement (*cf.* Moffatt, 'You ought much rather to be mourning the loss of a member!'). Paul uses the conjunction *hina*, which, in this context, may indicate contemplated result, *i.e.* what the result of the mourning would have been, the removal of the offender. Or it may be equivalent to an imperative, 'Let him . . . be taken away' (*cf.* RSV, Moffatt).

2. The punishment of the offender (5:3–5)
Matters cannot be allowed to rest there. Paul proceeds to the punishment that must be given to the offender.

3. 'For' (which NIV omits) links this with the foregoing; what follows arises out of what Paul has already said. *I* is emphatic. The Corinthians had failed in their duty, but the apostle's attitude is in sharp contrast. Those who were present and might have been expected to take action had done nothing. He who was absent, and might have pleaded distance as an excuse for inaction, was taking strong measures. Paul has a striking description of a disciplinary assembly. He himself is *not physically present*, but he is there *in spirit* (*cf.* Col. 2:5). He has *already passed judgment*, where the perfect tense of his verb gives an air of finality to the sentence. He does not name the offender, but characterizes him from his deed.

4. Verses 3–5 are one long and difficult sentence in the Greek. The biggest problems arise from the fact that we can take *in the name of our Lord Jesus* and 'with' (which NIV omits) *the power of our Lord Jesus* with more than one part of the sentence. Conzelmann lists six possibilities and there are others. Here are seven possible views.
   1. We could take 'in the name' with 'when you are assembled', and 'with the power' with 'hand over' ('assembled in the name . . . and hand over with the power . . .').
   2. Both could go with 'are assembled' ('assembled in the name and with the power').
   3. Both could go with 'hand over' ('hand over in the name and with the power').
   4. Both could go with both.

5. 'In the name' could go with 'hand over' and 'with the power' with the participial clause 'when you are assembled' ('when you are assembled with the power . . . to hand over in the name . . .').

6. 'In the name' could go with 'passed judgment' and 'with the power' with 'you are assembled' ('I have passed judgment in the name . . . when you are assembled with the power . . .').

7. 'In the name' could go with 'passed judgment' and 'with the power' with 'hand over' ('I have passed judgment in the name . . . with the power you are to hand over . . .').

It is not possible to rule out any of these absolutely and we can only assume that with the knowledge the Corinthians had of Paul and of the situation they knew which to choose. We do not. On the whole I favour no. 5 on the grounds that the solemn formula *in the name* is more likely to go with the main verb to *hand over* than with the subordinate participle ('being gathered together'), and that the reference to *the power* brings out the solemn nature of the assembly. It is not only a gathering of a few obscure Corinthians. The apostle is there in spirit and the Lord Jesus is there in power.

5. To *hand over to Satan* is a very unusual expression (elsewhere only in 1 Tim. 1:20). Whatever else it means, it seems to include excommunication (see vv. 2,7,13). The idea underlying this is that outside the church is the sphere of Satan (Col. 1:13; 1 Jn. 5:19; *cf.* Eph. 2:12). To be expelled from the church accordingly is to be delivered over into that region where Satan holds sway. It is a very forcible expression for the loss of all Christian privileges. Deissman argues, on the basis of certain heathen texts, that the words point to 'a solemn act of execration' (*LAE*, p. 303). More difficult is 'for the destruction of the flesh'. It is not easy to see how expulsion from the church could have this effect. Two solutions have won support. One sees 'the flesh' as the lower part of man's nature, and takes the passage to mean the destruction of the sinful lusts (so NIV, *that the sinful nature may be destroyed*; *cf.* Redpath, he 'is to be given over to Satan until that principle of yieldedness to the flesh is ended'). But it is difficult to see how handing a man over to Satan would have such a purifying effect; we would expect the reverse, the

stimulation of those lusts. Yet the possibility remains that Paul
has in mind the effect on the offender of being severed from
all that fellowship in the church means. The contrast between
a present experience of the things of Satan and the nostalgic
recollection of the things of God might cause a revulsion of
feeling and conduct, the fleshly lusts being destroyed.

The other view is that 'the flesh' is to be understood as
physical, the reference being to sickness and even death. The
difficulty is in seeing how this could be effected by excommunication. But Paul speaks of physical consequences of spiritual
failings (11:30). We see the extreme example of this in the case
of Ananias and Sapphira (Acts 5:1–10); *cf*. the blindness of
Elymas (Acts 13:8–11). Paul's own 'thorn in the flesh' was 'a
messenger of Satan' (2 Cor. 12:7). It may well be that Paul
envisages the solemn expulsion of this offender as resulting in
physical consequences. It is the effect of being withdrawn from
the secure realm of the church of God. On the whole this second
view seems the more likely. Chrysostom sees it this way, but
also understands the reference to the flesh 'to lay down regu-
lations for the devil', which prevent him from going too far.
Chrysostom cites the case of Job, where Satan could afflict Job's
body but not take his life (Jb. 2:6f.). Paul sees the punishment
as remedial: though the flesh be destroyed it is so that *his spirit*
may be *saved*. That this means saved in the fullest sense is made
clear by the addition, *on the day of the Lord*. At the final day of
judgment he expects to see the disciplined offender among the
Lord's people.

3. *Exhortation to clean out all evil* (5:6–8)
Paul insists that resolute action be taken to deal with the
offender, for the church must not countenance evil.

6. *Boasting* means strictly the matter of boasting, not the
activity (*cf*. 9:15; Rom. 4:2): 'what you boast about is not good'.
The Corinthians did more than acquiesce in the situation; they
were proud. Paul borrows an illustration from the kitchen to
show the dangers in their attitude. It requires only a very small
amount of yeast to leaven quite a large lump of dough (*cf*.
Mt. 13:33; Gal. 5:9). By keeping the offender within the fold

they were retaining the bad influence, and it would inevitably spread. Moffatt cites Thomas Traherne, 'Souls to souls are like apples, one being rotten rots another.' It is also the case that by their *boasting* the Corinthians were admitting evil into their own lives. In time it would work through their whole being. Sin must be put away resolutely, else in the end the entire Christian life will be corrupted.

7. There is a 'Become what you are' situation. The Corinthians are *a new batch without yeast*, they really are. But really to be that new batch they must *get rid of the old yeast*, where Paul's verb (*ekkathairō*) means 'clean out'. Sin is dirty and defiling, and like *yeast* it will work until it permeates the whole. The only remedy is to clean out the evil entirely. So Paul speaks of *a new batch without yeast*. The Christian church is not just the old society patched up. It is radically new (2 Cor. 5:17). The evil that characterizes worldly people has been taken away, and they are 'free from corruption' (Weymouth). Paul does not say 'You ought to be without yeast', but states it as a fact; that is what Christians actually are. Therefore they must not bring back *the old yeast*, which, in this context, of course, symbolizes evil.

For introduces the reason for this confident assertion. The great fact that makes all things new is that *Christ, our Passover, has been sacrificed* (it is astonishing that several translations insert 'lamb', as NIV; it is not in the Greek and it is incorrect, for the sacrifice might be a kid; Paul simply says *pascha*, 'passover'). Christ is for believers what the passover was for the Jews. In Egypt they had offered their sacrifice in order that the destroying angel might pass over them. They had been delivered, and a slave rabble emerged as the people of God. Paul is using this imagery to remind his readers that the death of Christ had delivered them from slavery to evil and made them the people of God. There is emphasis on emergence to new life, and here the symbolism of yeast makes an important point. Ancient Israel was commanded to remove all yeast before the sacrifice (Ex. 12:15; 13:7), and in Paul's day a feature of passover observance was a solemn search for and destruction of all yeast before the feast began. This had to be done before the *pascha*, the kid or lamb, was offered in the temple. Paul points out that *Christ, our Passover* has already been sacrificed. It is time and more than time that all yeast (*i.e.* all evil) was put away.

8. The Christian life is a continual *Festival* (*let us keep* is present continuous). The believer does not observe this feast according to the standards of the old life he has left. The *old yeast* is *the yeast of malice and wickedness*. Evil is characteristic of the old way of life. By contrast, the believer's perpetual festival is kept with *sincerity*, which refers to purity of motives, and with *truth*, which points to purity of action. Both are so characteristic of the Christian as to be compared to his necessary food, his *bread*.

4. *A misunderstanding cleared up* (5:9–13)
The Corinthians had misunderstood what Paul wrote on this subject in an earlier letter. He proceeds to make it clear.

9. Some take *I have written* as an epistolary aorist, in which case it refers to this letter. But Paul has not so far written about not associating with the *sexually immoral*, and anyway the Corinthians could not misunderstand this letter before it came to them (Lenski). It seems clear that Paul is referring to an earlier letter, now lost (see Introduction, pp. 22f.). The verb *to associate with* (*synanamignysthai*) is an expressive double compound, used outside this passage only once in the New Testament (2 Thes. 3:14; see note in *TNTC*, p. 149). It means 'to mix up yourself with'; Paul has forbidden them to have familiar intercourse with sexual offenders.

10. But his directions had been misunderstood or misrepresented, as though he meant that they must have no contact with this world's evil people. This was *not at all* his meaning. Circumstances would inevitably arise in which they must meet with gross sinners. He adds to 'fornicators' (*immoral*, NIV), *the greedy*, *i.e.* those possessed by the desire to have more, the spirit of self-aggrandizement. From the spirit Paul passes to the deed. *Swindlers* are those who seize something (*harpages*), robbers in any shape or form. They are linked with *the greedy* as one class (there is but one article, they are joined by *kai*, *and*,

and separated from the rest by *ē, or*). Such sinners have a wrong relationship to people, and Paul goes on to *idolaters* (incidentally the first occurrence of this word in literature), who have a wrong relation to God. Evil people abound and it is not possible to live without some contact with them. Paul is not forbidding that. For that they *would have to leave this world* (*cf.* Jn. 17:15).

11. There is a rather stronger case for holding that 'I wrote' is an epistolary aorist here than was the case in v. 9 (NIV so takes it with *I am writing*). But it is not likely that Paul would use the same expression in different senses so soon and in such close connection. Even the *now* does not require this. The sense will be 'But now (you see) I wrote . . .' ('What I meant when I wrote . . .', Bruce). His point had been that they must not maintain intimate fellowship (the same picturesque word as in v. 9) with *anyone who calls himself a brother*, but denies his profession by the way he lives. He is not really *a brother*, but 'a fornicator' or the like. To the evils already castigated Paul adds two more, the *slanderer* (*loidoros*, one who abuses others, *cf.* Mt. 5:22), and the *drunkard*. That such people should be found in the church shows the background of some of the early converts. Small wonder that they found it difficult to enter all at once into all that the Christian way means. But Paul will not compromise for a moment. Believers are to have no intimate intercourse with people who continue in such practices. *Do not even eat* will refer primarily to ordinary meals (*cf.* 2 Jn. 10), not to Holy Communion, though that, too, would be forbidden. When we reflect that Jesus ate with sinners and that Paul regards it as permissible to accept invitations to eat in heathen homes (10:27), the detailed application of this injunction is not easy. But the principle is plain. Where anyone claims to be a Christian but leads a life that belies his profession, there is to be no such close fellowship as will countenance his sin.

12. The verse begins with 'for' (which NIV omits): two facts will validate what Paul has just said, judgment inside the church and outside it. There is a difference. It is no business of Paul's, or for that matter of the Corinthians, to judge outsiders, but the Corinthians must judge *those inside*. It was their responsibility to discipline their own members. The question looks for an affirmative answer and thus makes this responsibility plain.

13. Just as v. 12 insists that the church take action in discipline, so v. 13 limits the scope of that action. It is no part of the church's function to discipline those who are not its members. *God will judge* (the verb could be present or future) outsiders. Paul ends with a quotation from Scripture (Dt. 17:7, *etc.*). They are to expel the offender, and leave him to God's judgment, he having now become one of *those outside*.

The application of all this to the modern scene is not easy. Our different circumstances must be taken into account. But Paul's main point, that the church must not tolerate the presence of evil in its midst, is clearly permanently relevant.

B. LAWSUITS (6:1–11)

Some of the Corinthians were going to law with one another. Paul rebukes them for this (1–6), and then for actually defrauding one another (7–8); he goes on to speak of the kind of conduct that excludes people from the kingdom of God (9–11).

1. Paul recognizes that disputes will occur, but these should be settled within the brotherhood. He uses a strong word for *dare* (*cf.* Héring, 'has the audacity'); it is far from the conduct looked for in believers. *Dispute* (*pragma*) is common in the papyri in the sense 'lawsuit' (MM). The *ungodly* (*adikoi*, the 'unjust' or 'unjustified') means those outside the church. Paul is not saying that the secular courts in Corinth were corrupt, but that they were composed of unbelievers. Such courts did not regulate their thinking or actions by the law of God. He is not complaining that believers would not obtain justice in heathen courts, but saying that they had no business being there at all. This was a principle to which the Jews adhered firmly. We read in the Talmud, 'R. Tarfon used to say: In any place where you find heathen law courts, even though their law is the same as the Israelite law, you must not resort to them' (*Gitt.* 88b; the Qumran community had a similar law, Millar Burrows, *The*

Dead Sea Scrolls (Secker & Warburg, 1956), p. 235). Paul says Christians should do no less.

2. Paul's *Do you not know . . .?* occurs six times in this chapter; it emphasizes that the Corinthians should know better than to do what they are doing. That *the saints* will assist in the final judgment of *the world* goes back to the teaching of Jesus (Mt. 19:28; Lk. 22:28ff.); indeed it occurs in Old Testament prophecy (Dn. 7:22). There is no passage where Jesus explicitly says that all believers (*the saints*) will share in the judgment, but Paul appeals to it as well known. The reference to angels (v. 3) shows that *the world* (*kosmos*) has the same wide sense as in 4:9, the entire universe of intelligent beings. Some hold that *judge* is to be taken in the Hebraic sense of 'rule'. This is possible, but the context deals with lawsuits, not government. *Cases* translates *kritērion*, a word which signifies 'a means of judging, test, criterion', then 'a tribunal, law-court' (AS, who notes that the meaning 'law-case' is 'doubtful'). 'Court of justice' is a frequent meaning in the papyri (MM). Here the sense will be, 'are you unworthy to judge in the least important courts?' (so Bruce, Barrett, and others).

3. *Angels* is without the article, which directs attention to their quality or character. They are by nature the highest class of created beings. Yet the saints *will judge* them. Accordingly the Corinthians should have realized that they were quite capable of judging *the things of this life*. This translates one Greek word, *biōtika*, which means the ordinary things of common life. *How much more* (*mēti ge*) is a strong expression, occurring only here in the New Testament. The conclusion is inescapable.

4. The *if*-construction (*ean* with the subjunctive; contrast *ei* with the indicative in v. 2) carries the delicate implication that such lawsuits should not arise. *Disputes* is *kritēria* (see on v. 2), and should be understood as 'if you do have courts' (Barrett), though several translations agree with NIV. At the end of the verse NIV takes the verb as imperative, *appoint as judges*; it is then a direction to the community to appoint judges from among their own number, and in doing so to choose *men of* *little account in the church.* This would indicate contempt for the judicial process – even 'the despised' (so the expression is translated in 1:28) are good enough for that! But it is question-able whether Paul really regards judges in this way, and it is not easy to think that he would seriously call any believer 'despised'. It is better to take the words as a question: 'how can you entrust jurisdiction to outsiders, men who count for nothing in our community?' (NEB; so RSV, Conzelmann, *etc.*). In accepting Christ believers deliberately rejected the standards of the world. It is completely out of character for them to go to law by such worldly standards and to submit to the judgment of 'men who count for nothing' among them.

5. 'I say to you, "For shame!" ' (Orr and Walther). Earlier Paul was not writing to shame his readers (4:14), but it is different here. It appears from his treatment of wisdom at the beginning of the letter that the Corinthians prided themselves on their wisdom. But now the apostle can ask whether they have even one wise man among them. *To judge* is an aorist infinitive with the meaning 'to give a decision' (rather than 'conduct a trial'). The word implies not litigation, but 'an amicable settlement by means of arbitration' (Grosheide). *Between believers* is really 'between his brother', where we should supply 'and another'; NIV misses the point that it is 'brothers', people who should be united, who are in dispute.

6. A string of argumentative questions is typical of Paul's style, and this may be another in the chain, 'Does brother go to law . . .?' (NIV's *instead* is not in the Greek). The question is broken with *and this*. It is extraordinary that brother should want to go to law with brother at all. But if he did, it was even more extraordinary that he should do so before *unbelievers*. This last word is without the article: it is their quality as lacking faith to which Paul draws attention.

7. To go to law with a brother is a defeat in itself, whatever the outcome of the legal process. *You have lawsuits* might be translated 'you get judgments (*krimata*)'. The gaining of the verdict matters little. The cause is already lost when a Christian institutes a lawsuit. The injurious effects are implied in the expression 'among yourselves'; the injury is to the body of Christ, not to outsiders. More biting questions drive home the point that a real victory might be obtained rather by choosing to *be wronged*, to *be cheated*. Jesus taught his followers to turn the other cheek, and, when sued at law for their tunic, to yield up their cloak as well (Mt. 5:39–40), and he set them an example (1 Pet. 2:23). But the Corinthians were far from basic Christian principles. Indeed, they were far behind the best Greek thought, for Plato can say that it is better to suffer wrong than to do wrong (*Gorgias* 509C).

8. They were even farther away than all this implies. Not only were they not ready to suffer wrong, but they were actively doing wrong, defrauding their fellows. Sharp practice is not uncommon in society at large, but there is no place for it among Christians. The addition *to your brothers* does not imply that the sin was not very serious when committed against unbelievers. It is serious no matter who is wronged. But the Christian, besides exercising love towards all people, must exercise 'love of the brothers'. Those in Christ have a special care for one another. The Corinthians were thus committing a double sin. They were sinning against ethical standards, and they were sinning against brotherly love.

9–10. Paul again appeals to what is common knowledge (see on v. 2). *Wicked* lacks the article in Greek, thus putting emphasis on the character of these people, not the unrighteous as a class. The word *God* immediately follows *wicked* in the Greek; the two are set in sharp contrast. Wicked people cannot be found in that kingdom that is *the kingdom of God* (see on 4:20). *Inherit*, as often in the New Testament, is not used in the strict sense, but with the meaning 'enter into full possession of'. Paul proceeds to list ten forms of evil that are incompatible with the kingdom, six being repeated from 5:11. He adds *adulterers* and two words denoting the passive and active partners in homosexuality. The inclusion of *idolaters* in a part of the list stressing sexual vice may point to the immorality of much of the heathen worship of the day. The second part of the list puts the emphasis on

93

sins against others. *Thieves* (*kleptai*) are petty pilferers rather than brigands. For the other offenders see the notes on 5:10–11. Paul's point is that people who practise such vices have no part in the kingdom of God.

11. The tremendous revolution brought about by the preaching of the gospel comes out in the quiet words, *And that is what some of you were*. It was no promising material that confronted the early preachers, but people whose standards were of the lowest. It had required the mighty power of the Spirit of God to turn people like that away from their sins, and to make them members of Christ's church. Three times Paul uses the strong adversative *alla*, *but*, to stress the contrast between the old life that they had left, and the new life in Christ. The first verb, rendered *you were washed*, is in the middle voice, and while some take it as equivalent to a passive (as NIV), it is better to retain the middle force, 'you got yourselves washed' (as in Acts 22:16). It may be, as many recent commentators think, that this refers to baptism, but if so, it will be the inward disposition and not the outward action that the verb denotes. But there is nothing in the context to point to baptism and Paul may have in mind a metaphorical washing (*cf.* 'To him who loves us and has washed us from our sins by his blood', some MSS of Rev. 1:5). The prefix *apo* points to the complete washing 'away' of sins. The tense is past, the aorist referring to one decisive action. *You were sanctified* is in the same tense and will here indicate God's act in setting them apart to be his. *You were justified* is another aorist; it looks back to the time when they were accepted as just before God. It is a legal term used of acquittal, 'reckon as righteous', 'declare righteous', 'acquit'. Paul uses it for the act of God whereby, on the basis of Christ's atoning death, he declares believers to be just, and accepts them as his own. It is unusual to have a reference to justification following one to sanctification. There may be a certain emphasis on the character involved in sanctification. Or, as Calvin held, all three verbs may refer to the same thing, though from different angles.

The *name* brings before us all that is implied in the character of the Lord, while the full title, *the Lord Jesus Christ*, brings out the dignity of him whom we serve. To this is joined *the Spirit of our God*. There is a power manifest in Christian living, and that power is divine, given by the very Spirit of God. Notice what has been called the 'unobtrusive Trinitarianism' of these words. It was from such statements that the doctrine of the Trinity would in due course develop.

C. FORNICATION (6:12–20)

Paul has spoken of a specific case of incest (ch. 5). Now he deals with the general principle governing sexual practices. First he shows that what the Christian does with the body is determined by what God has done for him (12–14). Then he goes on to apply this to the specific evil of sexual sin (15–20).

12. *Everything is permissible for me* occurs twice here and twice more in 10:23. It looks like a catch-phrase the Corinthians used to justify their conduct, possibly one they had derived from Paul's teaching when he was among them. He would perhaps have said something like this by way of an assertion of Christian freedom over against Jewish legalism and the like. Other religions laid down rules that must be kept if people were to be saved (food laws were especially common). To abstain from specified forbidden things was a necessary part of attaining salvation. Not so Christianity. The believer will avoid evil things, but this is not a path of merit, earning salvation. Salvation is all of grace. It depends on what God has done in Christ. The believer is not hedged around with a multitude of restrictions. All things are lawful. But this liberty must be lived out in the spirit of Augustine's maxim, 'Love, and do what you will.' If we love, in the sense in which the New Testament understands love, we need no other guide. The Corinthians, however, were taking Christian liberty to mean, not an unbounded opportunity to show the scope of love, but an incredible means of gratifying their own desires.

Paul agrees with the statement of Christian freedom, but he immediately goes on to an important qualification: *not everything is beneficial*. Some things are not expressly forbidden, but their

95

results are such as to rule them out for the believer. There is a second reason for caution, *I will not be mastered by anything*. There is a play on words which Edwards (following Chrysostom) renders, 'All things are in my power, but I shall not be overpowered by anything.' There is some emphasis on 'not I'. Paul would not allow himself to be brought under the control of anyone or anything. How could he when he was 'the slave of Christ' (7:22; Rom. 1:1, *etc.*)? There is an ever-present danger that we bring ourselves into bondage to the very things we do by way of asserting our Christian freedom.

13. *'Food for the stomach and the stomach for food'* looks like another expression used by the Corinthians. Eating is a natural activity, and they apparently held that one bodily function is much like another. Fornication is as natural as eating. Paul rejects this with decision. The belly and food are transient ('God has no permanent plans for the stomach!', Wilson); in due course God will do away with both (for *destroy* see note on 'nullify' in 1:28). But the body is not destined to be destroyed. It is to be transformed and glorified (15:44,51; *cf.* Mt. 22:30; Phil. 3:21). There is no such connection between *the body* and sensual lusts as between *the stomach* and *food*. God did not design *the body* for *sexual immorality* as he did *the stomach* for *food*. Rather the connection is between *the body* and *the Lord*. Most agree that whereas *sarx*, 'flesh', expressed for Paul thoughts like those of man in his weakness, his sin and his fallen estate, *sōma*, 'body', is rather the whole personality, man as a person meant for God. 'While *sarx* stands for man, in the solidarity of creation, in his distance from God, *sōma* stands for man, in the solidarity of creation, as made for God' (J.A.T. Robinson, *The Body* (SCM Press, 1952), p. 31). The body cannot be dismissed as unimportant; the body is *for the Lord*. It is the instrument wherein we serve God. It is the means whereby we glorify God. *The Lord for the body* shows that just as food is necessary if the stomach is to function, so is the Lord necessary if the body is to function. It is only as God enables us that we can live the kind of life for which we were meant.

14. The resurrection dominated early Christian thinking, as we see from the early chapters of Acts, and, indeed, from the whole New Testament. That the Father raised the Son from the dead, and did not simply cause his soul to persist through bodily dissolution, shows something of the dignity of the body. Bodily life enshrines permanent values. The resurrection forbids us to take the body lightly. Here, as usually in the New Testament, the resurrection is attributed to the action of the Father (though occasionally we read of Jesus rising). Closely connected is the future resurrection of believers, a subject Paul will deal with at greater length in ch. 15. Here it is enough for him to draw attention to the fact of the resurrection as showing the importance of the body. If it is to be raised it must not be put into the category of things that will be destroyed. That this is due to the divine initiative is stressed in the reference to *his power*. There is an exact correspondence. Food is for the stomach and the stomach for food, and the end of both is destruction. The body is for the Lord and the Lord for the body, and resurrection is the destiny of both. In passing we notice that Paul classes himself with the dead at the parousia (as in 2 Cor. 4:14); he can also put himself among the living (1 Thes. 4:15). It is precarious to draw inferences from such statements about whether he thought he would live until the parousia or not.

15. For the fourth time in this chapter Paul appeals to what his readers know with *Do you not know . . .?* Members (*melē*) is the ordinary word for parts of the body (*cf.* Rom. 6:13,19). That believers are the body of Christ is more fully developed elsewhere (12:12ff.; Eph. 5:23ff.). The point here is that believers are united to Christ in the closest fashion; they are 'in Christ'; they are members of his body. It is this that makes sexual vice so abhorrent. The word rendered *take* (*airō*) means 'take away'; the horrible thing about this sin is that *the members of Christ* are taken away from their proper use (the service of Christ) and made 'members (*melē* again) of a prostitute'. The sinner is, of course, not 'a member' of a prostitute in the same sense as he is 'a member' of Christ. But the use of the same word both times brings out something of the intimacy and incongruity of the union with the prostitute. There is a horrible profanation of that which should be used only for Christ. This would be even more so if the Corinthian prostitute was connected with the temple, for then the act would form a link with the deity. Paul recoils from it with an emphatic *Never!* This renders *mē genoito*, 'may it not be'. All but one of the New Testament occurrences of this expression are in the Pauline writings, though this is the only example in this epistle. It is a strong repudiation of the suggestion that has been made. Paul will have nothing to do with it. 'Perish the thought!'

16. Yet again Paul appeals to what his readers know. The view he is expounding of the nature of the sexual act is no private opinion, but one known and accepted by the Corinthians, and one found in Scripture (Gn. 2:24). D. S. Bailey says that Paul's application of this passage 'displays a psychological insight into human sexuality which is altogether exceptional by first-century standards' and he goes on to speak of the act as 'an unique mode of self-disclosure and self-commitment' (cited by Bruce). The Corinthians had not thought through the implications of their sexual laxity. Anyone who unites with a prostitute by that act becomes one with her. 'Casual sex' is anything but casual. It is an act of sacrilege. Temples like our bodies are not meant for profanations like this.

17. As in v. 16, Paul uses the strong verb *kollaō* (*unites*), a word used of close bonds of various kinds. In the literal sense it means 'to glue'; it comes to have metaphorical meanings, but clearly it points to a very close tie, indeed. In v. 16 Paul uses it of the physical bond with the harlot. Those who share the sexual act become 'one body'. Now he uses the same verb for the spiritual tie that links the believer to the Lord. Those joined by the spiritual tie become 'one spirit'. Believers are one with their Lord. They have 'the mind of Christ' (2:16). They react the way the Lord would react.

18. *Flee* fornication, says Paul. The present imperative indicates the habitual action, 'Make it your habit to flee'. It cannot be satisfactorily dealt with by any less drastic measures. The believer must not temporize with it, but flee the very thought. Paul goes on to suggest that this sin strikes at the very roots of our being. He does not say that it is the most serious of all sins, but that its relation to the body is unique. Other sins may have effects on the body, but this sin, and this sin only, means that a man takes that body that is 'a member of Christ' and puts it into a union which 'blasts his own body' (Way). Other sins against the body, *e.g.* drunkenness or gluttony, involve the use of that which comes from outside the body. The sexual appetite arises from within. They serve other purposes, *e.g.* conviviality. This has no purpose other than the gratification of the lusts. They are sinful in the excess. This is sinful in itself. And fornication involves a man in what Godet calls 'a degrading physical solidarity, incompatible with the believer's spiritual solidarity with Christ'. The sexual sinner sins *against his own body*. Moule suggests that *All sins* (*other* is an insertion of NIV) *a man commits are outside his body* is the slogan of some of the Corinthians, meaning 'physical lust cannot touch the secure "personality" of the initiated'. To this Paul retorts: 'on the contrary: anyone who commits fornication *is* committing an offence against his very "personality" ' (*IBNTG*, pp. 196f.). J. Murphy-O'Connor rejects the idea that 'body' can mean 'personality' and holds that the Corinthians were saying that 'the body has nothing to do with sin . . . sin takes place on an entirely different level of one's being' (*CBQ*, 40, 1977, p. 393). Whichever way we take it, Paul's rejoinder is that the body is sacred. And the resurrection shows that it has permanent values.

19. For the sixth time in this chapter Paul drives home his appeal to what the Corinthians know so well with his argumentative question, *Do you not know . . .?* Earlier he had referred to the church as a whole as God's temple (3:16), but here *body* is singular, so that each believer is a *temple* in which God dwells. The word is *naos*, which means the sacred shrine, the sanctuary, the place where deity dwells, not *hieron*, which includes the entire precincts. This gives a dignity to the whole of life, such as nothing else could do. Wherever we go we are the bearers of the Holy Ghost, the temples in which God is pleased to dwell. This rules out all such conduct as is not appropriate to the temple of God. Its application to fornication is obvious, but the principle is of far wider application. Nothing that would be amiss in God's temple is seemly in the child of God.

This verse sheds light on the way Paul regarded the Spirit. The *temple* is the place where God dwells; that is its distinguishing characteristic. Now the One who dwells in this *temple* is *the Holy Spirit*, who is thus seen to be divine. This comes out also in the expression, *whom you have received from God*. The Spirit within man is the gift of God, not the result of some man-induced experience. And because the *temple* is God's and because the believer is that *temple* it follows that the believer is God's.

20. The reason is *you were bought at a price* (Goodspeed, 'you have been bought and paid for'). There is possibly an antithesis to the price paid to a prostitute (Ruef thinks that this 'is not a very delicate way of putting it, but the Corinthians were probably not very delicate people'). The verb is in the aorist tense, which points to a single decisive action in time past. Paul mentions neither the occasion nor the price, but there is no need. Clearly he is referring to Calvary, where Christ gave his life to purchase sinners. The imagery is that of redemption, perhaps what scholars call 'sacral manumission'. By this process a slave would save the price of his freedom, pay it into the temple treasury of a god, and then be purchased by the deity. Technically he was the slave of the god, but as far as men were concerned he was free. Deissmann says that the words used here are 'the very formula of the records' (*LAE*, p. 324). Of course Paul is not saying that Christ's redemption corresponded exactly to sacral manumission; it is the terminology, not the precise process that is significant. And the price paid for sinners was no pious fiction, but the very real price of the death of the Saviour. The result is to bring us into a sphere where we are free (*cf.* 'Everything is permissible for me', v. 12). But we are God's slaves. He has bought us to be his own. We belong to him. Héring comments on this appeal to act in accordance with the truth that the body is God's temple: 'we are probably witnessing here the first attempt in the history of moral thought to refute libertinism in some other way than by the arguments of an ascetic, legalistic or utilitarian type'. We should miss neither the originality nor the force of Paul's argument.

The obligation now rests on us to *honour God* (*cf*. Rom. 12:1). This is the positive where 'flee fornication' is the negative. The prime motive in the service of the Christian is not the aim of accomplishing purposes attractive to him personally, but the glory of God. *Therefore* translates *dē*, a shortened form of *ēdē*, 'already'. It is sometimes added to an imperative to give it a note of greater urgency. 'Do it so speedily that it is already done!' The use of the aorist rather than the present imperative agrees with this. There is an urgency about it. Let there be no delay.

IV. MARRIAGE (7:1–40)

A. THE GENERAL PRINCIPLE (7:1–7)

Paul turns to the specific subjects on which the Corinthians had written to him, the first of which is marriage. In antiquity some people had a deep admiration for ascetic practices, including celibacy, and clearly some of the Corinthians shared this view. Paul makes every concession to their point of view. He agrees that celibacy is 'good', and he points to some of its advantages. But he regards marriage as normal, and he will later make the point that, though there are some advantages in celibacy, there is a greater completeness in marriage (11:11). Celibacy requires a special gift from God, and Paul is not unmindful of the stresses involved in living the Christian life in Corinth, with its constant pressure from the low standards of pagan sexual morality, and what he calls 'the present crisis' (v. 26). He himself prefers celibacy, but his advocacy of that state is very moderate. He does not command a celibate life for all who can sustain it, nor does he say that celibacy is morally superior to marriage. He regards marriage as the norm, but recognizes that there are some to whom God has given a special gift, who should remain unmarried.

1. 'Now concerning' (*peri de*), which begins this verse, is a formula introducing topics raised in the letter from the Corinthians (again in v. 25; 8:1; 12:1; 16:1,12). It is possible that we should take the words *It is good . . .* as a quotation from what the Corinthians had written (Bruce notes that this view is as old as Origen). It is possible, also, to see it as a question (Orr and Walther). *Good* does not here mean 'necessary' or 'morally better' (*cf.* vv. 8,26; Gn. 2:18; Jon. 4:3,8). It is simply something to be commended, rather than blamed. *Not to marry* is NIV's interpretation of what is more literally 'not to touch a woman' (RSV). 'Touch' in such a context is often used of sexual relations (*e.g.* Gn. 20:6; Pr. 6:29). It is possible that some of the Corinthians thought it advisable for believers to have no sexual relations in marriage. Paul, however, would not have called this good; he saw sexual relations as a necessary part of marriage (vv. 3–4).[1] NIV's interpretation seems better. Paul's view is that the unmarried are freer to serve God, since they are without the cares attendant on the married state (vv. 32ff.). But this does not imply that the married state is not also *good*. Our Lord commanded the rich young ruler to sell all that he had, but this does not imply that all ownership of goods is an evil.

2. The general rule is that people should be married and the expressions *his own wife* and *her own husband* point to monogamy. Paul is agreeing that celibacy is good, but he is also pointing out that temptation abounded: *there is so much immorality* (the word is plural, pointing to many acts). In the face of such temptation *each* should be married. *Should have* is an imperative, a command, not a permission. There will be exceptions (v. 7), but Paul leaves no doubt as to what is normal. Since fornication was so common at Corinth it was hard for the unmarried to remain chaste and hard for them to persuade others that they were, in fact, chaste. Some complain that Paul is here giving expression to a low view of marriage. But, of course, he is not here expounding his view of the married state (*cf.* Eph. 5:28ff.). He is not saying that this is the only reason for marriage; he is dealing with a specific question in the light of an actual situation. Calvin comments, 'the question is not as to the reasons for which marriage has been instituted, but as

---

[1] W. E. Phipps argues that the words refer to sexual relations, but he thinks that they are a quotation from the Letter of the Corinthians and that Paul quoted it in order to rebut it (*NTS*, 28, 1982, pp. 125–131).

to the persons for whom it is necessary.' Conzelmann thinks Paul's words 'unfashionable, but realistic'.

3. Each partner in a marriage has rights and Paul calls on each to pay what is due (*tēn opheilēn*). Each owes duties to the other. Paul does not stress the duty of either partner at the expense of the other, but puts them on a level, a noteworthy position in the male-dominated society of the time. His verb is the present imperative, which indicates the habitual duty. It is significant that he stresses the importance of giving rather than getting. Marriage is the giving of oneself to another.

4. Paul makes this more explicit. NIV paraphrases with *does not belong to her*, for the verb *exousiazō* means rather 'to exercise authority over' (*cf.* Lk. 22:25, 'those who exercise authority over'). Bengel sees 'an elegant paradox' in the conjunction of her 'own' body with 'does not exercise authority over'. Paul is saying that neither wives nor husbands have the right to use their bodies completely as they will. They have obligations to one another. Two things are noteworthy: the putting of the sexes on an absolute equality in this matter, and the indispensability of the sex act in marriage. Paul will have no truck with a view of marriage that leaves the sex act in the sole control of the male, nor with a view of marriage that sees sex as defiling.

5. There may arise occasions when the partners to a marriage agree to abstain for a time from normal intercourse in order to give themselves whole-heartedly to *prayer*. But this is clearly exceptional. Each belongs to the other so fully that Paul can call the withholding of the body an act of fraud (*apostereite*). *That you may devote yourselves* (*hina scholasēte*; we get our word 'school' from this verb) is literally 'that you may have leisure for'. Prayer must be unhurried. In the rush of life it may be necessary sometimes to take exceptional measures to secure a quiet, leisurely intercourse with God. But for married people the breaking off of normal relations, even for such a holy purpose, can be only by mutual consent. Then the couple must *come together again*. Otherwise the strength of their natural passions means that they will place themselves at Satan's mercy.

6. Not many take *this* to refer to what follows (though that is a possible understanding of the text). It is much more likely that it refers either to v. 5, or to the whole of the preceding section with its acceptance of marriage. It makes good sense to say that the suspension of intercourse is the *concession* (it is less likely to refer to the resumption of sexual intercourse). But it seems more in harmony with the general thrust to see Paul as saying that marriage is not a duty required of all. He has laid down the duties of all who are married, but he has not said that all should be married.

7. Paul's own preference is that *all men were as I am*. The chapter makes it clear that Paul was not married, but it is unlikely that he had never married. Jewish men were required to be married and beget children (Mishnah, *Yeb.* 6:6). R. Eleazar said, 'Any man who has no wife is no proper man' (Talmud, *Yeb.* 63*a*), while Raba and R. Ishmael taught that God watches a man to see when he will marry; then 'As soon as one attains twenty and has not married, He exclaims, "Blasted be his bones!" ' (Talmud, *Kidd.* 29*b*). Thus it is likely that Paul had at one time been married (and this is certainly the case if he had been a member of the Sanhedrin; *cf.* Acts 26:10), but clearly he was not in that state when he wrote this letter. He may have been a widower, or perhaps his wife had left him (when he became a Christian?). He had a number of special gifts (*charismata*), one of which enabled him to live the single life. He recognizes that continence is a divine gift. Those who have not received it should not try to remain unmarried. Each has *his own gift from God*. The question of whether to marry or not cannot be decided by applying one law to all. Each must consider what gift God has given, and marriage, just as much as celibacy, is a gift from God.

B. THE UNMARRIED AND THE WIDOW (7:8–9)

8. Having laid down the general principle, Paul now proceeds to deal with specific classes. He begins with those who have no marriage tie, *the unmarried and the widows*. Some have thought that the former term means 'unmarried men', others that it signifies 'widowers', the reasoning in both cases being that it is set over against *widows*. But this does not carry conviction. *Unmarried* (*agamois*) is a broad term; it includes all not bound by the married state. Then *widows* are singled out for special mention (*cf*. 'and Peter', Mk. 16:7), perhaps because of their particular vulnerability and the consequent temptation to remarry. Paul says that it is well for all such to remain as they are, just as he himself does.

9. But this depends on their having the gift of continence. If God has not given them this gift, *they should marry* (a command, not a permission), *for it is better to marry than to burn*. NIV adds *with passion*, which yields a good sense and may well be right. But the verb could be understood of burning in Gehenna (Bruce), and this is supported by the fact that there is no *cannot* in the original; the Greek means 'if they are not living continently' (Barrett). Paul has recently said that 'the sexually immoral' will not inherit the kingdom of God (6:9–10; *cf*. M. L. Barré, *CBQ*, xxxvi, 1974, pp. 193–202). Either view is possible.

C. THE MARRIED (7:10–11)

10. To *the married* Paul gives an authoritative command (*parangellō*; see notes in *TNTC* on 1 Thes. 4:2,11, pp. 80,87). He stresses that this is not a personal direction; it is *the Lord* who commands (Mk. 10:2–12). Paul is here speaking of marriages where both partners are Christians. He directs the wife not to *separate* (the verb is passive, 'not to be separated'; MM say that in the papyri it 'has almost become a technical term in connexion with divorce').

11. *But if she does* envisages the possibility that she will disobey the injunction. Or, as Conzelmann thinks, the aorist may refer to an already existing situation. The separated wife must then remain as she is *or else be reconciled to her husband*. Similarly, the husband is not to *divorce* his wife. The verb is different from that used of the wife, but the result is the same. Paul does not mention the exception Jesus allowed on the grounds of fornication (Mt. 5:32; 19:9). But he is not writing a systematic treatise on divorce. He is answering specific questions.

D. THE CHRISTIAN MARRIED TO AN UNBELIEVER WILLING TO LIVE WITH THE BELIEVER (7:12–14)

12–13. It is noteworthy that Paul gives these directions under the heading, *I, not the Lord*. He does not, of course, mean that this is contrary to what the Lord would have directed. But, whereas in v. 10 he could cite an express command of Christ, here he has no such express command and he makes the situation clear. But that does not mean that what he says lacks authority; he believes that he has the Spirit of God (v. 40). Moffatt points out that Paul's careful discrimination between a saying of the Lord and his own injunction tells strongly against those who maintain that the early church was in the habit of producing the sayings it needed and then ascribing them to Christ: 'It is historically of high importance that he did not feel at liberty to create a saying of Jesus, even when, as here, it would have been highly convenient in order to settle a disputed point of Christian behaviour.'

The rest must mean those not linked in Christian marriage, for apart from this all the cases have been dealt with, the unmarried, the widows, and the married. But some were married before they became Christians, and if one partner only became a believer there was a problem. Paul regards unions entered into as pagans as on a footing different from those contracted by Christians. Here everything hinges on the attitude of the pagan partner. If the unbelieving wife *is willing* (*syneudokei*, 'agrees with him') to continue the marriage, the *brother* (almost a technical term for a Christian) is not to *divorce her*. In exactly similar language Paul instructs the believing woman married to an unbelieving husband not to divorce him if he is agreeable to continuing the marriage (Greek and Roman law allowed women to divorce their husbands, though Jewish law did not).

14. *For* introduces a reason. Believers are 'saints', they are 'set apart' for God (see on 1:2). The basic idea in *sanctified* is that of relation to God, not that of moral uprightness (though this should follow). The believer's state of being set apart for God is not diminished because, before believing, he had contracted a marriage with a continuing pagan. Rather, the good prevailing against the evil, his sanctification in some way covers his wife. *Sanctified* is in an emphatic position (it is important), and it is in the perfect tense (which points to a continuing state). It is not possible to give a precise explanation of what this means. But it is a scriptural principle that the blessings that flow from fellowship with God are not confined to the immediate recipients, but extend to others (*e.g.* Gn. 15:18; 17:7; 18:26ff.; 1 Ki. 15:4; Is. 37:4). Thus the sanctification of the believing partner reaches out to the unbeliever. Paul sees this in what was clearly accepted with regard to the children of such a marriage. If the believer's sanctification stopped with himself, his children *would be unclean*. The word is used of ceremonial uncleanness, 'that which may not be brought into contact w. the divinity' (BAGD). This is an unthinkable position. Until he is old enough to take the responsibility upon himself, the child of a believing parent is to be regarded as Christian. The parent's 'holiness' extends to the child. The child is 'part of a family unit upon which God has his claim' (Mare).

E. THE CHRISTIAN MARRIED TO AN UNBELIEVER NOT WILLING TO LIVE WITH THE BELIEVER (7:15–16)

15. The case is different if the unbeliever is unwilling to continue the marriage. *Leaves* is in the middle voice, 'takes himself off' (it is the verb used in 10f. of the wife separating from her husband). If the unbeliever takes the initiative, then the believer *is not bound*. This appears to mean that the deserted partner is free to remarry; it would be a curious expression to use if Paul meant 'is bound to remain unmarried'.

God has called us to live in peace probably refers to the whole of the treatment of mixed marriages, not simply to the last clause. Paul's point is that the believer is called by God into a life where *peace* in the widest sense is his concern. In this matter of mixed marriages the line should be followed that conduces to *peace*. In some cases this will mean living with the pagan partner, in some cases it will mean accepting the pagan partner's decision that the marriage is at an end. The underlying concern for *peace* is the same in both cases.

16. It is uncertain whether a believer will succeed in 'saving' an unbelieving spouse if the marriage continues. Precisely opposite conclusions have been drawn from this. Most recent translators and commentators take the 'optimistic' view: a marriage should be kept up as long as possible in the hope of a conversion. Who can tell whether the other will not in due course be saved? But this is not soundly based. The grammar leaves it uncertain (as in Ec. 2:19; 3:21; and see Sakae Kubo, *NTS*, 24, 1977–78, pp. 539–544), and the context is against it. To cling to a marriage which the pagan is determined to end would inevitably lead to frustration and tension. The certain strain is not justified by the uncertain result. Marriage should not be seen simply as an instrument of evangelism. The guiding principle must be 'peace' (v. 15).

F. LEAD THE LIFE GOD ASSIGNS (7:17–24)

Paul turns from marriage to the wider question of living contentedly in whatever state God has set us. He relates this on the one hand to the equipment and call God gives us, and on the other to circumcision and to slavery, the great religious and social distinctions which divided the world of his day. Becoming a Christian means bringing what one is into the service of God, circumcision, uncircumcision, slavery, freedom, or whatever. Each has its own importance in the service of God. The slave, for example, can show how the believer can serve God under the limits imposed by slavery (as the free man cannot), while the free can show how to submit himself to voluntary service to God. Paul's point is that one can serve God in a variety of places and it is not necessary to leave one's station in life simply because one is converted.

17. *Nevertheless* (*ei mē*, 'but', BDF 376) is unexpected. Probably we should understand it as setting what follows in contrast to the preceding. Paul has asserted the freedom of the Christian (v. 15), but freedom is not licence. Over against the liberty the believer has in certain marriage situations Paul sets the maintenance of one's present state as the normal Christian practice. Barrett points out that throughout this paragraph Paul 'is not thinking primarily of a vocation *to* which a man is called, but of the condition *in* which a man is when the converting call of God comes to him'. Most modern translations paraphrase 'so let him walk' (AV), but we should not miss the point that walking is a favourite metaphor with Paul for the living of the Christian life with its idea of steady progress. Twice in this verse Paul has *each* in an emphatic position (NIV omits the second): he is stressing the duty of the individual. The verb *memeriken* (*assigned*) is often used of dividing things among people, though usually the things divided are mentioned. Here it points to our divine endowment; God has given some gift to each of us. *Called* (the Greek has no *to which*) reminds us of the priority of the divine call in salvation. We do not choose God; he chooses us. When he gives certain gifts and calls us in a certain state, we should live the life thus set before us, using the gifts God has given. This is no novelty produced for the special benefit of the Corinthians, but the rule *in all the churches*.

18–19. This has importance for the great religious division into the circumcised and the uncircumcised. For the Jews circumcison was of paramount importance, especially since the Maccabean struggle. They saw the uncircumcised as outside the covenant of God, people cut off from the blessings God has for his own. In a sense for them circumcision was everything. But for many of the Gentiles circumcision was a matter for scorn; it was the mark of a despised people. They saw it as a sign of enlightenment when a Jewish youth, by undergoing a surgical operation, tried to efface the marks of his circumcision in order to take his place in the wider world of Hellenistic culture (see 1 Macc. 1:15; Josephus, *Ant.* xii. 241). But Paul says firmly that these distinctions do not matter in the slightest. Both circumcision and uncircumcision are nothing; they do not matter at all (*cf.* Gal. 5:6; 6:15). Thus a man should not seek to change his state whatever it is. Over against both Paul sets *keeping God's commands*. No ritual observance can be set alongside the keeping of God's commandments.

20. The principle of v. 17 is stated again. Paul speaks of the divine call and relates it to the external circumstances of those called. People should serve God in that place in life in which it pleases him to call them. *Remain* is present imperative, with the thought of continuance.

21. Paul turns from religious to social divisions. The one *called* when *a slave* should not let that *trouble* him. If God has called him as a slave he will give him grace to live as a slave. The second part of the verse is something like 'But if also you can become free, rather use (it)', and the pundits are divided as to what this means. Some, impressed by the evidence throughout the paragraph on remaining in one's state, think Paul is saying, 'Even if you can gain your freedom, make the most of your present condition instead.' This is a possible understanding of the Greek, but against it is the aorist imperative, which more naturally signifies the beginning of a new 'use' than the continuance of an old one. It is also difficult to think that Paul, who held that marriage introduced difficulties in the way of Christian service, could have thought otherwise about slavery, which introduced much more serious difficulties. Paul seems to be saying: 'Your state is not of first importance. If you are a slave do not worry. If you can be made free, then make use of your new status. It is your relationship to the Lord that matters most.'

22. Paul employs paradoxical language to emphasize the point that the outward state does not matter. The slave who is *called* has entered the glorious liberty of the children of God. He has been freed from slavery to sin and this divine liberty matters so much more than his outward circumstances that he should see himself as *the Lord's freedman* (*freedman* means one set free from slavery; *free man* one who has not been a slave). *Called by the Lord* is better 'called in the Lord', *i.e.* called to be 'in Christ'. The addition is unusual (*called* is generally enough); it emphasizes the intimate relationship of the believer to the divine Lord. It is not without its interest and importance that Paul says this of the slave, the least esteemed of people in the first century. With this goes the complementary truth that he who was a *free man* when called is *Christ's slave*. Once more the point is that outward circumstances matter little. The important thing for the *free man* is his relationship to Christ; his whole life is to be lived in lowly service to his Master. Nothing matters alongside this.

23. Paul repeats *You were bought at a price* from 6:20 (where see notes). Believers have been bought by Christ's blood. They belong to the Lord. They should not then be the *slaves of men*. Deissmann reminds us that it was specifically provided in many documents of manumission (see note on 6:20) that the person who had been bought by a god to be the god's freedman should never again be brought into slavery (*LAE*, p. 325). Paul may have had this in mind. No-one could compel the Corinthian believers to be slaves again; let them then not put themselves into slavery. It is highly unlikely that he is speaking of literal slavery. But to live as free people demands a special temper of mind and spirit. It is easy to accept unquestioningly what others lay down, to subject oneself to some man-made system, and thus display the mentality of a slave. This is not the Christian way.

24. The section concludes with a reiteration of the principle already twice laid down (vv. 17,20), that *each man* (note the individual application) should remain in the state in which God called him (NIV's *to* is unwarranted). This does not forbid a man to better himself. But it cautions him against seeking a change simply because he is a Christian. Conversion is not the signal to leave one's occupation (unless it is plainly incompatible with Christianity) and seek something more 'spiritual'. All of life is God's. We should serve God where we are until he calls us elsewhere. As throughout the passage, the aorist *called* looks back to the time of God's call. *Remain* is present continuous. Paul rounds it all off with 'with God' (apparently NIV's *as respon-*

sible to God). He is not counselling an attitude of passive resignation, an acceptance of the established order at all costs. He is reminding his friends that they are not alone as they try to live the Christian life. God is with them, whatever their circumstances. Let them, then, seek first and always to remain with him.

G. VIRGINS (7:25-38)

25. *Now about* (*peri de*, see on 7:1) points to another matter on which the Corinthians had asked a specific question. *Virgins* (*parthenoi*) are usually female, though sometimes the word is used of men (in the New Testament only in Rev. 14:4). Some take it here as referring to both sexes (*e.g.* Bengel, Craig, Hurd, p. 68). J. K. Elliott sees in the plural a reference to engaged couples (*NTS*, 19, 1972-73, p. 220), while J. Massingberd Ford thinks of young widows or widowers (*NTS*, 10, 1963-64, p. 362). But the whole tenor of this passage shows that Paul is referring to young women only. Five times out of six his use of the feminine article shows that women are in mind, and the sixth, that here, should surely be taken in the same way. A girl's parent or guardian largely determined whether she should marry or not. Paul has no saying of the Lord on this subject; he says so plainly and gives his own advice. His description of himself in terms of *the Lord's mercy* emphasizes at one and the same time his own shortcomings and the centrality of his Lord. The perfect (*ēleēmenos*) indicates the permanence of the Lord's mercies, and *trustworthy* (*pistos*) the obligations this lays on the recipient of God's good gifts. It is possible to understand the word as 'a believer', but unlikely in this context.

26. Paul's advice is conditioned by *the present crisis* (*anangkē*). This is usually taken to mean the troubles preceding the second advent, and indeed this is often held to be self-evident. But the word is never used in the New Testament in this way; the nearest is a reference to the troubles preceding the fall of Jerusalem (Lk. 21:23). Paul often refers to Christ's return, but he does not associate *anangkē* with it. When he uses this word it has meanings like 'compulsion' (v. 37), 'compelled' (9:16), 'hardships' (2 Cor. 6:4), *etc.*, but never the events preceding the second coming. It seems here to denote more than the opposition the Christian always encounters. Some pressing constraint lay hard on the Corinthians at the time of writing (Bengel says firmly, 'The famine in the time of Claudius, Acts xi. 28'). Whatever the precise meaning, Paul's friends were at that time in unusually difficult circumstances, and in view of the troubled times Paul felt it best for them to stay as they were. When high seas are raging it is no time for changing ships.

27. Paul spells it out. The man who has *married* (the Greek means 'is bound to a wife') should not seek to loose the tie. The man who 'has been loosed' (which may mean divorced, that the spouse has died, or that he has never married) should not seek a wife. Both verbs are in the perfect tense and indicate settled states.

28. Paul has consistently maintained that, while it is good for some not to marry, yet marriage is the normal state. There is nothing sinful about it. He repeats this. Though in the prevailing troubles he advised a man not to marry, he says plainly that it is no sin if he does. And so with *a virgin*. Paul's reason for not advocating marriage is the *many troubles* (actually *thlipsis*, 'trouble' is singular) the married face, but he does not define the nature of the trouble. Robertson and Plummer appropriately cite Bacon, 'He that hath wife and children hath given hostages to fortune', and 'children sweeten labours, but they make misfortunes more bitter'. Marriage implies responsibility, and marriage in times of distress must lead to some kind of trouble. *In this life* is more literally 'in the flesh', an expression which here points to human weakness, 'the totality of the limitations under which we live' (Ruef). Paul's tenderness comes out in his refusal to pursue the matter further. His *I* is emphatic; he for his part is trying (conative present) to *spare* them.

29. *What I mean* ('But this I say') gives what follows a heightened solemnity. *Short* is a perfect participle: 'the time has been shortened'. Many see a reference to the second advent. This may be right, but though he often refers to the Lord's return, Paul never elsewhere gives this kind of counsel with regard to it. Both in his earlier and his later epistles he uses the second advent to inspire people to blameless conduct (*e.g.* 1 Thes. 5:1–11; Phil. 1:9–11). The note of present crisis, so marked here, is absent. Those who see the second advent here never seem to face the question of why the last generation should live differently from any others. We all face the same judgment. Calvin thought of the shortness of life (so also Robertson); but it is difficult to see how this justifies the following instructions. RSV has 'the appointed time', which raises the question, 'appointed for what?' It is best to see a reference to prevailing circumstances at Corinth (the 'crisis' of v. 26). The culmination was evidently not far off; in this troubled period many kinds of conduct must be transformed. In particular *those who have wives* must be 'as those who have none'.

30. So with other things. Mourners tend to be engrossed in their mourning. Those that rejoice are taken up with their happiness. Purchasers concentrate on their new possessions. In the prevailing distress and the shortened time all will be jolted out of their normal attitudes. Believers should accordingly not be preoccupied with their earthly circumstances; they should be detached from them all.

31. The whole is summed up in the expression *those who use the things of the world*. The construction is unusual (*chraomai* with the accusative, only here in the New Testament), but the meaning is clear. Paul speaks of those who make any use of the things of time and sense. *Engrossed* translates the compound verb, *katachraomai*, of which the uncompounded form has just been used. The prefix *kata* sometimes gives the simple verb a sinister twist ('use wrongly', AV 'abuse'). But it often simply intensifies the meaning ('use to the full'), though the intensification is sometimes not marked (*i.e.* the simple and compounded verbs may differ little). In this context NIV seems to have the sense of it. Those who make use of the things of this world should not be *engrossed* in them, overlooking the transitoriness of earthly things and the importance of what is eternal. *Schēma* (*present form*) denotes the outward shape, especially when there is some idea that this is changeable. It is adapted to the thought of fickleness, the changing fashion. There is nothing solid and lasting in this world system; it is its nature to pass away. It is folly for believers to act as though its values were permanent.

32. Paul repeats his thought of vv. 27f. that he wishes his friends to be *free from concern* ('anxieties', RSV). The trying nature of the times meant that the married must take anxious thought for their partners: 'A man who is a hero in himself becomes a coward when he thinks of his widowed wife and his orphaned children' (Lightfoot on v. 26). This *concern* would distract from that perfect service of the Lord at which Paul aimed. But the *unmarried man* is *concerned about the Lord's affairs*. Paul may see this as desirable (as most commentators hold). But he has just said that he wants his readers to be *free from concern*; he may thus mean that he wants their service of the Lord to be a relaxed acceptance of God's will for their lives rather than a worried preoccupation with personal holiness and the like. MM shows that the verb *areskō* (*please*) includes the thought of service in the interests of another, in this case, of God. This is the extent of Paul's preference for celibacy. He wants people to be given to the service of God without distraction.

33. The *married man*, by contrast, must have a certain concern about *the affairs of this world*. This does not, of course, mean 'worldliness', but is a reminder that the married man must take thought for the interests of his family. He has obligations, and their discharge demands some attention to the things of this world. He must face the question of *how he can please* (*areskō*, as in v. 32) *his wife*. We should probably take 'and he is divided' here rather than in v. 34. The man wants both to please the Lord and to please his wife. He 'is divided'.

34. Some take the verb *divided* with this verse and see a difference between a wife and a virgin (as AV). But this is not a natural reading of the Greek. Rather Paul moves on to show that there is the same kind of difference between married and unmarried women as he has just shown exists between married and unmarried men. The *unmarried woman* may be a widow or divorced or, of course, a *virgin*, who is thus singled out for special notice. The woman who is not bound by the marriage tie is able to concentrate on the things of God without distraction. She can give herself over to being 'holy in body and spirit' (RSV). 'Holy' here refers not to ethical achievement, but to consecration. The virgin is no more righteous than the wife, but her consecration is unmodified by family responsibilities. The married woman, by contrast, must take into account the needs of her husband. Just as he does, she must give attention to *the affairs of this world* in order to *please* her partner.

35. The apostle insists that he has the best interests of the Corinthians at heart. He is seeking what is for their *own good* ('benefit' or 'advantage'). *Not to restrict you* employs a metaphor from hunting, 'not to throw a lasso over you'. Paul is not trying to capture and constrain them. He wants that which makes for 'good order' (*euschēmon*, 'of good shape') and which provides for constancy (*euparedron*). There need be no intermission in the service offered by the unmarried, no distraction of any sort.

36. As he has done repeatedly, Paul qualifies a statement pointing to the advantages of celibacy by making it clear that marriage is not to be despised. There is no sin if the *virgin* gets married. This verse is very difficult and three explanations have won support.

(*a*) *Anyone* means the parent or guardian of a girl, and *acting improperly* means not providing for her marriage. The parent has acted on the view that celibacy is to be preferred to marriage and has kept her unmarried (whether with or against her will is not clear). He now wonders whether he is doing the right thing. To withhold marriage from a girl of marriageable age and anxious to marry would have been to court disaster in first-century Corinth and bring dishonour on both father and daughter. *Getting on in years* renders a very unusual term (*hyperakmos*). It seems to mean 'past the stage of being fully developed' (*akmē* = 'highest point', 'prime'; Plato speaks of a woman as at her *akmē* at the age of twenty, *Rep.* V. 460.E); she is, then, at or past the age when marriage would be expected. Paul adds a further point, if 'it has to be' (RSV), which probably means that she does not have the gift of continence (cf. v. 7). If the parent sees all this, he may do what he wants. There is no sin. Let them marry. The principal objections are two. 'His virgin' is not common for 'his daughter' (but it does occur; LSJ cites Sophocles as saying 'my virgins' for 'my daughters'). It would be a quick way of including guardians as well as fathers. The other is that 'let them marry' is most naturally taken as referring to the man and the virgin spoken of earlier in the verse. This is so, but the grammarian, A. T. Robertson, sees the subject of the verb here as 'drawn from the context (the two young people)' (*Grammar*, p. 1204). AV and JB take this view.

(b) The view behind NIV (RSV, GNB) is that *anyone* refers to a young man and *the virgin* to his fiancée; the pair have agreed to remain celibate. Paul tells them that there is no sin if they change their mind and decide to marry. But this may be reading modern ideas of engagement into the text. The Greeks do not appear to have had an 'engagement' at all (Conzelmann). There was a betrothal among the Jews and the Romans, but this was more than our 'engagement'; it was in effect marriage, stage 1, and could be broken only by divorce proceedings. And it was not brought about by an agreement of the couple; it was an arrangement made by the parents. Even if we allow the possibility of an 'engagement' the question arises, 'Engagement for what?' 'Engagement' surely means 'engagement to marry'. Why should people get engaged at all unless they mean to marry? It is, moreover, difficult to put meaning into *acting improperly towards the virgin* on this hypothesis. There is nothing 'improper' in his not marrying a girl he has agreed not to marry. Again, 'his virgin' (NIV translates the Greek for 'his' by *he is engaged to*) is a very strange designation for a man's fiancée. For all its popularity in some circles, Hillyer is probably right in saying that this view reflects 'a more recent and western situation'.

(c) Many commentators think that Paul is referring to 'spiritual marriage', whereby people went through the form of marriage, but lived together as brother and sister. From highly spiritual motives they abstained from sexual intercourse. They sought a union of spirit, but not of bodies. Those who take this view often take *hyperakmos* as referring to the man (as is grammatically possible), and give it the meaning 'over-passionate' or the like. Paul gives permission to such people to marry if they find the strain too great. The decisive objection to this is that Paul regards the withholding of sexual relations by married people as an act of fraud (v. 5; few of those holding this position discuss this point). It may be done by mutual consent 'for a time', and the couple must then 'come together again'. It is impossible to think that a man who valued the sex act in marriage so highly would acquiesce in a situation where it was done away with. Again, this view has to take the verb *gamizō* ('give in marriage') in the sense 'marry' (v. 38, where see note). Robertson and Plummer regard this as 'decisive'. Further, it is more than doubtful whether *hyperakmos* can mean 'over-passionate'. Moffatt says that it denotes 'the surge of sexual passion', but he gives no reason and it does not seem natural. If we feel that there is no change of subject and that it must apply to the man, this meaning is perhaps inevitable, but we would not expect such a meaning for the word. Finally, the earliest date at which 'spiritual marriage' is attested is well into the second century, and then it is vigorously opposed. There is no reason, in our present state of knowledge, for holding that it existed as early as this, or that Paul would have countenanced it.

None of the explanations is without substantial objection. But the first view should probably be accepted because the objections to it do not seem as forceful as those urged against the other two.

37. Paul reaffirms his preference that *the virgin* be not given in marriage, but lists four conditions before this course be followed.

(*a*) The man *has settled the matter in his own mind*; he is clear that this is the right course. (*b*) There is *no compulsion*, no external obligation such as a marriage contract. (*c*) He has 'authority' (*exousia*), *i.e.* 'the right to give effect to his own purpose' (Parry). Slaves, for example, would not have this right. (*d*) He has 'made a judgment' (*kekriken*) to keep his virgin (as a virgin). If these four criteria are fulfilled, then the man *does the right thing* in keeping her from marriage.

38. Paul concludes that the man who gives his daughter in marriage 'does well', while he who does not 'will do better'. The verb 'gives in marriage' (*gamizō*) is not found before the New Testament. The *-izō* termination points to the meaning 'gives in marriage' (not 'marries'), and this does not sit well with a reference to engaged couples or spiritual marriages (which requires the meaning 'marry'). Those who hold such views point out that in the New Testament period the *-izō* termination was losing its force in many verbs. It was, but no-one seems to have shown that this is true of *gamizō*. Those who hold such views maintain that *gamizō* here has the same meaning as *gameō* in earlier verses. But why should Paul change his verb? And why do it just here? Why use a verb which elsewhere always means 'give a woman in marriage'?

H. WIDOWS (7:39–40)

39. Christian marriage means that a wife is bound to her husband as long as he lives. If he dies (*koimēthē*, 'falls asleep'), she is free to remarry if she will. NIV is a trifle over-definite with the rendering, *he must belong to the Lord*. While this is often accepted as the meaning, Paul says no more than 'only in the Lord'. In marriage as in all else, the Christian must remember that he acts as a member of Christ's body.

40. Right to the end Paul refrains from saying anything to indicate that there is something morally higher about celibacy. He thinks that the widow is *happier* if she refrains from remarriage. We must, of course, read this in the light of the special circumstances mentioned earlier in the chapter. There is nothing tentative about the authority with which Paul speaks. He has sometimes been able to quote a saying of Jesus, sometimes he has given his own opinion. But in doing this he holds that he has *the Spirit of God*. He is conscious of the divine enablement; what he says is more than the opinion of a private individual.

His *I too* may imply that some of the Corinthians had claimed inspiration. Paul is no whit behind any of them.

V. MEAT SACRIFICED TO IDOLS (8:1 – 11:1)

Christians today are apt to find it a little strange that there could be doubt about the attitude of believers to meat offered to idols. It seems to us so obvious that they could have no truck with idolatry. But it was not as easy as that to a new convert at Corinth in the first century. The situation was complicated by two facts. First, it was an accepted social practice to have meals in a temple, or in some place associated with an idol. 'It was all part and parcel of the formal etiquette in society' (Moffatt). The kind of occasion, public or private, when people were likely to come together socially was the kind of occasion when a sacrifice was appropriate. To have nothing to do with such gatherings was to cut oneself off from most social intercourse with one's fellows. People from the lower classes, moreover (and *cf.* 1:26ff.), 'knew meat almost exclusively as an ingredient in pagan religious celebrations'. Some of them would not want 'to miss out on what little bit of meat was offered to them by pagan feasts and institutions' (Theissen, pp. 128f.).[1] But some Christians might well eat it with a guilty conscience. Others, firmly convinced that there was but one God, might well reason, 'How can there possibly be any harm in eating before a block of wood or stone? What difference can it make if meat has been offered to a non-existent deity?'

Secondly, most of the meat sold in the shops had first been offered in sacrifice (see *SPC*, p. 33). Part of the victim was always offered on the altar to the god, part went to the priests, and usually part to the worshippers. The priests customarily sold what they could not use. It would often be very difficult to know for sure whether meat in a given shop had been part of a sacrifice or not. Notice that there are two separate questions:

---

[1] C. K. Barrett quotes H. D. F. Kitto: 'Barley-meal, olives, a little wine, fish as a relish, meat only on high holidays – such was the normal diet. As Zimmern has said, the usual Attic dinner consisted of two courses, the first a kind of porridge, and the second, a kind of porridge' (*NTS*, 11, 1964–65, p. 145).

the taking part in idol feasts, and the eating of meat bought in the shops, but previously part of a sacrifice. Many things might be said. Paul begins with the obligations of Christian love.

A. KNOWLEDGE ABOUT IDOLS (8:1–6)

1. *Now about* (*peri de*) is the formula that introduces matter raised by the letter from the Corinthians (see on 7:1). This is another topic that gave them difficulty. *We know that we all possess knowledge* may be a quotation from the Corinthians' letter (so NEB, GNB). Paul agrees. Knowledge is important and he associates himself with his readers in its exercise. The use of *all* may be a gentle reminder that the knowledge on which the Corinthians prided themselves was by no means unusual, but the common possession of Christians. But love is more important. *Knowledge puffs up* (see note on 'take pride' in 4:6). Knowledge is so often accompanied by pride, which is the very antithesis of the genuine Christian spirit. While knowledge may make people proud, *love builds up* (*cf.* Phillips, 'while knowledge may make a man look big, it is only love that can make him grow to his full stature'). *Builds up* (*oikodomei*) properly applies to the erection of buildings; Paul is fond of using it metaphorically for the development of Christian character (see *TNTC* on 1 Thes. 5:11, p. 102).

2. Knowledge here on earth is, at best, incomplete. No matter what a man *thinks he knows* (the perfect tense implies full and complete knowledge), *he does not yet know* (if the aorist is inceptive, he has not even begun true knowledge) *as he ought* ('must', *dei*). There is no point in priding oneself on what is inevitably partial and incomplete (*cf.* 13:9). There is probably also the thought that he who thinks he knows really does not know (*cf.* 3:18). As Kay says, 'Knowledge is proud that it has learnt so much. Wisdom is humble that it knows no more.'

3. Love, by contrast, has permanent effects. Paul surprises us here. After 'If anyone thinks he knows something he knows nothing. If anyone loves God' we expect something like 'he has real knowledge'. Instead we read, he *is known by God*. The really important thing is not that we know God, but that he knows us: 'The Lord knows those who are his' (2 Tim. 2:19; *cf.* Gal. 4:9). People who truly love God are brought within the sphere of those on whom God is graciously pleased to set his knowledge.

In these three verses Paul has given a very gentle rebuke to those who gave too high a place to knowledge. Love rather than knowledge is the Christian's guide.

4. Returning to the subject of idol meats, Paul agrees with the Corinthians that *an idol is nothing at all in the world* (or 'there is no idol in all the world'; *cf.* JB, NEB). He may well be quoting the Corinthians again, as many think. He is certainly not giving his own full idea on the matter, for he later says that what is sacrificed to idols is actually sacrificed to devils (10:20). There are spiritual beings behind the idols, though not the ones their worshippers thought. But here this is not the point. Paul is prepared to agree that the gods the heathen worship are no gods. In all this ordered universe there is no reality corresponding to idols. This is a necessary consequence of the assertion that *there is no God but one*. One of the first things a little Jewish boy was taught was the *Shema*, 'Hear, O Israel: The LORD our God, the LORD is one' (Dt. 6:4). It was absolutely fundamental, and the Jew clung to it with a fierce tenacity. The Christian was no less sure of it than the Jew.

5. Paul allows that there are *so-called gods*. Idol worshippers referred to the objects of their worship as 'gods', and really believed them to be such. But *so-called* indicates their unreality. All are dismissed, whether their abode was thought to be *in heaven or on earth* (Chrysostom sees those in heaven as the sun, moon and stars, those on earth as demons). There is probably no great difference between *many 'gods'* and *many 'lords'*. 'Lord' was a common way of referring to deity in the cults of the time (which makes Paul's frequent application of the term to Jesus Christ significant). Paul is simply making it clear that the heathen world worshipped a multitude of deities, none of which was real.

6. *Yet* is the strong adversative *all'*, and *for us* is in an emphatic position. In sharp contrast to the idolaters, Christians are essentially monotheistic: *there is but one God*. He is given his characteristic title, *the Father*, partly to point to his relationship to the Son, and partly to indicate his tender care for his people (both are mentioned in the following clauses). Pagans divided up creation among their gods and goddesses, each having his own sphere. But the one God, says Paul, is responsible for *all things*. We came *from* him and we live *for* him; he is our origin and goal. The preposition *eis*, *for*, indicates the set of the life. The believer lives for God.

Paul thinks also of the Son, the *one Lord, Jesus Christ*. *One* draws attention to Christian monotheism over against the plurality of the gods of the heathen, and *Lord* to the deity of Christ. So, of course, does the fact that he is mentioned in this way in the same breath as the Father. Paul does not stay to examine the relationship between them (and thus sets later theologians many a problem!). But clearly he is saying that there is but one God, and just as clearly he is including the Lord Jesus within that one Godhead (*cf.* Moffatt, 'For Paul the *one Lord* is vitally one with the *one God*'). *Through whom all things came* points to Christ as the Agent in creation; the Father created *through* the Son (*cf.* Jn. 1:3; Col. 1:15f.). *Through whom we live* means that Christians have their being only through him. It is a reference to the new creation in Christ (*cf.* 2 Cor. 5:17).

B. THE WEAK BROTHER (8:7–13)

Paul has more than one thing to say about idolatry. He sees it, for example, as an evil from which believers must flee and as an association with demons (10:14,20). But his first point is that Christian love means that in this as in other matters strong Christians must act with consideration for the weak.

7. Paul has been speaking of the knowledge that enables a believer to see an idol as 'nothing at all'. Now he makes the point that such knowledge is not universal among Christians. There is no contradiction with v. 1. There Paul said that knowledge was not confined to the Corinthian élite; in principle it is open to every believer. But not every believer has risen to it and he now points to some who, from the habit of their pre-Christian days, were *so accustomed* to thinking of the idols as real that they could not completely shake off such thoughts. It is not unlike the situation in the modern mission field, where some converts find it very hard to rid themselves completely of a belief in witchcraft (to say nothing of the superstitions that linger on even in 'enlightened' communities!). At Corinth something of the old way of thinking persisted. When *some people* eat meat that has come from an idol temple their long-standing attitude to idols leads them to think that they are in some way participating in idolatry. *Their conscience is weak*, Paul says, and accordingly *it is defiled*. What one of the strong Corinthians might do without a tremor, fully assured that the idol is nothing, is a sin to the weaker brother.

8. *But* (the adversative *de*) the eating of any particular food is a very minor matter. Those who advocate eating food from the temples are not contending for some great principle (as Paul was when he stoutly refused to accept the necessity of circumcision). The eating of *food* is a thing indifferent. It does not *bring us near to God*, where the present tense points to what happens here and now (some MSS have the future; food will not bring us before God for praise or blame at the day of judgment). Eating food makes us no better and abstaining makes us no worse. It may be that Paul is quoting the Corinthians again. The strong perhaps held that the Christian should assert his freedom by eating what has been offered to an idol; it shows that he has a full understanding of the truth that an idol is nothing. As long as scruples hold him back, they may have said, he is a *worse* Christian, but when he eats he is a *better* one. If so, Paul is accepting what they say about food, but applying it the other way round. Eating does not matter either way. It must not be insisted on.

9. The person who insists on doing anything allowable has not learnt the Christian way of love. Every believer must have a concern for *the weak*. The strong at Corinth claimed their 'right' (*the exercise of your freedom* translates *exousia*, 'authority' or 'right'); they could do as they pleased in the matter of idols. Paul reminds them that no Christian is at liberty to assert his 'rights' if that means doing harm to other people. A *stumbling block* (*proskomma*) is a stone in the pathway, an obstacle, something that trips one up and makes progress difficult. The actions of the strong must never be such as to offer a hindrance to the progress of the weak. What one person sees as right may well be quite wrong for another. No-one should try to force his standards of right and wrong on others, whose consciences react differently.

10. Paul points to the kind of thing that can happen. The man with *knowledge* is pictured as taking part in a meal in the temple of an idol, a common social practice. Many commentators draw attention to an invitation in the Oxyrhyncus papyri: 'Chaeremon invites you to dine at the table of the lord Sarapis in the Sarapeion (*i.e.* temple of Sarapis) tomorrow. . . .' For the arrangements in a typical temple in Corinth see Figs. 1 and 2 (pp. 126, 127). *Eating* means 'reclining at table'; the man is taking his ease in a place dedicated to an idol. Paul asks whether the weak person's conscience will not be *emboldened* by this so that he will do the same. The verb is that translated 'builds up' in v. 1. The strong had evidently spoken of the necessity of 'building up' the weak by encouraging them to do such things. Paul takes up their word and points out the harm. 'By setting such an example will you "build up" the weak brother? You will "build him up" only to destruction!' (*cf.* Lenski, 'A demolition calling itself edification').

11. Paul brings out the consequences. The *knowledge* on which the strong pride themselves is the means of doing tremendous harm to the *weak* (the change to the participle may stress the continuing state of weakness). *Is destroyed* (*apollytai*) is a strong term (*cf.* Phillips, 'bring spiritual disaster to'). The strong inflicts ruinous disaster on the weak by inducing him to sin where otherwise he would not. Paul is speaking of a present activity (the tense is present, not future): 'It is not the man's eternal perdition, but the stunting of his Christian life and

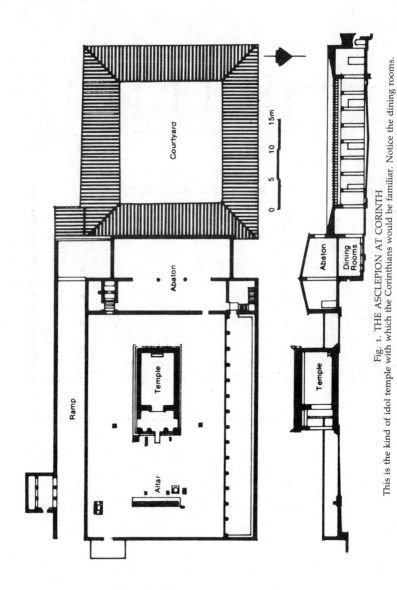

Fig. 1. THE ASCLEPION AT CORINTH

This is the kind of idol temple with which the Corinthians would be familiar. Notice the dining rooms.

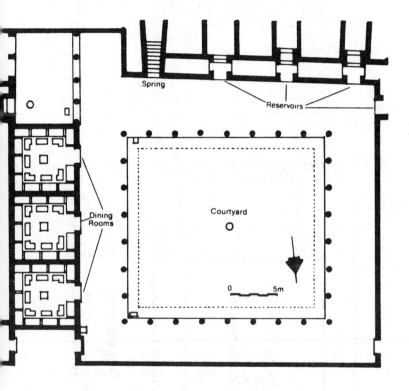

Fig. 2. THE DINING ROOMS OF THE ASCLEPION

Each of the three rooms could take eleven diners. Cooking was apparently done in the square space in the centre of the room. The courtyard formed a 'perfect little piazza' which could be used by anyone and which gave access to the dining rooms (cf. 8:10). It is not completely certain that these actual rooms were in use in the time of Paul, though it is probable. In any case there would have been a similar arrangement in the temples of his day generally.

127

usefulness' (Bruce). The word order is unusual. Paul emphasizes 'the brother for whose sake (*di' hon*) Christ died', by putting it right at the end. 'The last clause could hardly be more forcible in its appeal; every word tells; "the brother," not a mere stranger; "for the sake of whom," precisely to rescue him from destruction; "Christ," no less than He; "died," no less than that' (Robertson and Plummer).

12. The harm done to the weak is bad enough, but even that is not the whole story. To sin *against your brothers* means nothing less than to sin *against Christ* (a lesson brought home to Paul long since, on the Damascus road, Acts 9:4f.). They are 'in Christ', and anything done against them is therefore done against him (*cf.* Mt. 25:42-45). There is a high dignity in being Christian. It is easy to look down on some church members as unimportant. But they are not so. No temple of the Holy Spirit (6:19) is unimportant. God lives in the weak. We must honour them as members of Christ, and beware of sinning against the Lord. *Wound* renders *typtō*, used metaphorically only here in the New Testament. Its customary use is for striking vigorous blows, for beating. The strong 'hit' the weak conscience, and thus do great harm.

13. Paul himself will do his utmost to see that he does not hinder the weak. In this context he might have confined himself to 'meat offered to idols', but he speaks simply of 'food' (NIV, *what I eat*). If need be he will become a vegetarian and *never eat meat again*. The important thing is not his own rights, nor his own comfort, but the well-being of the brotherhood. There is emphasis on *brother*; it occurs four times in the last three verses (NIV makes the last one *him*). *Cause to fall* renders *skandalizō*, a verb difficult to translate. It means something like 'to set off a trap' (from *skandalon*, used in 1:23, the bait stick, *i.e.* the stick that sets the trap in motion when a bird or animal touches it). It is used metaphorically for trouble of various kinds. Paul's negative is the emphatic *ou mē*, and he follows it with 'into the age', *i.e.* the coming age. It is a strong expression for *never*.

The principle laid down in this chapter is one of great practical importance. It is always easy for the strong Christian to see no harm whatever in actions which the weak can only regard as sinful. While it would not be true to say that the robust Christianity of the New Testament envisages the strong as permanently shackled by the weak, yet the strong must always act towards the weak with consideration and Christian love. In cases like the one dealt with here the strong must adapt their behaviour to the conscience of the weak. No good purpose is served by asserting their 'rights' (*cf.* Paul's treatment of the same general subject in Rom. 14).

C. THE EXAMPLE OF PAUL (9:1–27)

1. *Paul's rights* (9:1–14)

At first sight this appears to be a different subject altogether and not a few have thought that it is an insertion from another letter, or that it is a parenthesis in which Paul temporarily leaves his subject. But there is no need of such hypotheses. Paul has been dealing with the strong who asserted their rights even when that harmed others. He has told them that this is wrong. He now proceeds to show that he himself has consistently applied this principle. He practises what he preaches. From what he says it is plain that some of his critics held that Paul's acceptance of restrictions on his liberty showed that he was no apostle. They had not learnt that 'Freedom is not licence to do what I want, but liberation to do what I ought' (Green, p. 94). Paul argues strongly for two things: (*a*) he really is an apostle in the fullest sense; (*b*) neither he nor any other believer should assert Christian liberty to the detriment of others.

1. Paul begins with four questions, each expecting the answer 'Yes'. The order of the first two, referring to the liberty of the Christian then the rights of the apostle, suggests that he has done more than he has been urging the Corinthians to do. He has forgone not only the general rights that all Christians have, but his special rights as an apostle as well. Paul rarely uses the name *Jesus* without 'Christ'. We must assume that here he wishes to place some emphasis on the human nature of the

Lord. That he has seen *Jesus* brings out one of his qualifications as an apostle. Apostles were authoritative witnesses to the facts of the gospel, more especially to the resurrection (Acts 1:21f.; 2:32; 3:15; 4:33, *etc.*; notice the words of Ananias to Paul, 'the God of our fathers has chosen you . . . to see the Righteous One', Acts 22:14; *cf.* 26:16). As Paul was not one of the original apostolic band, some may have questioned his right to bear such witness. But on the Damascus road he was granted a special privilege – he saw the Lord (15:8). This qualified him to bear witness to the resurrection. He puts some emphasis on this (*not, ouchi,* is more emphatic than the negatives in the other questions). That the Corinthians are Paul's work *in the Lord* arises from the fact that it is not the servant but the Lord who 'makes things grow' (*cf.* 3:5-7). *Cf.* Calvin, 'we must always speak of the efficacy of the ministry in such a manner that the entire praise of the work may be reserved for God alone.' Paul has not only seen the risen Jesus, but the Lord has enabled him to do apostolic work.

2. Others might call Paul's apostleship in question, but the Corinthian church ought to be the last to do this; 'If it denies *his* standing, then it abrogates its own' (Conzelmann on v. 1). No-one else had the same relationship to them as did he. They were a living proof of the effectiveness of his work. A *seal* was important in an age when many could not read. The impress of a *seal* in clay, wax, or the like, was a mark of ownership. All could see the mark and know what it meant. It came to be a means of authentication. The Corinthians had been won for Christ by Paul, and they were thus the sign that he was an apostle ('the certificate of my apostleship', Goodspeed). Their very existence as Christians proved his point.

3. In the Greek these words can be taken either with what precedes or with what follows. Despite the fact that most recent translations agree with NIV in taking them with what follows, the words go better with the preceding. What follows does not in fact prove Paul's apostleship (for that see vv. 1-2); it brings out the consequences when that apostleship is accepted. *Defence* translates *apologia*, the term for a legal defence against a charge, while *sit in judgment* is another legal word (see on 2:14). There is emphasis on both *my* and *me*.

4. *The right (exousia)* was used of the Corinthians in 8:9 (where see note). As the previous chapter was concerned with the eating of certain foods, it may be that Paul is reminding his friends that he himself has full rights in such matters. But in this context most agree that we should understand *food and drink* to be 'at the church's expense'; it is the right to maintenance that is mainly in mind. Paul's refusal to exercise this right is not a confession of ineligibility. The use of the plural may be epistolary (='I'; it is often difficult to be certain whether *we* in Paul's letters extends to others than the apostle). However, the transition from the singular in the earlier verses leads many to think that Paul is associating others (specifically Barnabas) with him here.

5. It is not the right of apostles to marry that this verse asserts. Nobody would have queried this in the apostolic age. It affirms rather the right *to take a believing wife along* on apostolic journeys, that is to say, a married apostle is entitled to take his wife with him at the church's expense. That *the other apostles* do this indicates that most were married (as we might have expected). Paul singles out *Cephas* (Peter) as a specially important case (*cf.* Mk. 1:30). The most natural interpretation of *the Lord's brothers* is that they were the children of Joseph and Mary. The views that they were the children of Joseph by a former marriage, or cousins of Jesus, do not rest on evidence, but are conjectures apparently based on the assumption that it would not have been seemly for Mary to have had children other than Jesus. But the repeated use of *brothers* without qualification is against such views.

6. *Only* is singular, which makes it seem as though *Barnabas* was added as an afterthought. Paul speaks of Barnabas and himself as two apostles (for Barnabas as an apostle, *cf.* Acts 14:4,14) who did not refrain from earning their own living while preaching. This seems to imply that it was the custom of others to do so.

7. From three diverse human activities Paul shows his right to be maintained. The soldier, the man who plants a vineyard, and the shepherd all draw their sustenance from their occupation, and the inference is that Christian apostles are entitled to do the same. Notice the differing status: the soldier was commonly paid wages, the man who plants a vineyard may here be the owner (he eats 'the grapes', not *of* them as NIV), while the shepherd more often than not was a slave. Yet all were fed from their occupation.

8. The argumentative questions continue. The first is introduced by *mē*, indicating that a negative answer is expected. Paul rejects the thought that the principle he is enunciating and illustrating from various fields of human endeavour rests simply on human wisdom (it is not *a human point of view*). He can show it in *the Law* (his question expects the answer 'Yes'). The Jews used *Law* strictly for the first five books of our Old Testament, but sometimes more loosely for the whole of sacred Scripture. But whichever the usage, the *Law* is always regarded as authoritative.

9. In ancient Israel an ox was used in threshing; the animal trampled the corn, thus shaking the grain loose from the husks. The mixture was tossed up in a breeze so that the wind blew the chaff away, while the heavier grain fell straight down. *The Law* provided that while the ox trod the grain he was not to be muzzled (Dt. 25:4), which meant that he could eat some of it. The question *Is it about oxen that God is concerned?* looks for the answer 'No'. This does not mean that Paul held that God was indifferent to the needs of oxen (*cf.* Mt. 6:26; Lk. 12:6–7), nor that the verse does not apply to them. We should bear in mind, though, that it occurs in a passage dealing with people, not animals, and may have been meant figuratively from the first. Be that as it may, the Rabbis could argue from this verse that what is true of oxen is all the more true of men (Talmud, *BM* 88*b*). Paul is doing something like that. He is asking where the primary application of the words lies, and denying that it is with oxen. There is a principle; the worker shares in the fruit of his work, a principle that applies to oxen. And to apostles.

10. Paul maintains that the words he has quoted apply first and foremost to the preacher of the gospel. We may gather the force of it from Knox's translation, 'Is it not clear that he says it for our sakes?' So the Christian worker, be he ploughman or reaper (cf. 3:6), should do his work in hope. God provides for his needs from the fruits of his labour.

11. Paul becomes specific. The opening conditional clause implies that the condition has been fulfilled: 'If, as is the case, we sowed. . . .' Paul's sowing was his preaching at Corinth which had established the church there. He speaks of sowing, and he might have added that he did some reaping. But the precise function exercised is not important at this point. His concern is rather with the fact that anyone who labours to produce the harvest is entitled to a share in that harvest. Paul had laboured in *spiritual* things among them. He was fully entitled to receive from them *a material harvest*.

12. Others, it seems, had in fact exercised the right Paul speaks of. Perhaps Peter or Apollos or someone else had received gifts from the Corinthians. Paul did not. Some Corinthians evidently regarded this as proof that Paul was not a real apostle. They may have argued that Paul implicitly recognized his inferiority by not attempting to obtain the sustenance to which apostles were entitled. Paul counters that the founder of the church at Corinth has far more right to this sort of thing than anyone else (*we* is emphatic). Paul's word for *hinder* is unusual (here only in the New Testament). It means 'a cutting into', and was used of breaking up a road to prevent the enemy's advance. Paul had avoided doing anything that might prevent a clear road for the gospel advance.

13. *Don't you know* (see on 3:16) indicates that they ought to have known. It was common knowledge that those whose work was in sacred things received their livelihood from it. More particularly, those who *serve at* ('sit beside'; the word denotes habitual service) *the altar* receive their portion of what is offered on the altar (Lv. 7:6, 8–10,14,28–36, *etc.*).

14. In conformity with this, *the Lord*, none less, *has commanded that those who preach the gospel should receive their living from the gospel*. No command of the Lord has been preserved in precisely these terms. One may have been given, or Paul may be thinking of such words as 'the worker deserves his wages' (Lk. 10:7; *cf.* Mt. 10:8,10; 1 Tim. 5:18). Theissen thinks that by eschewing 'charismatic poverty' Paul could be charged with lack of trust in God's grace, for a true apostle would go out with nothing, and rely on God to supply his daily needs (Theissen, p. 43). Paul counters that charismatic poverty is a privilege, not a requirement.

2. *Paul's refusal to exercise his rights* (9:15–18)

Paul was in no doubt about his rights. But he had not always used them, and he proceeds to develop the point.

15. Paul's *I* is emphatic. Whatever the practice of others, *he* has not exercised his rights. Nor is his purpose in writing in this strain to establish a basis for a change of practice. So fiercely does he hold this conviction that he says *I would rather die* than change it. The text here is very difficult. Paul appears to break off his sentence and never complete it: 'It would be better for me to die than — No-one will make this boast of mine an empty one!' The break in construction marks Paul's deep emotion, and his emotion shows the importance he ascribed to his practice.

16. Preaching the gospel is no matter for boasting (there is *woe* for Paul if he does not preach it). He can claim no particular credit for this, for he is *compelled* to preach (*cf.* Je. 20:9). Not all are called to a ministry like Paul's, but none is exempt from the requirement of letting the grace of God be known. Paul thinks of some undefined disaster (*woe*) as coming to him if he does not preach. This is perhaps all the more effective in not being closely defined. These days we are not good at emphasizing duty, and we do not like the thought of punishment. Paul is clear about both.

17. There is more than one way of understanding this

difficult verse. Paul may mean that if (as he does) he preaches willingly, he merits a reward (or 'wage', *misthos*), whereas if he is not willing he must still do it, for an obligation is laid on him. Or he may be starting from the fact that he is 'compelled to preach' (v. 16). If his preaching were in fact voluntary, he would merit a reward; but as it is, he has no choice. He is Christ's slave (7:22; Rom. 1:1, *etc.*). He must preach. There is nothing of grace in *misthos*, *reward*, which rather signifies 'wages', 'the payment of what is due'. Paul can claim nothing, for he has done no more than he should and is an 'unprofitable servant' (Lk. 17:10). For *discharging the trust* (*oikonomia*) see the note on 'those entrusted' (*oikonomos*) in 4:1. The thought is that Paul is responsible to God; he must discharge the commission God has given him.

18. Paul had to preach. But he did not have to preach without charge. He did not see this simply as good strategy. He has already said that it is his boast (v. 15), something he delights in. Now he says it is his *reward*: his pay is to serve without pay! Preaching without pay is his privilege. The gospel gave him rights, but he chose not to use them.

3. Paul's service of all people (9:19–23)
The apostle did not stand on his dignity, but adapted himself to the position of his hearers in a whole-hearted determination to win them for Christ.

19. Nothing could more strongly show his abandonment of his rights than this astonishing statement. He was a *free* man (and proud of his Roman citizenship), but made himself *a slave to everyone* (and specifically to those very Corinthians, 2 Cor. 4:5 where 'servant' translates *doulos*), so that he could gain the more.

20. Paul could assert his Jewishness (2 Cor. 11:22; Phil. 3:5), but here he speaks of becoming *like a Jew*. His prime relationship was to Christ, and he saw himself accordingly as *not under the law* (the law of Moses). For him 'Christ is the end of the law' (Rom. 10:4); the believer is 'not under law, but under grace'

(Rom. 6:14). But in approaching Jews he conformed to practices that would enable him to win *those under the law*. The sort of thing in mind is his circumcision of Timothy (Acts 16:1-3) and his joining in Jewish 'purification rites' (Acts 21:23-26). He always respected Jewish scruples. He asked Jews not so much to give up the practice of the law as their confidence in it (Phil. 3:3ff.). Their trust must be in Christ.

21. *Those not having the law* are the Gentiles, those not bound by the law mentioned in v. 20. Paul met them on their own ground (*cf.* Acts 17:22ff.). D. Daube points out that Jewish rabbis such as Hillel made the law no more burdensome than necessary in their endeavours to win people for Judaism (*The New Testament and Rabbinic Judaism*, Athlone, 1956, pp. 336ff.). Paul went further. He did not bring them under Jewish law at all; he became *like one not having the law*. He does not mean that he was a lawless person; he was *not free from God's law*, but was *under Christ's law*. His disavowal of subjection to the Jewish law is emphatic. But equally emphatic is his commitment to ethical ends in the service of God (Rom. 7:22; Gal. 6:2). He is not making Christianity into a 'new law'; he is affirming his commitment to the kind of life that befits the servant of God. And as far as this service allows he says he conformed to Gentile practice *so as to win* Gentiles.

22. This whole discussion has underlined Paul's tender concern for *the weak*. But, unlike the Jews and the Gentiles of the previous verses, *the weak* were already Christians. He does not seek *to win* them in the same sense, but to win them for greater strength, or perhaps simply to keep them from slipping. He respected their scruples and conformed his behaviour to theirs to help them. He sums it all up with *I have become all things to all men*. This does not, of course, mean that his conduct was unprincipled. On occasion his principles led him to follow courses of action in the teeth of strong opposition. But where no principle was at stake he was prepared to go to extreme lengths to meet people. Personal considerations are totally submerged in the great aim of by all means saving some. H. Chadwick finds in this sort of thing evidence that Paul 'had an astonishing elasticity of mind, and a flexibility in dealing with situations requiring delicate and ingenious treatment' (*NTS*, 1, 1954–55, p. 275).

23. Paul's conduct was determined by the gospel. That was what mattered, not the preacher. Yet he is not unmindful of his own need, and he looks to *share in its* (the gospel's) *blessings*. Yet even here he thinks of others, for *share* points to partnership.

4. Paul's self-control (9:24–27)
Athletic contests were common in the Greek world, and the Isthmian Games, second only to the Olympic Games, were held every two years at Corinth. Paul often uses imagery from the Games.

24. A foot race yielded but one winner. Therefore the runners must make every effort. Winning is more than simply starting in the race. The parallel with the Christian way is not complete, for many are saved, not just one winner. Paul's point is that, like the runner, the Christian must give of his best.

25. *Competes in the games* renders *agōnizomai*, which gives us words like 'agony' and 'agonize'. It does not mean a half-hearted effort. Every competitor had to undergo *strict training* for ten months, during which he was 'temperate in all things' (AV). After all this, his reward if he won was *a crown that will not last* (in the Isthmian Games it was a pine wreath at first, later celery was used, and towards the end of the first century, pine again; *SPC*, p. 101). The Christian has before him something much more worth while, *a crown that will last for ever* (*cf.* 2 Tim. 4:8). The strenuous self-denial of the athlete as he sought a fleeting reward is a rebuke to half-hearted, flabby Christian service. The athlete denies himself many lawful pleasures and the Christian must similarly avoid not only definite sin, but anything that hinders spiritual progress.

26. The imagery from the Games continues. Paul is not like a runner who does not know where the finishing-line is, or a boxer who hits nothing but air (either shadow-sparring or missing his opponent). Paul's Christianity is purposeful. He puts everything into direct and forceful Christian endeavour.

27. Paul refuses to be bound by bodily desires. In picturesque language he speaks of the way he disciplines himself. *Beat* renders *hypōpiazō*, a verb from boxing, with the meaning 'give a black eye to'. This, coupled with *make it my slave*, leaves no doubt as to the vigour with which Paul subdues his body. This does not mean that he saw the body as evil. That is not a Christian position. Paul is saying emphatically that the body must be controlled. *Disqualified* translates *adokimos*, which means 'which has not stood the test'; it was used of disqualification in the Games. Paul's fear was not that he might lose his salvation, but that he might suffer loss through failing to satisfy his Lord (*cf.* 3:15).

D. THE EXAMPLE OF THE ISRAELITES (10:1–13)

1. A reference to history (10:1–5)
Paul has argued that the strong should have a concern for the weak, and has emphasized his own example. Now he shows from the history of the people of God that the enjoyment of high privilege does not guarantee final blessing. The Israelites of old experienced redemption, baptism and God's continuing help. But they flirted with idolatry and nearly all of them perished in the wilderness. It may be that some of the Corinthians felt that their baptism and their use of Holy Communion guaranteed their final salvation, no matter what they did. Paul warns them that this is not so. Idolatry brings ruin.

1. *For* ties this section to the preceding. The danger of being 'disqualified' is very real, as the case of the Israelites in the wilderness shows. *I do not want you to be ignorant* is a formula Paul uses to introduce something new and important (Rom. 1:13; 11:25; 1 Cor. 12:1; 2 Cor. 1:8; 1 Thes. 4:13). It is interesting that in writing to a Gentile church he speaks of *our forefathers*. Clearly he sees the church as the true Israel. The word *all* occurs five times in vv. 1–4 (NIV omits the word before *drank*); the Israelites, without exception, received the tokens of God's good hand on them. The fact that most perished (v. 5) comes accordingly with greater force. *The cloud* was the means of divine guidance at the time of the Exodus (Ex. 13:21–22), when the people *passed through the sea* (Ex. 14:21–22).

2. The experiences linked with the cloud and the sea (Ex. 13:21–22; 14:21–22) united Israel to Moses in such a way that *they were all baptised into Moses.* NIV accepts the passive, but, with Metzger, it is likely that we should see the verb as middle with a force like 'they got themselves baptized' (Goodspeed, 'all, as it were, accepted baptism as followers of Moses'). It is startling for the Christian, who is 'baptised into Christ' (Rom. 6:3; Gal. 3:27), to read of baptism *into Moses*. Probably we are to think of Moses as a type of Christ. Just as baptism in one aspect brings people under the leadership of Christ, so participation in the great events of the Exodus brought the Israelites under the leadership of Moses (*cf.* 'they believed in the Lord and in his servant Moses', Ex. 14:31, RSV). They were united to him, though we should not press this, for no other union can be anything like as close as that between Christians and Christ. All the Israelites shared the common baptism, but that did not prevent most of them from perishing on account of their subsequent sin.

3. They were all likewise sustained by the manna (Ex. 16:4,13ff.), here called *spiritual food*. The adjective does not mean that Paul doubts the physical reality of the manna. It is his way of directing attention to the heavenly origin of this food (*cf.* Ps. 78:24); RSV has 'supernatural'.

4. When he refers to their *spiritual drink* Paul adds an explanation, as he did not do with his reference to food. Moses got water from a rock at the beginning and end of the wilderness wanderings (Ex. 17:1–7; Nu. 20:2–13), and this apparently was the origin of a Jewish legend that a rock travelled with the people. Paul may have had this legend at the back of his mind, but he does not refer to it. He refers to Christ and sees him as following the Israelites and continually giving them drink. He transfers to Christ the title, 'the Rock', used of Yahweh (Dt. 32:15; Ps. 18:2, *etc.*), a transfer that is significant for Christology, as of course is the clear implication of Christ's pre-existence (*cf.* Conzelmann, 'The "was" . . . means real preexistence'). The reference to spiritual food and drink is surely made (as Calvin and others have thought) in the light of the Holy Communion. Israel had her equivalents of both sacraments.

5. *Nevertheless* (the strong adversative *alla*), although God had given them such signal manifestations of his power and goodness, the majority failed to enter the Promised Land. God was *not pleased* with them. *Most of them* is a masterly understatement. Of all the hosts of Israel only two men entered Canaan; the rest perished in the wilderness. Paul's verb *katastrōnnymi* adds a picturesque touch; he sees the wilderness as strewn with bodies ('their corpses littered the desert', JB). This is not simply natural death. It is God's sentence against the rebels.

2. Idolatry and its lessons (10:6–13)
Paul brings out the fact that we are to see these events as history indeed, but as more than history. They are 'types' conveying spiritual lessons.

6. *Examples* renders *typoi* (see *TNTC* on 1 Thes. 1:7, p. 46). The meaning is that certain things in the history of Israel prefigured spiritual realities in the Messianic age. God had a purpose in them both at the time they happened and for later generations. In this case it was *to keep us from setting our hearts on evil things*. No-one who seriously considers what God did to the sinning Israelites will lightly follow their example.

7. The warning against idolatry is very relevant to conditions in Corinth. Paul quotes Exodus 32:6, where the eating and drinking and dancing point to a typical idol festival. Often such a festival degenerated into a debauch. There was no sense of serious purpose in idol worship (how could there be?). The lowest passions might be, and often were, unleashed in the very act of worship.

8. This is not a new subject, for fornication (*sexual immorality*) formed part of much idol worship. Sacred prostitutes were found at many shrines, and Corinth had an unenviable notoriety in this respect. But Paul's primary reference is to the incident in which Israel 'began to indulge in sexual immorality with Moabite women', and 'joined in worshipping the Baal of Peor' (Nu. 25:1,3). Judgment came in the form of a plague, and twenty-four thousand people perished (Nu. 25:9). Paul speaks of *twenty-three thousand*, but both are obviously round numbers, and in addition Paul may be making some allowance for those slain by the judges (Nu. 25:5). The words emphasize that idolatry exposes people to serious danger.

9. So we should not *test the Lord* (the verb (*ek*)*peirazō* means 'to test' but usually with a view to the person failing; thus it has a secondary meaning 'tempt'). The idea in 'testing' or 'tempting' God is that of seeing how far one can go (*cf.* Acts 5:9; Heb. 3:9). Paul urges the Corinthians not to *test the Lord* (many MSS have 'Christ'); Israel did this of old when the people complained about food, with the result that God sent fiery serpents among them (Nu. 21:5–6; *cf.* Ps. 78:18).

10. The verb *grumble* is used a number of times of the Israelites complaining against God (Nu. 14:2,36, *etc.*), a complaint followed in each case by suitable punishment. Here the reference is probably to the overthrow of the company of Korah (Nu. 16). *The destroying angel* (Phillips, 'the Angel of Death') does not occur in exactly that form in the Old Testament (though *cf.* Ex. 12:23; 2 Sa. 24:16; Is. 37:36), nor in the New (though *cf.* Heb. 11:28). But the meaning is clear enough. Grumbling about God calls down divine punishment.

11. Paul sums up by saying that these things are *examples*, recorded as *warnings*. *The fulfilment of the ages* is a curious expression (which many oversimplify, as JB, 'at the end of the age', or GNB, 'when the end is about to come'). It appears to mean that the culmination of all past ages has arrived. The coming of Christ has decisive significance. All previous ages come to their appointed end in him. Those ages are now completed and the lessons they teach are open to us. We should then reap the fruits of the experience of those ages.

12. The Corinthians were very sure of themselves. But then, so had the Israelites been. They had dallied with idolatry and reaped nothing but disaster. Let the self-confident take heed lest they fall.

13. *Temptation* (see on v. 9) is sometimes understood simply as 'test' (GNB, Héring), a meaning it certainly has on occasion. But here it is used in a broad sense which includes both 'test' and 'temptation'. Nothing exceptional in either way had happened to the Corinthians. They had experienced only *what is common to man*. And God is not simply a spectator of the affairs of life; he is concerned and active. Believers can count on his help. He will always make *a way out*. This word (*ekbasis*) may denote a mountain defile. The imagery is that of an army trapped in rugged country, which manages to escape from an impossible situation through a mountain pass. The assurance of this verse is a permanent comfort and strength to believers. Our trust is in the faithfulness of God.

E. THE INCOMPATIBILITY OF CHRISTIAN AND IDOL FEASTS (10:14-22)

14. *Therefore* (*dioper*), a stronger particle than that in v. 12, indicates a very close logical sequence. *My dear friends* (*agapētoi mou*, 'my beloved') is not a common form of address; it indicates Paul's deep emotion as he counsels these dear friends to take the right course. He had urged them to 'flee fornication' (6:18), and he now says *flee from idolatry*. Here, as there, the present imperative signifies the habitual practice. There is to be no leisurely contemplation of the sin, thinking that one can go so far, and be safe from going further. The only wise course is to have nothing to do with it. 'They must not try how near they can go, but how far they can fly' (Robertson and Plummer; *cf.* Chrysostom, 'he did not say, simply, depart, but "flee" '). Paul has just assured them of God's help in time of temptation. But that does not give them licence to dally needlessly with it. They must *flee* from it.

15. The Corinthians prided themselves on their wisdom (2 Cor. 11:19); now Paul appeals to it. They are *sensible people* (*phronimos*, not *sophos* as in 1:20ff.), and *yourselves* is emphatic. Paul does not need to demonstrate the point. They can see it for themselves.

16. 'The cup of blessing' (NIV *thanksgiving*) is the name the Jews gave the cup at the end of a meal, over which a thanksgiving was said; it was also used of the third cup at the Passover feast. It is possibly this cup with which Jesus instituted the sacrament of Holy Communion (though Rabbi Dan Cohn-Sherbok thinks that Jesus' blessing was over the fourth cup and that Paul means simply 'the cup which Jesus blessed', *NTS* 27, 1980–81, pp. 704–709). 'Bless' does not mean that a blessing was somehow attached to the cup; it means that a prayer of thanksgiving was said over it (hence the translation of NIV). Among the Jews the usual form of thanksgiving began, 'Blessed art Thou, O Lord', after which came the matter for thanksgiving. Paul is referring then to the prayer of thanksgiving said over the cup at Holy Communion. Chrysostom comments, 'he called it a cup of blessing, because holding it in our hands, we so exalt Him in our hymn, wondering, astonished at His unspeakable gift. . . .' The cup is mentioned before the bread, though when Paul comes to deal with the institution (11:23ff.) the bread comes first. The order here may be due to a desire to stress the shedding of the blood of the Lord, or it may be due to the prominence of the cup and the insignificance of bread in the pagan sacrifices to which Paul is leading up. In Holy Communion there is *a participation in the blood of Christ* ('The basic idea is that of the atoning power of the blood', Conzelmann). Those who receive the cup rightly receive Christ. They are bound together in fellowship with Christ. 'The soul has as truly *communion in the blood*, as we drink wine with the mouth' (Calvin). Such reception is, of course, a spiritual process, and therefore takes place by faith. Paul says that the faithful communicant receives Christ, but nothing about the 'how' of it. Hodge points out that Roman Catholics, Lutherans and Reformed all agree 'that a participation of the cup is a participation of the blood of Christ'. But doctrines like transubstantiation or consubstantiation cannot be demonstrated from these words. 'All that the passage asserts is the fact of a participation, the nature of that participation must be determined from other sources.' The statement about *the bread* is to be understood similarly: the broken loaf means *a participation in the body of Christ*.

17. This is a difficult verse to interpret in detail, but the stress on unity is clear. The *one loaf* at Communion symbolizes and brings about unity. Believers are *many*, but they are *one body*. The word *for* points to the place of Holy Communion in bringing about unity. Communicants are united to Christ and united to one another.

18. Paul develops his point from the example of *the people of Israel* ('Israel according to the flesh'). The expression distinguishes physical Israel from the true Israel, the church (*cf.* Gal. 6:16). Jews *who eat the sacrifices* by that very fact *participate* (the word is cognate with 'participation' in v. 16) *in the altar*. Those who receive the food of sacrifice enter into fellowship with all that the altar stands for.

19. The problem before the Corinthians was a difficult one. To eat idol meat might be held to sanction idolatry; not to eat it might imply that the idol was real. Paul starts with vigorous questions that imply that the idol sacrifice and the idol are both shams.

20. *No* is the strong adversative *alla*. Far from the preceding, Paul affirms something that is nearly its opposite. He will not dispute the contention of the Corinthians that an idol is not a god at all. But he will not agree that therefore idols can safely be treated as nothing more than so many blocks of wood and stone. The *demons* use people's readiness to worship idols. Thus, when people sacrifice to idols, it cannot be said that they are engaging in some meaningless or neutral activity. They are sacrificing to evil spirits (*cf.* Dt. 32:16f.). Paul has shown from the usage of both Christians and Jews that to share food is to establish fellowship. Idol worshippers are entering into fellowship with *demons*. Paul does not wish this to befall his Corinthian friends.

21. He puts the alternatives in stark contrast. It is impossible for people to be participants in both the Holy Communion and idol feasts if they realize what they are doing. The one necessarily excludes the other. There is no room for compromise. *The Lord's table* reminds us that the Lord is the host at the sacrament. By parity of reasoning *the table of demons* indicates that there may be other hosts. But those who accept the Lord's invitation cannot in good conscience also accept the invitation of *demons*. If we are really in fellowship with the Lord we cannot also be in fellowship with demons. Some have thought that the reference to the two tables here shows that the Holy Communion is essentially a sacrifice (just as an offering to an idol is a sacrifice). But the inference is not valid. All that Paul is saying is that the Holy Communion, in one aspect, is a feeding at the table of the Lord, an enjoyment of fellowship with him. Similarly participation in an idol feast means having fellowship with demons. There may be many other aspects to either. Identity of principle is neither asserted nor implied.

22. 'Or' at the beginning of the verse in the better mss brings us to an alternative. Paul has been assuming that the Corinthians do not realize the significance of taking part in idol feasts and has therefore explained it. But suppose they did understand what they were doing? Then they would be wilfully provoking the Lord (Dt. 32:21). The second question brings home the weakness of us all before our Maker and therefore the incredible folly of the kind of action of which he speaks.

F. THE PRACTICAL OUTCOME (10:23 – 11:1)

23. '*Everything is permissible*' repeats a statement already made (6:12, where see notes). As before, Paul repeats it, but this time follows the repetition with *not everything is constructive* ('not all things build up'; for 'build up' see on 8:1). Christian liberty is important, but there are some things that are not wise. They neither build the believer up in the faith, nor help other people (v. 24). It is more important to avoid such actions than to assert one's rights.

24. The Christian has a concern for the well-being, *the good*, of others. It is important to promote the best interests of other people, not selfishly to seek our own.

25. Paul has refused to countenance attendance at idol feasts. Now he turns to *the meat market*, where food of all kinds was sold. We saw earlier (on 8:1–6) that it would be difficult if not impossible to know for certain whether a particular piece of meat had or had not been offered to an idol. Paul sees no point in raising the issue: 'don't ask fussy questions' (Barclay). This is in sharp contrast to the Jewish approach. Jews were very scrupulous and made searching inquiries before they would eat meat. Paul's attitude was revolutionary. He took seriously the truth that an idol is nothing. This refusal to ask questions shows it did not matter to him whether a piece of meat had been offered to an idol or not. He discouraged over-scrupulousness.

26. The reason is that everything belongs to God (Ps. 24:1). Whatever the pagan may do before his idol, the believer knows that the meat comes from the goodness of the Lord and from no other source. Therefore, even though there may be some doubt as to what has happened to it on the way, its divine origin means that the Christian may eat it.

27. Paul gives a similar ruling about an invitation to a meal. A meal in a private home is meant, for eating in idol temples has already been dealt with. When invited by a pagan a Christian is at liberty to accept, and to eat whatever is provided without asking where it came from. That is his host's business.

28. The situation is different if someone expressly says, '*This has been offered in sacrifice.*' Earlier Paul has used the term *eidōlo-*

thytos of meat sacrificed to an idol (8:1,4,7,10); now he uses *hierothytos*, 'devoted, offered to a god' (LSJ), the term a pagan would naturally use (Theissen, indeed, thinks only a pagan would use the word, p. 131). Paul does not say who would make this remark. Some think he means the host, some a pagan fellow-guest, some a 'weak' Christian at the table. There is no way of being sure, but perhaps the last mentioned is most likely (who else would have a 'conscience' about idol meat?). By whomever made, the remark alters the situation. Now the meat is not simply a good gift of God that has passed through unknown channels. It is the end-product of idolatry and known to be such. To eat under such circumstances, some would think, would be to countenance idolatry. The Christian must therefore not eat *for conscience' sake*.

29. This means *the other man's conscience*. The strong Christian knows that offering meat to an idol cannot really alter its character, for the idol is nothing; his conscience is clear. But a pagan observer thinks the idol is a god, and thus sees the Christian who eats the meat as sanctioning his idolatry. A weak Christian observer will be in danger of being harmed in the way noted earlier (8:10ff.). Whatever the status of the informer, then, the wise and kindly course for the strong Christian is to abstain from eating. Godet explains the question at the end of the verse: 'For what advantage can there be in my liberty being condemned. . .?' The action, which to the strong is a simple exercise of *freedom*, must not be made the means of offence to another.

30. *With thankfulness* translates *chariti*, which may be understood as 'by grace' (AV). Most recent translations agree with NIV, but Orr and Walther see 'Paul's declaration of his *share in grace*' as 'the clue to the understanding of how he is consistent through this whole discussion'. It is because of what the grace of God means that the strong Christian can give thanks for such meat and eat it. Paul does not want an action done in this spirit to be the occasion for evil-speaking on the part of people who do not understand. It is better to abstain. What the believer eats does not matter; that he avoids giving offence does.

31. The principle is clear. The Christian is not concerned with his rights, but with *the glory of God* (*cf.* Col. 3:17). Eating, drinking, everything must be subordinated to this.

32. Paul urges his friends to have a tender concern for all, *Jews*, *Greeks* and *the church of God*. Their conduct might have repercussions in any of these groups, and they should try to give no offence to any.

33–11:1. As elsewhere, Paul appeals to his own example. He is not guided by personal advantage but consideration for *the good of many*, specifically their salvation. He calls on his converts to imitate him, but in the very act of saying this he points them away from himself. The reason they should imitate him is that he imitates Christ. His example points them to the Saviour.

VI. DISORDERS IN PUBLIC WORSHIP (11:2 – 14:40)

The Corinthians had asked Paul about one aspect of public worship at least, as we see from the 'Now concerning' of 12:1. Paul makes comments on other aspects, which the Corinthians may have mentioned in their letter, or the visitors (16:17) may have reported to Paul.

A. THE VEILING OF WOMEN (11:2–16)

Evidently some 'emancipated' Corinthian women[1] had dispensed with the veil in public worship, and Paul argues that they should not do this. Jewish women were always veiled in public in the first century, but it is difficult to be certain about what was done elsewhere. A. Oepke thinks that customs varied (*TDNT*, iii, p. 562), but Conzelmann can say, 'It can be assumed

---

[1] It is a mark of the outlook of women at Corinth in New Testament times that they competed in the Games. Murphy-O'Connor cites an inscription referring to a number of women, including a redoubtable Hedea, who won the war-chariot race at the Isthmian Games in AD 43, the 200 metres at two other Games, and a prize for young lyre players (*SPC*, p. 16).

that respectable Greek women wore a head covering in public.' If so, the practice of the Corinthian Christian ladies outraged the proprieties. Paul rejected it with decision. It is no part of the life of the Christian needlessly to flout accepted conventions.

2. Paul begins with praise. Perhaps the Corinthians had said that they remembered what he had told them, and the apostle expresses his pleasure. The *teachings* (*paradoseis*) were the 'traditions', the oral teaching that formed such an important part of early Christian instruction. They were not Paul's own, but teachings handed down to him and which he passed on. The term stresses the derivative nature of the teachings in question, and particularly of the gospel (15:1ff.). It did not originate in the fertile mind of the teacher (see further, *TNTC* on 2 Thes. 2:15, p. 138).

3. It is easy to be too definite in interpreting *head* in this verse. We use the term often for a person in authority (*cf.* 'Heads of State'), but this usage was unknown in antiquity (except for a few passages in LXX). LSJ note usages of *kephalē* for the whole person, for life, extremity, top (of wall or column), source, *etc.*, but never for the leader of a group. S. Bedale reminds us that the functions of the central nervous system were not known to the ancients, who held that we think with the midriff, the *phrēn* (*JTS*, n.s., v, 1954, pp. 211–215). The head was thus not the controlling factor (as GNB takes it with the translation 'supreme over'); we must seek its significance elsewhere. 'Head' was used of the 'source' (as 'head' of a river), and LSJ cite an appropriate passage which says, 'Zeus is the head, Zeus is the middle, in Zeus all is completed' (II.d; they note that *archē*, 'beginning', is a variant for *kephalē* in some MSS). It seems that it is this meaning 'source' that is required here (so Bedale, Barrett, Bruce, and others; H. Schlier says, 'Paul could have used *archē* if there had not been a closer personal relationship in *kephalē*', *TDNT*, iii, p. 679). Paul is saying that the woman derives her being from man (Gn. 2:21–22), as man does from Christ and Christ from God. But we must be cautious in pressing these words, for none of the relationships mentioned is exactly the same as either of the others. Some translations speak of the husband here (*e.g.* RSV, GNB), but it is surely the relation of men and women that is in mind, not husband and wife. Marriage is not mentioned. Paul has just used the same word in the expression *every man*, which plainly refers to mankind, not husbands (*cf.* 8:6). Further, to understand *woman* here as 'wife' raises the question of unmarried women. Are they to worship with uncovered heads? It seems clear that it is 'man', not 'husband', that Paul means.

4. The order of creation has consequences for worship, but Paul's precise meaning is not easy to see. NIV, as many translations, sees the unusual Greek to mean *with his head covered*. But what Paul says is 'having down from (his) head' (*kata kephalēs echōn*), and not a few argue that this means 'having long hair' (which hangs down from the head). J. Murphy-O'Connor favours a reference to long hair, more precisely 'an un-masculine hair-do', with a possible reference to homosexuality (*CBQ*, 42, 1980, pp. 482–500). But, while long hair fits the Greek of v. 4, it runs into a problem with the use of 'cover' and 'uncover' in later verses. On the whole it seems that we should understand the apostle to refer to a covering on the head of the man. He will go on to speak of the man as 'the image and glory of God' (v. 7), and now he says that if he *prays or prophesies* with covered head he *dishonours his head*. The one who is God's image and glory must not veil that glory in the act of worship. It is not unlikely that the dishonoured *head* is both the man's physical head and also Christ, 'the head of every man' (v. 3). For *prophesies* see on 12:10.

5. This verse plainly indicates that some Corinthian women prayed or prophesied in public worship. That Paul does not criticize the practice, but on the contrary lays down the way women should be dressed when engaging in it, shows that he accepted it (which raises a problem with 14:34–35, where see notes). Here his point is that a woman must have a head-covering when engaging in prayer and prophecy. Otherwise she *dishonours her head* (which seems to mean her physical head). It is as bad for her to pray or prophesy in this way as it would be if she were *shaved*. Moffatt cites evidence for the shame of a shaven woman (including a comedy of Menander, set in Corinth).

6. Paul drives his point home. If a woman will not cover her head, then let that head be shorn. If she counts it *a disgrace* for her head to be shorn or shaven, let her understand that it is equally a shame to have her head uncovered at worship.

7. The reason a man should not cover his head is that he is *the image and glory of God*. In the creation story we read that God made man in his own image (Gn. 1:26–27). Genesis makes no distinction between the sexes at this point, but Paul understands it particularly of the male. *Glory* is not mentioned in the Genesis story (though *cf.* Ps. 8:5, and passages where 'heart' or 'soul' renders the Hebrew for 'glory', *e.g.* Pss. 16:9; 57:8). Man shows forth God's *glory* as does nothing else; the expression may also be meant to direct attention to the state of man before the Fall. When people worship, this high dignity must be recognized; *the glory of God* is not to be obscured in the presence of God (by covering the head of its bearer). The woman is not made in the image of man (it was Seth, not Eve, who was in the image of Adam, Gn. 5:3). Her relationship to man is not the same as that of man to God. She has a place of her own, but it is not the man's place. She stands in such a relation to the man as does nothing else, and thus she is called *the glory of man*. And it is precisely the glory *of man* that should be veiled in the presence of God. In worship God alone must be glorified.

8–9. *Man did not come from* (*ek* denotes the source) *woman*; he was the result of the direct creation of God. *But woman from man* refers to Eve's being made from a rib taken from Adam's side (Gn. 2:21ff.). The same passage explains *neither was man created for woman, but woman for man*. God said, 'It is not good for the man to be alone. I will make a helper suitable for him' (Gn. 2:18; D. Kidner comments, 'the sexes are complementary: the true partnership is expounded by the terms that are used', *TOTC, Genesis*, p. 65). Neither in her origin, nor in the purpose for which she was created, can the woman claim priority.

10. This verse is very difficult. What Paul says is something like 'the woman ought to have authority on her head', but most translations understand this of the subjection of the woman (JB, 'covering their heads with a symbol of the authority over them'; GNB, 'to show that she is under her husband's authority'; RSV, 'a veil on her head', rewrites rather than translates). But *exousia* means 'authority', not 'subjection'; when anyone is said 'to have authority' it does not mean that the person is set under someone. W. M. Ramsay poured scorn on the idea that the term can indicate woman's subjection, seeing this as 'a preposterous idea which a Greek scholar would laugh at anywhere except in the N.T.' (cited in Robertson and Plummer). Paul appears to be saying that there is a new view of women in Christianity. They are not to be regarded as an inferior species, as was generally the case in the ancient world. Christ's new creation makes everything new (2 Cor. 5:17), and distinctions that matter so highly to men, including that between male and female, no longer count (Gal. 3:27–28); Paul will insist on equality in v. 11. He has said that women pray and prophesy in worship (v. 5). For that they need *authority* and he is saying that their head-covering is their *sign of authority*. As M. D. Hooker puts it, 'Far from being a symbol of the woman's subjection to man, therefore, her head-covering is what Paul calls it – authority: in prayer and prophecy she, like the man, is under the authority of God' (*NTS*, 10, 1963–64, p. 416).

In Judaism women had a very minor place; they were not even counted in the number required for a synagogue (ten males). Christianity gave them a new and significant place, and their head-covering is a mark of their new authority. The differences arising from creation remain; Paul is not trying to obliterate them. But he is clear that Christian women have *authority*. The idea that the covering of the woman's head is a sign of subjection to her husband runs into another difficulty. In praying or prophesying she is acting in obedience to God; why should she demonstrate subordination to a man in such an activity? Her head-covering, her authority for praying or prophesying, is the veiling of 'the glory of man' (v. 7).

There is a further problem in the expression *because of the angels*. Paul probably means that there is more to worship than the people in the congregation see. Good angels are there. *The angels* observe, and *the woman* must not be unseemly before them.[1] This is the more appropriate in that angels serve believers (Heb. 1:14) and do not rebel at the task. Some have thought that Paul has in mind bad angels who will lust against unveiled women (in the spirit of Gn. 6:2), but this seems unlikely. *The angels* without qualification would not be understood as evil spirits. Moreover there seems no reason why such angels should be tempted only during worship.

11. Paul makes it clear that what he has been saying is not meant as an undue subordination of women. There is a partnership between the sexes and *in the Lord* neither exists without the other (NEB, 'in Christ's fellowship woman is as essential to man as man to woman'). The man must not exaggerate the significance of his having been created first. There is a fundamental equality.

12. Paul repeats the point that *woman came from man* (v. 8). Now he supplements it by pointing out that *man is born of woman*, more literally, 'the man is through (*dia*) the woman'. The reference is no longer to the Genesis story, but to the ordinary processes of birth (so NIV). In this sense every man is 'through' the woman. The addition *everything comes from God* is a typical Pauline reminder of the priority of the divine. *From* is *ek*, denoting origin; the source, the origin of all things and all people is God. Neither man nor woman is an independent being. The implications for conduct are plain.

13. Paul makes an appeal to the Corinthians' own understanding of the fitness of things. *Yourselves* is emphatic both from its position and also because *autois* is added to *hymin*. They can surely work out for themselves what is *proper*. They need not rely on Paul to direct them.

[1] J. A. Fitzmyer draws attention to passages in the Dead Sea Scrolls in which men with any blemish (cripples, diseased, *etc.*) are excluded from the army or from the assembly, because of the presence of angels (*NTS*, 4, 1957–58, pp. 48–58). No unseemliness must come before them.

14-15. Paul proceeds to appeal to nature. Nature gives women longer hair than it does men, a difference which has usually, though not universally, been reflected in hair-styles. Some of the ancient Greeks had long hair, for example the Spartans and some of the philosophers. But generally speaking men have reflected the distinctions made in nature by using shorter hair-styles than those of women. This certainly must have been the case in first-century Corinth and in the places known to those who lived there, else Paul could not have couched his appeal in these terms. By contrast *long hair* is a glory to a woman. The precise length is not specified and it is not important. Paul simply says that it is longer than that of the man and this is accepted as *her glory*. Nature is giving a hint at the need for a woman to have her head covered on appropriate occasions. Indeed her hair is given to her *as a covering*.

16. But Paul has no intention of arguing the matter with anyone given to wordy battles (*contentious, philoneikos,* means someone who loves strife). Such people are capable of prolonging an argument indefinitely. In the face of such an attitude Paul points to universal Christian custom; Christians have *no other practice*. Exactly who he means by *we* is not clear; it may mean Paul himself, or the apostles generally, or those with him when he wrote the letter. But the addition *nor do the churches of God* shows that what he has outlined is the common practice throughout the churches.

This section of the letter raises the perennial question of the relationship of current social customs to Christian morality and practice. Behind all that Paul says is the principle that Christians must always act in a seemly manner: 'everything should be done in a fitting and orderly way' (14:40). The application of this principle to first-century Corinth yields the direction that women must have their heads covered when they worship. The principle is of permanent validity, but we may well feel that its application to the contemporary scene need not yield the same result. In other words, in the light of our totally different social customs, we may well hold that the fullest acceptance of the principle underlying this chapter does not require that in

Western lands in the twentieth century women must always wear hats when they pray. 'We must remember that when Paul spoke about women as he did in the letters to the Corinthians, he was writing to the most licentious city in the ancient world, and that in such a place modesty had to be observed and more than observed; and that it is quite unfair to wrest a local ruling from the circumstances in which it was given, and to make it a universal principle' (W. Barclay, *Letters to the Seven Churches* (SCM, 1957), p. 75).

B. THE LORD'S SUPPER (11:17–34)

1. The offences (11:17–22)

Accustomed as we are to the service of Holy Communion as the most solemn and dignified of services, this passage comes as something of a surprise. Clearly the service was far from being edifying, or even dignified, in first-century Corinth. The passage is of interest as the earliest account we have of a Communion service. It also contains significant teaching on the theology of Holy Communion.

17. There is nothing in the Greek corresponding to *following* (as NIV, RSV, GNB, *etc.*); Paul says, 'commanding you this', where 'this' would naturally refer to the preceding (*cf.* NEB, 'In giving you these injunctions'). Then he goes on to a further matter. His verb (*parangellō*) is authoritative; Paul is not offering a few academic comments, but giving a firm directive. He goes on to the supreme condemnation of any assembly for worship: *your meetings do more harm than good.* Instead of Holy Communion being supremely an act of edification, it was disruptive.

18. *In the first place*, says Paul, but he never gets round to 'secondly' or the like. There is no article with *church*, and some hold that the word is used here in the older sense of 'assembly' (as in Acts 19:32,39,41). It is the coming together of believers that is in mind. But, even when people met for worship, Paul has heard that there were *divisions* (*schismata*). The word is that used in 1:10, but the divisions are probably not the same. Those were based on loyalties to teachers, these were economic (some had food and some had none). *To some extent I believe it* shows that Paul was not credulous. He recognized that there was some exaggeration in the account that had reached him, but he recognized also an unpleasant amount of truth.

19. He accepts the inevitability of *differences* (*haireseis*). The word has to do with choosing and means those who have chosen in the same way, *e.g.* the Sadducees (Acts 5:17), the Pharisees (Acts 15:5), and the Christians (Acts 24:5,14). But the choosing can be disruptive; it may be one of 'the works of the flesh' (Gal. 5:20), which is the sense here. It does not differ greatly from 'divisions' (v. 18). It is only as those who choose in a self-willed manner make their appearance that those who *have God's approval* (*hoi dokimoi*, 'those who have stood the test') are made manifest.

20. The adjective *kyriakon* (only here and Rev. 1:10 in the New Testament) stresses the connection with the Lord. The disorders at Corinth are so serious that it is not *the Lord's* supper that is eaten; it has a different character (*cf.* 10:21). Chrysostom points out that what is the master's is common to all the servants; to make a difference means that it is no longer the master's.

21. Clubs and associations in antiquity often had communal meals, sometimes paid for out of group funds. It was not uncommon for the food served to the diners to differ in quality and amount. Theissen cites associations where officials by regulation received more than others, some one and a half times, some twice, and some three times the normal (p. 154). He also draws attention to hosts who had better food for privileged guests (pp. 156ff.). Clearly at Corinth the Holy Communion was a full meal, of the type called a 'love feast' (Jude 12; some MSS of 2 Pet. 2:13). But what happened at Corinth was a travesty of love. The wealthier members of the congregation clearly provided most of the food, and this could have been a marvellous expression of Christian love and unity. But it was degraded into the very opposite. The poor would have to finish their work before they could come, and slaves would find it particularly difficult to be on time. But the rich did not wait. They ate and drank in their cliques ('divisions', v. 18), each eating 'an own dinner' (*idion deipnon*). The food was gone before the poor got there! *One remains hungry, another gets drunk.* There was a sharp contrast between the hungry poor, lacking even necessary food, and the drunken rich. There was no real sharing, no genuinely common meal.[1]

22. A typical series of rhetorical questions hammers at the evil of the practice. Home is the place to satisfy one's hunger and thirst. To behave like the Corinthians is to despise *the church* which is no less than the church *of God*. It is to despise the poor (notice the connection between the poor and the church). There is no place whatever for praise.

2. A reminder of the institution (11:23-26)
This is the earliest account of the institution of the Holy Communion. Indeed, it is the earliest record of any words of Jesus, and one of very few incidents in his earthly life which Paul describes. There are some features of this account which we do not find elsewhere, such as the command to continue the service 'until he comes' (v. 26).

23. The verbs *received* and *passed on* (*paralambanō* and *paradidōmi*) are almost technical terms for receiving and passing on traditions (*cf.* v. 2). This, taken with the general probability, leads most commentators to the view that Paul means 'I received a tradition which goes back to the Lord'. Against this is the emphatic *I* (*egō*); why should Paul say '*I* received of the Lord' if he meant 'I received from other men a tradition that derives ultimately from the Lord'? Revelations were made directly to Paul (Acts 18:9f.; 22:18; 23:11; 27:23-25; 2 Cor. 12:7; Gal. 1:12; 2:2). The use of *apo* rather than *para* for *from* does

---

[1] It is even possible that they were physically separated. There was limited accommodation in private homes and the church would have met in the triclinium (dining-room) and/or atrium (courtyard). See Fig. 3, p. 242. It would be difficult to fit in as many as fifty people in the average large house (*SPC*, p. 158), and it is not unlikely that the first-comers (wealthy friends of the owner?) would go into the triclinium and later arrivals would have to be content with the atrium.

not necessarily indicate an indirect report (though it would be consistent with it), for it sometimes refers to direct communication (Col. 1:7; 3:24; 1 Jn. 1:5). Paul seems to be referring to a direct revelation (*cf.* Craig, 'Paul may still be asserting that his *interpretation* of the Lord's Supper was received by him from the risen Lord'). It all started *on the night he was betrayed* (better, 'he was being betrayed'). Paul brings out the poignant truth that that feast of love that was to bring such strength and consolation to Christians was instituted at the very time when human malignancy was engaged in betraying the Saviour to his enemies.

24. Matthew and Mark use the verb 'bless' of the bread, though Luke employs Paul's verb. All three use 'give thanks' of the wine. There is no important difference, for the prayer of thanksgiving would have begun, 'Blessed art Thou, O Lord' (see on 10:16). Jesus broke the bread and said, '*This is my body*' (Moffatt, 'This means my body'). These words have been made the proof text for doctrines such as transubstantiation and consubstantiation with their realistic identification of the bread with the body of Christ. But *This* is neuter (*touto*), not masculine as it should be if it referred to the masculine word for bread (*artos*). It may refer to the whole action, as the second *this* does. Further, *is* can denote various kinds of identification (see Jn. 8:12; 10:9; 1 Cor. 10:4, to name no others). Moreover, in the next verse the cup is not 'my blood', but 'the new covenant in my blood'. The words do not prove all that the advocates of such theories claim. On the other hand they should not be minimized into a 'Zwinglian' view, that the service is no more than an occasion when we remember Christ. There is a very real gift of the Saviour in the sacrament, none the less real for being essentially spiritual. 'The sacrament is a medium of communion with the body and blood of Christ, and a real means whereby faith appropriates the blessings which flow from the glorified Christ in virtue of His death' (Edwards, on v. 25).

The body is *for you* (some MSS insert 'broken' or 'given', but Paul has neither word). The emphasis is on the vicarious work of Christ; what happened to the body was *for* us. There was purpose in his suffering, a purpose of blessing for his people. *Do this* is present continuous: 'Keep on doing this.' If it be judged that these words are no part of the true text of Luke 22:19, this is the sole record of the command to continue the Communion (though we should not pass over the significance of the regular practice of the church from the very first, Acts 2:42). *Remembrance* (*anamnēsis*) is the activity of recalling to mind. By breaking and receiving the bread we recall Christ's sufferings for us.

25. There is no *took* in the Greek (*cf.* RSV); the language is terse and vivid. The impression left is that the bread was broken and shared during the course of the meal, and the cup was taken at the end. The word *covenant* (*diathēkē*) presents problems, too complex to be discussed here.[1] Briefly, it is the normal Greek word for 'last will and testament', but in the Greek Old Testament it is used regularly to translate the Hebrew for 'covenant' (277 times). The question in the New Testament is, 'Is *diathēkē* to be understood as in Greek generally, or as in the Greek Old Testament?' Probably it is sometimes one and sometimes the other. Here *covenant* is the meaning, with special reference to the 'new covenant' (Je. 31:31ff.). The idea of covenant dominates the Old Testament. The people entered into a covenant with the Lord (Ex. 24); they were God's people. But they broke that covenant consistently and Jeremiah looks for a new covenant, one based on forgiveness of sins and with the law of God written in the hearts of the people. Jesus is saying that the shedding of his blood is the means of establishing that new covenant. It provides forgiveness of sins and opens the way for the activity of the Holy Spirit in the heart of the believer. The whole Jewish system is replaced by the Christ, and everything centres on the death of the Lord; it is that death which establishes the new covenant.

26. The important word here is the one translated *proclaim* (*katangellō*). It has sometimes been made the proof text for positions like that expressed in W. Bright's hymn:

[1] The word is discussed in ch. II of my *The Apostolic Preaching of the Cross* (Tyndale Press, 1955), and in ch. 1 of *The Atonement* (IVP, 1983).

> We here present, we here spread forth to Thee
> That only Offering, perfect in Thine eyes,
> The one true, pure, immortal Sacrifice.

This, however, is quite unscriptural. In the Communion we receive Christ. We present neither him, nor his sacrifice, to the Father. We present, and can present, only ourselves. *Katangellō* means 'announce', 'proclaim'. In the New Testament it is mostly used of proclaiming the gospel. It always denotes an activity exercised towards people, never one towards God. The solemn observance of Holy Communion is a vivid proclamation of the Lord's death; in word and symbol Christ's death is set forth before people. 'The Eucharist is an *acted* sermon, an *acted* proclamation of the death which it commemorates' (Robertson and Plummer). Deluz reminds us that 'we do not commit ourselves very far by listening to a sermon but a communicant both commits himself and confesses his faith'. *Until he comes* looks forward to the Lord's return. Holy Communion has an eschatological aspect. It will not be necessary in the new order, but until then it keeps us mindful, not only of Jesus' first coming, when he suffered for our sins, but also of his second coming, when he will take us to himself. A. C. Thiselton thinks that the revelling Corinthians had missed this. They evidently saw Holy Communion as 'feasting at the eschatological banquet of the Messiah'. But the Lord's Supper 'has a distinctly *interim* character' (*NTS*, 24, 1977–78, pp. 521f.). There is a 'not yet' about it, as well as a 'now'.

3. The practical outcome (11:27–34)

Paul goes on to the way communicants should receive the sacrament. His exposition of the meaning of the service shows that it is a most solemn rite, instituted by the Lord himself, and charged with deep and sacred meaning. It should accordingly be observed with unfailing reverence.

27. *Therefore* (*hōste*) introduces the consequence. Because the Lord's Supper is what Paul has just shown it to be, people must observe it with due care. There is, of course, a sense in which we all partake unworthily, for none can ever be fully worthy.

But in another sense we can come worthily, in faith and with a due performance of all that is fitting. It is when we neglect this that we come *in an unworthy manner*, and sin *against the body and blood of the Lord*. Instead of proclaiming the Lord's death, we then misuse the symbols of that death, and share the guilt of those who put Jesus to death. *Cf.* 8:12.

28. *Examine* is *dokimazō*, 'test' (often used of the testing of metals). Holy Communion is not just another service. It is a solemn rite, instituted by our Lord himself, and charged with deep significance. Before taking part in such a service it is important to conduct a rigorous self-examination (*cf.* 2 Cor. 13:5f.), so that we avoid communicating unworthily (v. 27). In passing we notice that the reference to *the bread* (not 'the body') does not accord with theories like transubstantiation. The bread remains bread at the moment of reception.

29. *Without recognising the body of the Lord* is a difficult expression. The verb *diakrinō* means 'distinguish' and thus 'discern', 'separate'. Here it will mean distinguishing the Lord's Supper from other meals; the offender is one 'not bearing in mind, as he ought, the greatness of the things set before him' (Chrysostom). Some think *the body* (*of the Lord* is absent from the better MSS) to be the church (as in 12:13; Col. 1:18). But there seems no real reason for thinking of a change of meaning from that in v. 27. At the same time, there is a marked stress throughout this passage on the corporate nature of the service, and on the responsibility of each to all.

30. Spiritual ills may have physical results. The ill health and even the deaths of some of the Corinthians had spiritual causes. Some see the results of excessive drinking (v. 21), but Paul seems not to be referring to the 'natural' results of excesses, but to the chastening hand of the Lord (v. 32). He does not say that all illness comes about in this way; there are other causes. But this is a real one, and it took place even though some of the Corinthians had 'gifts of healing' (12:9,28).

31–32. Paul points to the value of 'judging' ourselves. We should make a practice (such is the force of the imperfect tense) of 'distinguishing' (*diakrinō* again; see on v. 29) ourselves, *i.e.* distinguishing between what we are and what we ought to be. Barclay translates, 'if we truly discerned what we are like'. Then we *would not come under judgment* (*krinō*), the kind of judgment mentioned in v. 30. *Being disciplined* means that these judgments are not nameless evils, but the tokens of God's love. They are meant to bring us back from the wrong way, so that we will not *be condemned with the world*.

33-34. *Hōste* introduces the logical conclusion. *Wait for each other* at the meal means the end of the disgraceful scramble of v. 21. The Lord's Supper takes the form of a meal, but its purpose is not to satisfy physical hunger. If a man is really hungry, *he should eat at home*. If people act in this way, then when they come together for worship, the result will not be *judgment*.

There were apparently other matters concerning Holy Communion, but they were not so urgent. They could wait until such time as Paul came to Corinth. *When* is the indefinite *hōs an*; Paul would come, but he did not know when it would be.

C. SPIRITUAL GIFTS (12:1 – 14:40)

It was universally accepted in antiquity that some people, who were in specially close touch with the divine, had special spiritual endowments. At times they behaved in unpredictable ways, threw themselves about, spoke in a frenzied manner, and so on. Their 'enthusiasm' was the mark of the presence of the divine spirit within them. From the day of Pentecost on, some within the Christian church manifested unusual spiritual gifts. They did things like speak in a tongue they did not understand. To many early believers this kind of thing was pre-eminently the mark of a 'spiritual' person. By comparison the practice of Christian virtue seemed staid and colourless. Paul's discussion of this subject is epoch-making. In contrast to the usual idea, he was clear that the Holy Spirit comes not only on a few outstanding people, but on all believers (Rom. 8:9,14). And the presence of the Spirit is to be seen characteristically in what he calls 'the fruit of the Spirit', qualities like love, joy, peace, and so on (Gal. 5:22–23), not ecstatic behaviour. Here he begins by showing that it is the Lordship of Christ that is the touchstone. If the exercise of 'spiritual gifts' does not make for the Lordship of Christ, they are not from God. He proceeds to the point that there are many gifts of the Spirit, and that all are necessary. He lists some of them and proceeds to 'the most excellent way', the way of love. Then he relates the exercise of the spectacular gifts to the conduct of public worship and insists that all must be done in an orderly fashion. He agrees with the Corinthians that the spectacular gifts have their place. But he does not accord them the pre-eminent place. That place belongs to love.

1. The variety of gifts (12:1–11)
Paul begins with the importance of a clear recognition of the Lordship of Christ. There are many spiritual gifts and they all bring glory to Christ; they never oppose him.

1. *Now about* introduces another of the topics in the Corin-thians' letter (see on 7:1), though exactly what they had asked is not clear. Whether *gifts* should be added after *spiritual* (as NIV, AV, *etc.*) is not certain. Paul's word (*pneumatikōn*) might be masculine, 'spiritual men', or neuter, 'spiritual things'; most take it in the latter sense and understand 'things' as 'gifts'. There is not a great deal of difference in this context, for both Paul and the Corinthians are thinking of the men who exercise the gifts. The adjective *pneumatikos* ('spiritual') is unusually common in this letter (15 times, out of 24 times in Paul; no more than 3 times in any other letter). It is not the usual word for 'spiritual gift', which is *charisma* (vv. 4,9, *etc.*). Notice the affectionate address, *brothers*, introducing a section where there may be much rebuke. For *I do not want you to be ignorant* see the notes on 10:1. It indicates that the subject thus introduced is important.

2. As it stands this verse in the Greek is ungrammatical. Two suggestions have won support. One is that of Hort, that for *hote* we should read *pote*, when the sense would be, 'You know that formerly you were Gentiles, carried away. . . .' The other is that we supply another *you were* (*ēte*) with the participle *apagomenoi* (*led astray*) at the end of the Greek sentence. This would yield the meaning, 'You know that, when you were Gentiles, you were carried away. . . .' The difference is not great and it does not matter much which we adopt. Usually in the New Testament *ethnē* (NIV *pagans*) means non-Jews, but it can mean those not Christian (*e.g.* 1 Thes. 4:5), as it does here. The characteristic of these people is that they are *led astray* to idols. The verb is often used of leading away a prisoner or condemned person (*e.g.* Mk. 14:44; 15:16). The pagans are seen, not as men freely following the gods their intellects have fully approved, but as under constraint, people who know no better. There is something pathetic about idol worship. *Dumb idols* characterizes their deities as totally unable to answer those who call upon them. They could make nothing known to their worshippers. There is a very unusual construction in the Greek that NIV renders *somehow or other you were influenced*; it seems to convey the idea of repetition (*Prolegomena*, p. 167; *Grammar*, p. 974); the pagans were continually led about. And no matter how they were led, they were brought only to dumb deities.

3. Because of this background, the Corinthians could not be expected to know everything about Christianity, and more particularly about 'spiritual men'. So Paul makes his first point, that the genuinely spiritual man is known by his utterances. *Cursed* translates *anathema*, 'something laid up', *i.e.* laid up in a sacred place. It thus came to mean what is given to a deity, and since this is totally lost to the giver, the word came to have the meaning 'that which is destroyed'. Particularly was this the case when the destruction was itself a religious act, for example when Jericho was totally destroyed at the Lord's command. So the meaning passes over to 'accursed', and this is the usual sense of the term in New Testament days. The natural meaning of these words is that someone had called Jesus accursed, but who or why or how we cannot say. Some point out that a Jew is more likely to use the term *anathema* than a Gentile and point to Jewish cursing of Christians (and *cf.* Acts 26:11). Others remind us that pagans in times of persecution called on the accused to curse Christ, which Pliny tells us those who are really Christians cannot be made to do (*Epistles* 10:96). Others again think no-one used the words; Paul is simply making up a suitable antithesis to *Jesus is Lord*. But perhaps we should start with Paul's teaching that Christ became 'a curse for us' (Gal. 3:13). It is not beyond the bounds of possibility that some excitable and imperfectly instructed Corinthian had distorted the thought in an ecstatic utterance. The Corinthians may have wondered whether the excitement under which the statement was made was evidence of divine inspiration. Paul firmly denies this. The content shows that the words are not from God. It is an assertion that Jesus is rejected by God, a denial of the Lordship of Christ. That is not the way the Spirit leads people. On the contrary, it is only *by the Holy Spirit* that anyone can hail Christ as Lord. Obviously a mocking unbeliever can mouth the words *Jesus is Lord*. Paul is not denying this. He is saying that the words can be uttered with full meaning only under the influence of the Holy Spirit. The Lordship of Christ is not a human discovery. It is a discovery that is made and can be made only when the Spirit is at work in the heart.

4. *Different kinds* (*diaireseis*) is from a root expressing the idea of division. It might mean 'apportionment' (Orr and Walther) or 'distribution' (Barrett), though most take it as NIV. *Gifts* renders *charismatōn*, the usual word for the extraordinary endowments the Spirit confers on chosen people. The word is from the same root as 'grace' (*charis*). It points to the freeness, the bounty of the gift. It might be used in a general sense of God's good gifts (Rom. 11:29), or of the 'spiritual gift' Paul wanted to impart to the Romans (Rom. 1:11). But characteristically it is used, as here, for the special operation of the Holy Spirit within people. The Corinthians had evidently regarded the possession of such *gifts* as a matter for pride and had set one believer against another on the basis of the possession of this or that gift. They had created division. Paul insists that this is the wrong attitude. There is diversity in the endowments the Spirit gives, but it is *the same Spirit*, and the Spirit does not fight against himself. All the gifts are to set forward the same great divine purpose.

5. There are different kinds of *service* (*diakonia*; see note on the cognate word *diakonos* in 3:5). But the differences are not important. It is *the same Lord*. As usually in Paul, *Lord* refers to Christ, and the passage reveals something of the high place Paul assigns to him. He places him here between the Holy Spirit and the Father. This is not a formal enunciation of the doctrine of the Trinity, but passages like this are distinctly Trinitarian in character. The *service* might be service rendered to Christ. But since in the previous and following sections it is the action of the divine within the believer that is mentioned, we should probably understand this verse to mean that the indwelling Christ enables his people to render service, or perhaps calls them to service. Conzelmann points out that 'everyday acts of service are now set on a par with the recognized, supernatural phenomena of the Spirit'. Humble, everyday service is not to be despised.

6. *Working* is something like 'activity'; it is God's power in action. The divine activities are manifold, but it is *the same God*. For the third time Paul brings out his point that there can be no division among Christians on the ground of the 'gifts', because it is one and the same God who provides the gifts in all their diversity. He *works all of them in all*. NIV is probably right in adding *men*, but the gender is indeterminate, and some prefer to add 'things'. But the emphasis in this passage is on what God does in believers.

7. *To each one* is important; everyone has some gift from God. *The manifestation of the Spirit* may mean 'that which the Spirit makes manifest' or 'that which makes the Spirit manifest'. Either way the thought is of the spiritual gifts, and of the exercise of those gifts as something public and open which others than their possessors perceive. The gifts are not given for rivalry and jealousy but *for the common good*. That is the point of it all. Spiritual gifts are always given to be used, and to be used in such a way as to edify the whole body of believers, not some individual possessor of a gift. A schismatic individualism contradicts the purpose of the gifts.

8. What has been put shortly in vv. 4–6 is now expanded, and some of the gifts the Spirit gives are listed, together with a repetition of the truth that it is the one Spirit who provides them all. There are other lists of the gifts (v. 28; Rom. 12:6–8; Eph. 4:11–12), but the lists are different; the only gift in all four is prophecy. Clearly the Spirit gives many gifts and there is no one definitive list. What most of these gifts were is uncertain. Long ago Chrysostom lamented that the passage is obscure on account of the cessation of the gifts, 'being such as then used to occur but now no longer take place.' The first two are 'word of wisdom' and 'word of knowledge'. 'Word' may mean *the message*, as NIV, but that is far from certain. And, while it is not difficult for us to differentiate between *wisdom* and *knowledge*, we cannot be sure that our difference is the one Paul meant. Some find no difference other than stylistic (Barrett, Conzelmann). It is true that *wisdom* denotes the highest mental excellence (see on 1:24), and that this has been prominent in the early chapters. But does Paul mean the same thing here? BAGD point out that Paul sometimes associates *knowledge* with mysteries, revelations and prophecy (13:2; 14:6). They suggest that he thus 'invests the term with the significance of supernatural mystical knowledge', a meaning common in Hellenistic Greek, more especially among the mystery religions. But is that what Paul means here? Paul certainly thinks of all the *wisdom* and all the *knowledge* the Christian has as coming from the Spirit. But here he is talking of special gifts, gifts moreover of 'a word' of wisdom and of knowledge, not wisdom and knowledge themselves. It is not easy to see what they are.

9. The difficulty here is that, whereas *faith* is characteristic of all Christians (they may be spoken of simply as 'believers'), Paul is limiting it to a certain group who have this special gift. There is no difficulty about faith being a gift; all faith must be seen as God's good gift to us. The difficulty is in seeing what this special faith is over against the common faith that all believers have.[1] Unfortunately there is little to guide us. Paul proceeds to speak of healing and the working of miracles, so he probably has in mind a special kind of faith associated with miraculous operations (cf. 13:2, 'a faith that can move mountains'). There is no article with *gifts of healing* (nor with any other item in this list). This fastens attention on the quality of the gift rather than its individuality. *Healing* is plural in the Greek, which perhaps means different gifts for different kinds of sickness.

10. *Miraculous powers* is more literally 'workings (cf. v. 6) of miracles', where miracles (*dynameōn*) stresses the element of power in the 'mighty works'. It is often used of the miracles of Jesus. We can only conjecture what is meant. As it immediately follows 'healings' and is preceded by *to another* it seems that miraculous cures are not in mind. Jesus did miracles like the stilling of the storm and the feeding of the multitude, but there is no record of any of his followers ever doing anything like that (though in the longer ending of Mark it is prophesied that they would 'drive out demons', 'pick up snakes', and 'when they drink deadly poison, it will not hurt them at all', Mk. 16:17f.). Calvin thinks of the smiting of Elymas with blindness (Acts 13:11), and the deaths of Ananias and Sapphira (Acts 5:1–11).

Prophecy is inspired speech. In the Old Testament the prophets spoke the word of God to their generation, sometimes predicting the future (which indeed is sometimes the mark of the true prophet, Dt. 18:21–22), more often speaking to the needs of the present. This, too, is the function of the prophets of the New Testament; they were engaged in 'forthtelling the present' rather than 'foretelling the future' (Redpath; though cf. Acts 11:28, *etc.*). Prophecy might be occasional (Acts 19:6), or a settled office (vv. 28f.). Here Paul probably has in mind mostly

---

[1] W. Schmithals argues that faith here has its usual Pauline sense and that the apostle is opposing the Gnostic view that only a few are Pneumatics ('spiritual'). Paul is saying that all Christians have faith and are thus Pneumatics (*Gnosticism in Corinth* (Abingdon, 1971), pp. 172f.). Whatever the truth of Schmithals's general position, this is surely not what Paul is saying here. Schmithals does not give sufficient attention to the expression 'to another'. This does not refer to a gift made to all Christians, but to one for a limited number.

the second class, though his expression is broad enough to include both. His point is that the Spirit gives to some the ability to utter inspired words, which convey the message of God to the hearers. Grudem points out that this does not necessarily mean more than 'a divine authority of general content' (p. 69), *i.e.* the general content is inspired, but the exact form of words cannot be put on the same level as that of the canonical prophets.

It must often have been difficult to be sure whether a man claiming to be a prophet should be believed or not. Every believer must 'test the spirits' (1 Jn. 4:1), because false prophets were many. But *the ability to distinguish between spirits* shows that to some was given a special discernment in this matter. The expression may be wider and include discerning demons. Again, our ignorance of the circumstances forbids us to be dogmatic.

The ability to speak in different kinds of tongues appears to have been a special form of speech when the person uttering the words did not know what they meant (unless he also had the gift of interpretation). Some have interpreted this from Acts 2, where 'tongues' seems to mean speaking in a foreign language. But it is difficult to see this here. Whereas in Acts 2 the characteristic is intelligibility (Acts 2:8–11), here the characteristic is unintelligibility ('no-one understands him', 14:2). The gift here is not part of the church's evangelistic programme (as in Acts 2), but one exercised among believers. It is not understood by people who speak other languages, but requires a special gift of interpretation. Without that gift of interpretation, the speaker in tongues is to speak 'to himself and God' (14:28), which is a strange way to treat one of the world's recognized languages. The gift was not one whereby people might be more readily understood by others, but one in which they did not even understand themselves. Utterances in no known language, but under the influence of the Spirit, seems to be Paul's meaning. *The interpretation of tongues* is added as the gift that makes the gift of tongues intelligible.

11. Some emphasis is put on the variety of the gifts by beginning the sentence with *all these* (the object of the verb 'works' in the Greek). The unity of the divine purpose comes out in the expression *one and the same Spirit*. The stronger form than that used in vv. 4,5,6 underlines the truth that the divergent gifts do not point to divergent divine purposes. It is the one God who gives them all. The gifts are thus not to be set over against one another as though their possessors were rivals. Those who have them are to co-operate in working out the one divine purpose. The Spirit gives them *to each man*, which reminds us that God deals with us as individuals. He does not hand out his gifts indiscriminately but meets the needs and the capacities of each. The personality of the Spirit is brought out in the concluding *just as he determines* (or 'wills'). This is a personal activity; the Spirit is to be thought of as a person, not a vague force or influence; as 'he' not 'it'.

2. *Diversity in unity* (12:12–31)
Paul sees the church not as 'a democracy, still less anarchy . . . . It is a Body' (Green, p. 93). Unity and diversity are both important. In antiquity quite a number of thinkers used the analogy of the human body, as in the Stoic idea of the world or of the state in which each citizen is a member (*cf.* Seneca, 'we are the parts of one great body' (*Epistles* 95:52). Many commentators cite the fable of Menenius Agrippa used in a plebs revolt in Rome: the stomach appeared to the other members of the body to be doing nothing but enjoy the food they put into it; so they agreed to starve it, only to find that they thereby enfeebled themselves (Livy, ii. 32). All the members of a body work for the common good.

12. It takes many different members (NIV *parts*) to make up a body. Inevitably the members differ, but their differences do not affect the fact that there is a fundamental unity. *So it is with Christ*. This is not the thought of Christ as the head of the body (as in Eph. 5:23; Col. 1:18; contrast v. 21). Rather, Paul's favourite concept that the Christian is 'in Christ' (see on 1:30) is at the basis of what he says. Since all believers are in Christ they are one body. There are *many parts* to the human body – and to the church. In both there is unity in diversity.

13. Baptism *into one body* symbolizes this truth (from other standpoints baptism is 'into Christ', Gal. 3:27, or 'into his death', Rom. 6:3). Early in this letter Paul appealed to baptism into Christ as pointing the Corinthians away from their factions and rivalries to their essential unity (1:13ff.). The same thought is put in a different form here. *Jews or Greeks, slave or free*, all alike are baptized into *one body*, and thus into a unity that transcends all human distinctions. Paul emphasizes what the Spirit does. *By one Spirit* is really 'in one Spirit' (the construction is the same as that in Mt. 3:11, 'with water', 'with the Holy Spirit'). It points to the Spirit as the element 'in' which they were baptized. It is only as there is an activity of the Spirit that baptism has meaning; 'the apostle refers to the spiritual reality of which their baptism in water was the symbol' (Wilson). From another point of view all Christians were *given the one Spirit to drink*. The Spirit has entered their innermost being and it is the same Spirit that has done this in all of them. The verb is sometimes used of irrigation, from which comes the thought of abundant supply (*cf.* Goodspeed, 'we have all been saturated with one Spirit').

14. Diversity is no accidental attribute of the body. It is of its very essence. No one member is to be equated with the body. It takes many members to make up one body.

15–16. Therefore individual members cannot contract out. The disputes at Corinth seem to have depressed some of the less gifted members of the church. They wondered whether they had any right to belong to so august a body, including as it did people with such wonderful and spectacular gifts. Paul gives encouragement to the lowly. *The foot* may very well be depressed at its inability to exercise the complicated functions of *a hand*, and may see its own function as a lowly one (always in the dust, and bearing the weight of the whole body). But that does not put it outside the body. As with *foot* and *hand*, so with *ear* and *eye*. Bodies need feet as well as hands, ears as well as eyes. Chrysostom acutely points out that the foot contrasts itself not with the eye, but with the hand. We are prone to envy those who surpass us a little, rather than those who are patently in a different class.

171

17. We should possibly omit *an* and read 'if all the body were eye . . .' for it is function that is stressed. No member of the body can perform the function of another. The ear cannot see, but then the eye cannot hear either. Both functions are necessary for a normal body. So with the *ear* and *the sense of smell*.

18. The whole discussion is placed on the highest level, for the members are not in the body haphazardly; *God has arranged* them, or better, 'put' them (JB). It is not only a matter of arrangement; God created the parts to make a body like this. *Every one of them* brings out the point that God's care does not extend only to the more important and spectacular. His oversight and creativity extend to every member of the body. He made them all *just as he wanted them to be* ('just as he willed').

19–20. The incongruity of the exaggerated reverence the Corinthians had for one or other of the gifts is brought out by a rhetorical question. No matter how important any one member may be, there can be no body formed from it alone. That would be a monster, not a body. But in fact, as things are, *there are many parts*, and together they make up but *one body*. This emphatic reiteration of the theme of unity in diversity rounds off this part of the discussion.

21. Now Paul looks at the other side of the coin. He turns from the humbler members, who thought their lack of the spectacular gifts might disqualify them from membership of the church, to those possessed of great gifts, who evidently looked down on their less gifted brothers. In their lofty eminence they thought that they could manage well enough without the unimportant contributions of lowly people. But *the eye* cannot do without *the hand*, nor *the head* without *the feet*. One member of the body may perform its own function well, but that does not mean that it can dispense with the services of other members which perform different functions, functions that it cannot perform. Barclay comments, 'Whenever we begin to think about our own importance in the Christian Church, the possibility of really Christian work is gone.'

22. From the negative Paul proceeds to the positive. Not only can no member do without other members, but even the parts *that seem to be weaker are indispensable*. *Weaker* is the comparative of *asthenēs*, 'sick'. The word emphasizes the apparently complete unimportance of these members. Yet even so Paul does not speak of them as an 'addition' or even 'a welcome addition'. They are *indispensable*. The body cannot do without them (like the stomach in Menenius Agrippa's fable). Robertson and Plummer comment that in society the humbler workers are more necessary than those with higher gifts. 'We can spare this artisan better than this poet; but we can spare all the poets better than all the artisans.'

23. Paul seems to be speaking about clothing here. There are some parts of the body thought to be *less honourable*. These we clothe in seemly fashion and thus give them *special honour* (the verb translated *treat* is often used of clothing, *e.g.* Mt. 27:28). In the same way our *unpresentable* parts (probably the reproductive and excretory organs) we treat *with special modesty* (BAGD, 'propriety, decorum').

24. *Our presentable parts* (those we think to be good looking) need no aid. Thus we do not adorn them as we do the other parts of the body; they get *no special treatment*. Again (as in v. 18) there is the thought that the composition of the body is not by chance, but is due to God's ordering. God gives honour to those parts of the body that naturally lacked it. *Combined* signifies a harmonious mixing; it is a word sometimes used of blending colours. God's arrangement of the members in the body does away with clashing and blends all into one harmonious whole.

25. The action of God is directed to the prevention of *division* (the word used in 1:10 of the dissensions that caused factions in the Corinthian church). In his perfect blending of the parts in the human body God provided against dissension. On the contrary (the strong adversative *alla*), it is his plan that the members *have equal concern for each other*. *Equal* (*to auto*, 'the same') guards against partiality. In the body all the members without distinction work for the good of the whole. No special care is lavished on one member to the detriment of other members. *Concern* (*merimnaō*) conveys the notion of anxiety. It is a strong term and denotes no tepid emotion.

26. The unity of the body is seen in both suffering and honour. The suffering of any one member means that the whole body suffers. It is impossible for one part of the body to be in pain and the remainder at peace. The existence of one trouble-centre means that the whole body is involved (we say 'I have a pain', not 'my toe has a pain'). Similarly when one member of the body *is honoured*, all share the joy. 'The head is crowned, and the whole man is honoured' (Chrysostom). Paul does not in fact speak of sharing the honour, but the joy. His choice of word emphasizes the impossibility of rivalry within the body.

27. *You* is the emphatic pronoun, put first for further emphasis. *Body* is without the article; it is the characteristic of the Corinthian believers that they belong to Christ's body (the article would have distinguished this body from other bodies). There is emphasis on the truth that the Corinthians are members of nothing less than Christ's body. All that Paul has been saying refers to them. The last part of the verse is more literally 'you are members in part' (*ek merous*, 'individually', Phillips; the same expression is translated 'in part' in 13:9). Paul's meaning is that each one of them belongs to the body. None can claim to be the whole, but none is excluded.

28. In the New Testament, *church* very often refers to the local group of believers. This is noteworthy as perhaps the earliest example of the use of the term for the church universal. Paul proceeds to list some of the parts of the body of Christ. He has made the point that in the natural body God puts the parts in place (vv. 18,24). So with the body of Christ. People do not choose to be *apostles*, *prophets*, and the rest, but God sets them in the church. *First of all . . . second . . . third* picks out three specially significant gifts (*cf.* Eph. 4:11). We cannot press the order throughout the list, though clearly none of the rest is to be ranked with the first three. It is probably significant that *tongues* (with interpretation), which the Corinthians valued so highly, comes last of all (as in vv. 8–10). *Apostles* were originally chosen by Christ to be with him, and that he might send them to teach and to cast out devils (Mk. 3:14f.). In time there were others than the Twelve, such as Barnabas, James, and Paul himself. They seem always to have been held in high esteem as custodians of the authentic gospel and witnesses to what God has done (see on 9:1f.). For *prophets* see on v. 10. Chrysostom remarks that every church 'had many that prophesied', which makes the prophets local officials, rather than belonging to the church at large as did the apostles. We would not have expected the *teachers* to rank so high. The fact that they do indicates the importance of teaching in the apostolic age. We must bear in mind that the cost of hand-copied books was high,[1] and few believers could look forward to owning a Bible. The function of a teacher in such a church must have been tremendously important, even if we do not know precisely what he did and why he needed a charisma.

From this point Paul speaks of the gifts rather than of the people who exercised them: 'then miracles, then gifts of healings' (see on vv. 9,10). The meanings of the words translated *those able to help others* (*antilēmpseis*) and *gifts of administration* (*kybernēseis*) are quite unknown. Commentators and translators guess at meanings like 'works of charity' (Héring) and 'gifts of support' (Barrett) for the first, and 'gifts of administration' (NIV, RSV) or 'good leaders' (JB) for the second. *Antilēmpseis* certainly means help of some sort, but what that kind of helping is that requires a special charisma we simply do not know. *Kybernēseis* is the activity of the steersman piloting a vessel (a cognate word is used of the 'pilot' or 'captain' of a ship, Acts 27:11; Rev. 18:17). It looks like a word of direction of some sort, but we have no way of knowing which. The two terms remind us of the immense amount about life in the apostolic church of which we are ignorant. For *tongues*, see on v. 10.

29–30. All the questions in these two verses are introduced with the particle *mē*, which indicates that the answer 'No' is

[1] A. Q. Morton estimates that 'a gospel represents in papyrus alone a year's wages and a New Testament about eight years' pay of a skilled workman' (*Penguin Science News*, no. 43 (Penguin, 1957), p. 26).

expected in each case. The series of rhetorical questions, quite in Paul's argumentative style, hammers home the fact of diversity. Christians differ from one another in the gifts they have received from God. No gift can be despised on the grounds that all have it, for all differ. Paul here omits 'helps' and 'governments' from the list, but adds, *Do all interpret?*

31. Paul has ranked some of the gifts in order. He has also indicated that even the humble parts of the body are necessary, and that all are set in the body by God. It is not inconsistent with this to suggest that the Corinthians do well if they *eagerly desire the greater gifts*. They cannot obtain them unless God chooses to give them, but presumably their earnest desire and their preparing of themselves is seen as a preliminary to reception, at least in some cases. Yet there is something higher than the greatest of all these gifts, and this is within the reach of the humblest and most ordinary believer. So Paul proceeds to unfold *the most excellent way*. Some suggest that he means that love is the more excellent way to the gifts. This is possible grammatically, but Paul's treatment of love does not leave the impression that it is simply a means to an end. Love is to be pursued for its own sake.

3. *In praise of love* (13:1–13)

Paul's 'most excellent way' is the way of love, which he proceeds to expound in a passage of singular beauty and power. Adolf Harnack called this chapter 'the greatest, strongest, deepest thing Paul ever wrote' (cited in Robertson and Plummer), and few would be prepared to contest this verdict. The chapter is not a digression, as some have thought, but is 'essential to Paul's argument' (Bruce, p. 117). He has not finished with the 'gifts', and he has much to say about them in the following chapter. But it is integral to his argument that the central thing is not the due exercise of any of the 'gifts'. It is love.

Some translations render the word *agapē* by 'charity' (AV, Knox), a translation derived from Wycliffe, who took it from the *caritas* of the Vulgate. We need not doubt that 'love' is the better rendering, but it is worth noticing that Jerome used *caritas* because the kind of love the Latins meant by *amor* was not what the New Testament meant by *agapē*. This Greek word was not in common use before the New Testament (it occurs twenty times in LXX and a few times in writings like *The Epistle to Aristeas*). But the Christians took it up and made it their characteristic word for love (it occurs 116 times in the New Testament, 75 being in Paul). Whereas the highest concept of love before the New Testament was that of a love for the best one knows, the Christians thought of love as that quality we see on the cross. It is a love for the utterly unworthy, a love that proceeds from a God who is love. It is a love lavished on others without a thought whether they are worthy or not. It proceeds from the nature of the lover, not from any attractiveness in the beloved. The Christian who has experienced God's love for him while he was yet a sinner (Rom. 5:8) has been transformed by the experience. Now he sees people as those for whom Christ died, the objects of God's love, and therefore the objects of the love of God's people. In his measure he comes to practise the love that seeks nothing for itself, but only the good of the loved one. It is this love that the apostle unfolds.[1]

1. Paul begins with some hypothetical possibilities (and his use of the first person probably means that he is preaching to himself, too). *The tongues of men and of angels* almost certainly refers to the gift of 'tongues', but the expression is general enough to cover speech of any kind (*cf.* JB, 'all the eloquence of men or of angels'). No language in earth or heaven is to be compared with the practice of love. It is easy enough to be fascinated by eloquent discourse, to be hypnotized by the magic of words, and to pass over that which matters most of all. Anyone who is taken up with saying rather than doing has become nothing more than sound. *A resounding gong* is really 'resounding bronze' (and Corinth was famous for its bronzes[2]).

[1] I have given a fuller exegesis of this chapter in *Testaments of Love* (Eerdmans, 1981), pp. 239–259.

[2] Murphy-O'Connor cites many passages referring to Corinthian bronze; clearly its reputation was widespread. He quotes Pliny the Elder, 'Corinthian bronze is valued before silver and almost even before gold' (*SPC*, p. 86). He also quotes *On Architecture*, a work of Vitruvius published before 27 BC, in which the writer describes how bronze vases were used as resonators in some theatres (*SPC*, pp. 75–77). According to Vitruvius some of the bronzes that Mummius took from old Corinth had been used in this way. Murphy-O'Connor is sceptical, but the passage is interesting and may illustrate Paul's 'resounding'.

'Bronze' may denote the metal itself or any object made from it. Here it clearly points to something noisy and *gong* is probably right (though some think a trumpet is meant). There may be plenty of noise in a gong, but there is nothing more. So is it with the *clanging cymbal*; it produces a loud, though harsh, sound. With both there is 'noise, but no melody' (Thrall). The gift of 'tongues' means noise, but, unless there is interpretation, no meaning. The sounds of gongs and cymbals would have been familiar at Corinth from their use by devotees of Dionysius or Cybele. Phillips perhaps has this sort of thing in mind with his unusual rendering: 'If I were to speak with the combined eloquence of men and angels I should stir men like a fanfare of trumpets or the crashing of cymbals, but unless I had love, I should do nothing more.' The best speech of earth or heaven, without love, is only a noise.

2. Paul moves from 'tongues' to knowledge, another important concept for the Corinthians. He has just ranked *prophecy* (see on 12:10) as second only to the apostolate (12:28), so that he cannot be accused of minimizing its importance. But loveless prophecy amounts to nothing. *All mysteries* (see on 2:7) and *all knowledge* point us to the sum of all wisdom, human and divine. It includes the knowledge people gather for themselves (*gnōsis*, *knowledge*, sometimes has a meaning not unlike our 'science'), and what they know only by revelation. *Mysteries* are truths that people could never find out for themselves. They know them only because it has pleased God to reveal them. *Faith* is, of course, the basic Christian attitude, but the term may also be used of a special gift of the Spirit (12:9), and here it is clearly this that is meant. It is the kind of *faith* that works miracles (*cf.* Mk. 11:22f.). Paul has 'all' before *faith* (*cf.* RSV); he is referring to faith in the fullest degree. The Corinthians clearly thought that the possessors of certain gifts were extremely important people. Paul stoutly maintains that if they have even the highest of gifts, and that in full amount, but lack love, not only are they not very important; they are actually *nothing*. His choice of words is very impressive.

3. From knowledge and deeds of power Paul turns to deeds of mercy and dedication. *Give* translates *psōmizō*, a verb connected with *psōmion*, used of the 'piece of bread' that Jesus dipped and gave to Judas (Jn. 13:26f.). Paul is speaking of giving one's goods in small amounts (JB, 'piece by piece'), *i.e.* to large numbers of people. Edwards thinks that the verb also conveys the idea that 'every gift is made by the man himself' (Chrysostom refers to 'the administering also with all care'), though this may be reading too much into it. The verb is in the aorist tense, pointing to a once-for-all action, the action of a man who, in one grand sweeping gesture, sells all that he has and gives it away. It is sobering to reflect that one may be generous to the point of beggary, and yet completely lacking in love. The Greek has nothing corresponding to *the poor*; the emphasis is on the giver, not the recipients. There is a difficult textual problem surrounding the next expression, where some MSS read 'give my body to be burnt' (as NIV), and others 'give my body that I may boast'.[1] On the whole it seems a little more likely that we should read 'boast', but giving oneself to be burnt is certainly one way the body might be given. The expression reminds us of the three youths who gave their bodies to the fire (Dn. 3:28, LXX), though there is, of course, no suggestion that they were lacking in love. Paul may have had a special case in mind, such as the Indian Calanus who burnt himself alive before Alexander (Strabo 15.1.68). If we accept the reading 'boast' we may perhaps think of people who sold themselves into slavery and used the money to provide food for the poor (1 Clement 55:2). Paul is saying that it is possible for a person to give his body up to burning or to slavery and make this spectacular sacrifice without love. That person may be moved by dedication to a high ideal, or by pride or the like. If so, he gains nothing. First-century people commonly saw great merit in deeds of charity and in suffering. Paul totally rejects all such ideas. Love is the one thing needful. Nothing can make up for its lack.

4. Paul has shown that even the highest gifts are worth

---

[1] See Metzger, pp. 563f. for the textual evidence and the reasons favouring 'boast'. There is a statement favouring 'burn' in R.V.G. Tasker (ed.), *The Greek New Testament* (Oxford and Cambridge, 1964), p. 436.

nothing at all if love is absent. Now he looks at the situation when love is present. Love *is patient*, he says, where his verb (*makrothymeō*) means the opposite of 'short-tempered'. It denotes patience with people rather than with circumstances (Barclay). The concept is often used of God (Lk. 18:7; 2 Pet. 3:9; the noun, Rom. 2:4; 9:22, *etc.*). It thus points to a godlike quality, and is eloquent of love's self-restraint. The other side of this is that love *is kind* (*chrēsteuomai*). This is the only occurrence of the verb in the New Testament and it is not found before this. Some have felt that Paul coined it. The corresponding adjective may be translated 'good' (15:33), or 'kind' (Eph. 4:32). Perhaps we are not wrong in suggesting that Paul's verb combines the two meanings. Love reacts with goodness towards those who ill-treat it; it gives itself in kindness in the service of others. Love *does not envy*; the verb is occasionally used in a good sense (as in 12:31, 'eagerly desire'), but more usually it means a strong passion of jealousy or the like. This is its meaning here. Love is not displeased at the success of others. Love *does not boast*, where Paul uses a picturesque word, the root pointing to what BAGD define as a 'wind-bag'. For *is not proud* see the note on 'take pride' in 4:6. The last two verbs remind us that there are many ways of manifesting pride. But love is incompatible with them all. Love is concerned to give itself, not to assert itself.

5. Love *is not rude*, where the verb (*aschēmoneō*) means 'what is not according to proper form (*schēma*)', and thus anything disgraceful, dishonourable, indecent. It is a general term with a wide range of meaning. Love avoids the whole range of unseemliness. Love *is not self-seeking* ('does not seek its own things'), which might be understood as 'does not insist on its own way' (RSV) or 'is not selfish' (GNB). Both arise from self-centredness and this is the very opposite of love. Love *is not easily angered*, 'is not touchy' (Phillips). There is, of course, a place for anger (*cf.* Eph. 4:26), but that is a passionate opposition to evil, not a selfish concern for one's own rights. Karl Barth reminds us that the neighbour 'can get dreadfully on my nerves even in the exercise of what he regards as, and what may well be, his particular gifts. . . . Love cannot alter the fact that he gets on my nerves, but . . . it can rule out . . . my allowing myself to be "provoked" by him' (*Church Dogmatics*, IV, 2 (T. & T. Clark, 1958), p. 834). Love *keeps no record of wrongs*. Paul uses this verb (*logizomai*) in the sense of the reckoning of righteousness to the believer. It is a word connected with the keeping of accounts, noting something down and reckoning it to someone. Love does not take notice of every evil thing that people do and hold it against them. Love takes no account of evil. It does not harbour a sense of injury.

6. It is all too characteristic of human nature to take pleasure in the misfortunes of others (*cf.* Smedes, 'We will enjoy our disgust so much that we would be furious were we to be deprived of it', p. 78). Much in our newspapers is the reporting of disaster or evil deeds, and our newspapers sell; plainly there is that in us to which reports of evil appeal. But love is not like that. Love takes no joy in evil of any kind. Rather it *rejoices with the truth*. Love shares truth's joy; it cannot rejoice when the truth is denied. There is a stern moral undertone throughout the New Testament, and nothing is ever said to obscure this. Love must not be thought of as indifferent to moral considerations. It must see truth victorious if it is to rejoice. *Truth* is often connected with the heart of Christianity (*cf.* Jesus' words, 'I am . . . the truth', Jn. 14:6; and Paul's words, 'as truth is in Jesus', Eph. 4:21). Truth is set over against unrighteousness a number of times (*e.g.* 2 Thes. 2:10,12), and we should probably understand this wide usage here. Love rejoices in the truth of God, in the truth of the gospel (*cf.* Jn. 8:56).

7. Now some positives to set over against the negatives. Love *always protects*. The verb (*stegō*) basically means 'cover'; this leads to 'hide by covering', or 'ward off by covering' and thus 'endure'. It is possible that it has the former meaning here (*cf.*, though with a different verb, 1 Pet. 4:8). Love conceals what is displeasing in another and does not drag it out into the pitiless light of public scrutiny. But it is more likely that it is the latter meaning that is in mind (as in 9:12, 'put up with'). Love does not give way easily; it endures. *Always trusts* points to the quality that is ever ready to allow for circumstances and to see the best in others (*cf.* Moffatt, 'always eager to believe the best'). This does not mean that love is gullible, but that it does not think the worst (as is the way of the world). It retains its faith. Love is not deceived by the pretences of any rogue, but it is always ready to give the benefit of the doubt. *Always hopes* is the forward look. This is not an unreasoning optimism, which fails to take account of reality. It is rather a refusal to take failure as final. It is the confidence that looks to ultimate triumph by the grace of God. *Always perseveres* brings the thought of steadfastness. The verb (*hypomenō*) denotes not a patient, resigned acquiescence, but an active, positive fortitude. It is the endurance of the soldier who, in the thick of the battle, is undismayed, but continues to lay about him vigorously. Love is not overwhelmed, but manfully plays its part whatever the difficulties.

8. Love is permanent; it *never fails*, where the verb commonly means 'to fall'. It comes to be used with the meaning 'collapse', 'suffer ruin'. Love will never suffer such a fate. 'Many waters cannot quench love' (Ct. 8:7). Over against this permanence of love Paul sets the certain passing away of gifts on which the Corinthians set so much store. *Prophecies* will *cease* (*katargeō*; see on 1:28). They are the setting forth of what God says to people through his prophet. But when we stand before God there will be no place for the prophet, no reason for his prophecies. *Tongues* likewise *will be stilled*. The same line of reasoning applies here. In the very presence of God there will be no reason and no place for the kind of revelation that *tongues* bring. *Knowledge*, the painfully acquired knowledge of earthly things, will *pass away* in the light of the immediate presence of God. The verb is the same as that used for *prophecies* (*katargeō*), though NIV translates it differently.

9–10. It is not difficult to understand *we know in part* (and the research in every laboratory in the world demonstrates the truth of the statement). The more we know the more we realize that we do not know. What is meant by *we prophesy in part* is not quite so clear. Probably the idea is that God does not reveal everything, so that the prophet, no less than the sage, gives but a partial glimpse of truth. *Perfection* (*to teleion*) conveys the idea of the destined end or aim. It points to God's plan. When the consummation is reached, all that is partial *disappears* (*katargeō* again; see on v. 8).

11. The contrast between the partial and the complete is illustrated from human life. It is natural enough for a child to act like a child, as Paul points out from his own experience. The verb *thought* (*phroneō*) is a word for general intellectual activity, and is not to be taken as 'feel' (as RV and others). It has to do with the intellect rather than the emotions. *Reasoned* (*logizomai*) takes it a step further. It means 'to reckon' (see on v. 5), from which we get the general idea of working things out or reasoning. For the child all talking, thinking and reasoning are done at the childish level. Paul contrasts this with man's estate. He was no Peter Pan, refusing to grow up. He exercised the functions of adulthood with determination; he *put childish ways behind* him (*put . . . behind* is *katargeō* once more; the fourth different translation of this difficult verb in four verses!). Paul does not mean simply that childish things passed away with the passing of time. His choice of verb indicates a determination on his part that he would not be ruled by childish attitudes. The tense is perfect, which shows that he put away childish things with decision and finality.

12. *Reflection* is really 'mirror' and this has occasioned some discussion. Some see a reference to revelation, some to the practice of certain magicians who used mirrors in their profession, others to a mere reflection of reality. But the double contrast in this verse surely puts the imperfect and the perfect in contrast. Our knowledge of God in the here and now is imperfect and is in contrast with what it will be in the hereafter. Mirrors in the first century were of polished metal. Corinth was famous for its mirrors, but few Christians would have been able to afford a mirror of good quality. In the nature of the case the reflection would not be very clear. It is, of course, also the case that a mirror always distorts to some extent: it reverses left and right, what it shows is limited by the frame, and it is always indirect. So Paul says we see *en ainigmati*, 'dimly' (RSV). The noun properly means 'a riddle' (we derive our word 'enigma' from it), so that the expression means 'in a riddle', *i.e.* 'indistinctly' (*cf.* NEB, 'Now we see only puzzling reflections in a mirror'). While we live out our lives on this earth our sight of things eternal is, at best, indistinct. But *then*, says Paul, it will be *face to face*. He does not define his *then*, nor does he say with whom we shall be *face to face*. But in neither case is there need. His meaning is plain enough.

As with seeing, so with knowing. All earthly knowledge is partial, a truth Paul has already laid down (v. 9). Over against it he sets the perfect knowledge when we shall know as we are known. The first *know* is *ginōskō*, but on the second occasion he employs the compound *epiginōskō* (used also when he says *I am known*). The use of the compound verb often signifies no more than that one's knowledge is directed towards (*epi*) a particular object. But it may mean a full and complete knowledge[1] which seems to be the force of it here (and which NIV brings out by inserting *fully*). *I am known* is in the aorist tense, which points in the same direction. The knowledge that God has of Paul is not something growing and becoming more and more perfect. God knows him through and through, with a knowledge that is perfect and complete.

13. If *and now* is understood in a temporal sense, 'now, at this present', Paul is contrasting life in the here and now with that in the hereafter. This, however, seems unlikely. He is not saying that faith, hope and love continue throughout this life, for that could equally be said of prophecy, tongues and the like with which he is contrasting them. It is more probable that the words are to be taken in the logical sense, 'now as things are', 'now in conclusion'. Over against the things that are temporary Paul sets these eternal verities. The verb *remain* is singular in the Greek. This may be only because the subject follows and the verb agrees with the nearest subject. But if it is significant Paul is seeing the three as in some sense one. They form a unity. By adding *these three* he effectively sets them apart from

---

[1] See Moulton, *Prolegomena*, p. 113. He paraphrases the present passage thus: 'Now I am acquiring knowledge which is only partial at best: then I shall have learnt my lesson, shall *know*, as God in my mortal life knew me.'

everything else. They are pre-eminent. Nothing may stand with them. We see this also in the fact that the three are often linked in the New Testament and early Christian literature (Rom. 5:2–5; Gal. 5:5f.; Eph. 1:15–18; 4:2–5; Col. 1:4f.; 1 Thes. 1:3; 5:8; Heb. 6:10–12; 10:22–24; 1 Pet. 1:3–8,21f.; *cf.* Barnabas 1:4; 11:8; Polycarp 3:2f.). Evidently it was an accepted practice in the early church to link these three.

Faith is one of Paul's dominant themes. He could write, 'The life I live in the body, I live by faith in the Son of God' (Gal. 2:20). The faith that was central to his living was central also to his teaching, as even a cursory acquaintance with his epistles reveals. Some have felt that faith essentially belongs to this life and they see no place for it in the hereafter. But faith means trust in God and commitment to him, and that surely lasts into the coming age.

It is a little surprising that *hope* should figure in this short list. And yet – we cannot live without hope. No movement has really gripped the hearts of significant numbers of people which has not given them hope. In the first centuries Christianity made a habit of taking people from the depressed classes, slaves, women, outcasts, and giving them a living hope. It is not a gain, but a grievous loss, that so often today Christians are people whose hope is no more than the mild optimism of the worldly. It is important to see that *hope* in the New Testament sense is one of the great, abiding realities. Hope is linked with God, who is 'the God of hope' (Rom. 15:13). And unless we think of the afterlife as a static, monotonous heaven, there will always be room for an eager hope based on the God of hope.

The last word in this chapter fittingly is *love*. Love occupies the supreme place. God cannot be said to exercise faith or hope, but he certainly loves, and indeed is love (1 Jn. 4:8,16). We should not press Paul's comparison too closely, nor waste our time inquiring into the precise manner in which love surpasses faith or hope (though it may not be without significance that in v. 7 these two are modes of love's outworking). It is not Paul's intention to rank the three in order. In the face of the regard the Corinthians had for the spectacular he is saying, 'The really important things are not "tongues" and the like, but faith and hope and love. And there is nothing greater than love.'

The commentator cannot finish writing on this chapter without a sense that soiled and clumsy hands have touched a thing of exquisite beauty and holiness. Here what is true of all Scripture is true in especial measure, that no comment can be adequate to so great a theme. Yet no commentator can excuse himself from the duty of trying to make plain what these match-less words have come to signify for him. And no Christian can excuse himself from the duty of trying to show in his life what these words have come to mean for him.

4. Prophecy is superior to 'tongues' (14:1–25)

Paul has dealt with the variety of spiritual gifts and the essential unity in the body of Christ of those who have them. He has shown that love is pre-eminent; it stands above all else. Now he concentrates on two of the gifts, 'tongues' and prophecy, and the length of his treatment shows the importance of the subject to his readers. From the way the apostle writes it is not unreasonable to deduce that there were some in Corinth who held that 'tongues' was the more important, perhaps even that those who spoke in 'tongues' were superior Christians. Paul is at pains to make it clear that the exercise of this gift is legitimate. It can be a mark of spiritual fervour, and in any case every gift of God is good and is to be used. But at the same time he curbs the exaggerated regard some of the Corinthians had for it. He steadily insists that the gift of prophecy is much to be preferred. Following on his demonstration of the importance of love, Paul insists that edification must be the prime consideration. Does one's gift help other people? That is the important thing.

1. The opening words sum up Paul's position. As he has stressed throughout chapter 13, the most important thing is the pursuit of *love* (the Greek has nothing to correspond to NIV's *the way of*). *Follow* (*diōkete*) has the idea of pursuit with persistence; it 'indicates a never terminating action' (Grosheide). Barrett translates, 'Pursue love as your aim.' With this Paul links *eagerly desire* (the same word as in 12:31) *spiritual gifts*; those gifts as the outworking of love will build up other believers. Among the gifts Paul gives the first place to *prophecy* (see on 12:10). This is something like our preaching, but it is not identical with it. It is not the delivery of a carefully prepared sermon, but the uttering of words directly inspired by God.

2. The reason for the inferiority of 'tongues' is its unintelligibility. Anyone exercising this gift is engaged in private communion with God. *No-one understands him*, which makes it plain that this gift differs from that in Acts 2, where everyone understood. Some think that *spirit* here refers to the Holy Spirit (*e.g.* RSV, 'in the Spirit'), but it seems rather to refer to the person's own spirit (*cf.* v. 14); his spirit as distinct from his understanding. *Mysteries* (see on 2:7) are matters which people could never know of themselves, but there is usually also the thought that God has now revealed them. Here it is the element of secrecy that is uppermost. Unless there is someone there with a special gift of interpretation, what is spoken in 'tongues' is quite unknowable to mankind.

3. By contrast the prophet edifies, exhorts, comforts. For *strengthening* (really 'edification' or 'upbuilding') see the note on the related verb in 8:1. The word for *comfort* (*paramythia*) is found only here in the New Testament, but the cognate verb is used of comforting the bereaved (Jn. 11:19,31). Prophecy, then, is a means of building up Christian character, of encouraging and strengthening people, and of giving them comfort in their distress.

4. Paul does not deny that 'tongues' have a value for edification. But (unless interpreted) they profit only the person who exercises the gift, whereas *he who prophesies* builds up the whole church. There can be no doubting which of the two acts is done in love.

5. Once again Paul stresses the importance of edification. He would like to see all the Corinthians speak with 'tongues'. Consistently he refuses to speak disparagingly of this gift. But even more would he wish to see everybody prophesying. The person prophesying *is greater* than the speaker in 'tongues' (would the Corinthians have put it the other way round?). The spectacular character of speaking in 'tongues' seems to have appealed to the Corinthians, but Paul roundly asserts the superiority of prophecy, unless there is interpretation. If 'tongues' are interpreted the hearers are *edified*, and there is no great difference from prophecy. Both are inspired speech, and both now convey a message to people.

6. As often, Paul softens his rebuke with the affectionate address, *brothers*. The construction is very condensed, being a mixture of 'If I come . . . what shall I profit you?' and 'What shall I profit you, except I speak . . .?'. Paul pictures his next visit to Corinth and supposes that he does nothing there except *speak in tongues. What good* would that be to anyone? The criterion is still edification, and the inferiority of 'tongues' is plain; it is a gift that does not profit the hearers. The things that do profit are gifts like *revelation*. This word is often used in the wide sense, of God's revelation of himself, but there is also a narrower use for some specific matter that God reveals to one of the believers (*cf.* Gal. 2:2), and which he might then pass on to others (*cf.* v. 25). In this sense *revelation* is closely related to *prophecy* (vv. 29–31). For *knowledge* (*gnōsis*) see on 12:8. *Word of instruction* (*didachē*) means 'teaching', instruction in the Christian faith.

7. Paul illustrates his point from other areas of life, first that of music. *Flute* will stand for wind instruments in general, and *harp* (*kithara*, from which we get 'guitar') for all stringed instruments. Neither flute nor harp makes sense unless there is a meaningful variation in the sounds produced. An aimless jangle means nothing.

8. So in the military realm. *The trumpet* conveys the commands of the leader to men remote from him. It is thus of the first importance that it should be blown so that it can be understood. If the sound is not *clear* (and the hearer does not know whether it means 'Advance' or 'Retreat'), it has failed of its purpose. It is useless.

9. *You* is emphatic. This applies to the Corinthians especially.

With your tongue is also in an emphatic position, which stresses the connection between the tongue and intelligibility. The Corinthians had delighted in unintelligible tongues, but speech is either intelligible or nothing more than *speaking into the air*.

10. There are some obscurities in the Greek here. *Undoubtedly* renders *ei tychoi*, which means 'if it should turn out that way, perhaps' (BAGD). Its use with numerals is to make them indefinite. Here it is probably meant to modify 'so many' (which it follows in the Greek). Barrett sees the meaning as 'I don't know how many', while Goodspeed translates, 'There are probably ever so many different languages in the world'. *Languages* translates *phōnōn* ('voices'), and *without meaning, aphōnon*; Paul is making a play on words. His point is that there is no real difference between being unintelligible and being dumb. The whole point of language is to communicate meaning.

11. *Meaning* translates *dynamis*, 'force', 'power'. Speech understood is effective communication, but speech not understood has no 'power' at all. *Foreigner* is perhaps not the best translation of *barbaros*, 'barbarian'. The word is onomatopoeic; it means someone whose language sounds like 'bar bar', *i.e.* whose language makes no sense. The word is often used in a derogatory fashion, of those beyond the pale of civilization (just as is the case with the English equivalent). It is this that *foreigner* misses. Paul's primary thought is that the person's speech is unintelligible, but the derogatory associations of 'barbarian' are in mind also. The speaking in 'tongues' that seemed to the Corinthians a matter for such pride turns out to be the means of making them nothing more than barbarians. This would be even worse for a Greek than for us.

12. Again an emphatic *you* drives home the relevance of what Paul is saying to his correspondents. *Are eager* is really a noun, 'zealots' (from the same root as 'eagerly desire', v. 1; 12:31). There is this difference that, whereas the verb is often used in a bad sense, the noun is usually used in a good sense, as here. *Spiritual gifts* is really 'spirits', but there is probably little difference (though some see a desire for supernatural gifts without much concern for their nature). 'Spirits' perhaps stresses a little more the 'spirit' character of the gifts for which the Corinthians were 'zealots', *i.e.* their origin in the Holy Spirit. Paul does not blame them for this desire, but urges them to seek *to excel in gifts that build up the church.* He keeps coming back to this thought. Edification, the building up of other believers, is what matters. 'Spiritual gifts are incompatible with spiritual selfishness' (Orr and Walther). While it is right to desire to excel in the exercise of spiritual gifts, it is those that build people up that are important. If they do not edify they do not matter.

13. *The man who speaks in a tongue* should not rest content with the gift. Its value is too limited, and he should pray for the gift of interpretation. Then what he says will help other people. There was apparently nothing static about possession of the gifts. Anyone who had the gift of 'tongues' need not take that as his end state. He might later receive other gifts, more particularly that of interpretation. He should pray to this end.

14–15. Up till this point Paul has concentrated on the value of the gifts to people other than those who exercise them. Now he looks within. Anyone who prays *in a tongue* is not using his *mind* (*nous*). The Christian life is considerably more than a mental exercise, but anyone whose mind *is unfruitful* is not being true to his Christian calling. This passage is very important for its insistence on the rightful place of the intellect. Notice that this is secured without any diminution of spiritual fervour. Paul is not arguing for a barren intellectualism. There is a place for the enthusiasm so strikingly exemplified in the use of 'tongues'. But it must be allied to the use of the mind, and this 'tongues' by itself does not provide. Paul singles out two activities specially appropriate in public worship: prayer and singing. Both must be done intelligently, with the *mind*. *Sing* (*psallō*) properly means 'sing to the accompaniment of a musical instrument', but here it is used quite generally (*cf.* v. 26, and for Paul singing, Acts 16:25). Clearly Paul is not looking for unintelligible prayers (prayers in a ritual, emotional jargon?) or hymns chosen on the basis of attractive tunes without regard to the theology they express. The *mind* is to be active in both.

16–17. Paul turns attention to one whom he calls *idiōtēs* (from *idios*, 'one's own'), a private person. It may mean 'unlearned' (Acts 4:13; *cf.* 2 Cor. 11:6), or it may be used for laymen over against priests, private citizens over against those in public life such as magistrates, men without military rank ('privates' or 'GIs') over against officers (see MM). It would be easy to understand the term here of the 'uninitiated', people not Christians, except that in v. 23 the *idiōtēs* is distinguished on the one hand from believers and on the other from unbelievers (*the whole church* is assembled and there come in some *idiōtai*, or *unbelievers*). It is, of course, possible that Paul uses the word in different senses in the two places, but they are close enough and similar enough for us to interpret the word in the same way both times if that is possible. In some religious associations the word was used for 'non-members who may participate in the sacrifices' (BAGD), and this may give us the clue. These are 'inquirers', people who had not committed themselves to Christianity, but who were interested and had thus ceased to be merely 'unbelievers'. Such people would not be able to give assent to a prayer of thanksgiving uttered in a 'tongue', for they would not understand it. *Amen* is our transliteration from the Greek of what was already a transliteration from the Hebrew. It is the participle of the verb 'to confirm', used adverbially in the sense 'truly'. It was employed as the congregation's response to prayers (*e.g.* Ne. 8:6), and that is its meaning here. By using it at the end of a prayer uttered by someone else the worshipper makes the prayer his own. The *idiōtēs* cannot do this with prayer in a tongue, since he is ignorant of the content of the prayer. Others would, of course, be in the same position, but probably everyone had a special concern for the *idiōtēs*, the man who might be won. It may be a perfectly good prayer (*You may be giving thanks well enough*), but it is unintelligible. There is thus no edification, and that, as Paul has been saying throughout this whole discussion, is the condemnation of 'tongues'.

18–19. Paul's minimizing of 'tongues' does not arise from 'sour grapes'. He himself exercises the gift more than all the Corinthians and that is something for which he thanks God. It is a good gift. But in *church* (= 'in assembly'; there is no *the* in the Greek) he would prefer to speak *five intelligible words* than to utter a torrent of words in a *tongue* (*cf.* Robertson, 'It is better to be useful than brilliant'). *In church*, of course, means 'in the assembly of Christians', not in a building, as our usage might suggest. There were no Christian buildings at this period.

20. The address *brothers*, a further reminder of Paul's affection, softens the rebuke and also serves to slow up the progress of the argument and to focus attention on what follows. *Stop thinking* (present imperative) *like children* implies that the readers were in fact doing this and Paul calls on them to cease. More literally, he says 'stop being children in mind', where his word for 'mind' differs from that in v. 14. Here he has the plural of *phrēn*, 'the midriff', 'the diaphragm'. The ancients located thought in this part of the body, so that the word came to mean much the same as our 'mind'. There is not a great deal of difference from *nous*. Paul just wants his friends to stop being infantile in their thinking. Godet comments: 'It is indeed the characteristic of the child to prefer the amusing to the useful, the brilliant to the solid. And this is what the Corinthians did by their marked taste for glossolalia' (glossolalia = speaking with tongues). It is good to be *infants* where *evil* is concerned; that is the place for the childlike attitude. But, when it comes to *thinking*, they should be *adults* (*teleioi*, 'mature').

21. *The Law* here is the Old Testament in general, not specifically the Pentateuch. Paul quotes Isaiah 28:11f., agreeing neither with lxx nor the Hebrew (it is not unlike the translation of Aquila). The reference is to the failure of the Israelites to heed the prophet. Their judgment will be to be delivered over to men of strange speech, the Assyrian invaders. The connection with the present argument is not obvious. Perhaps Paul means that, as those who had refused to heed the prophet were punished by hearing speech that was not intelligible to them, so would it be in his day. Those who would not believe would hear unintelligible 'tongues', but be quite unable to understand the wonderful meaning.

22. There is a problem in that at first sight what Paul says in this verse is contradicted by what follows. Here 'tongues' are for unbelievers, but in v. 23, when unbelievers are confronted with 'tongues', they think the speakers are mad. Again, prophecy is said to be for believers, but Paul speaks only of its effect on unbelievers (vv. 24–25). The meaning may be that 'tongues' are a judgment on wilful unbelief (as in v. 21), while prophecy is for believers in the sense that it 'makes believers of unbelievers' (Bengel). But perhaps the best suggestion is that of B. C. Johanson (*NTS*, 25, 1978–79, pp. 180–203), who argues that v. 22 should be seen as a rhetorical question (like that in Gal. 4:16, where the construction is similar). The Corinthians may well have argued that a man speaking in 'tongues' would be a sign to outsiders that God was at work, whereas prophecy did no more than convey a message to the believer. Paul asks, 'Are tongues, then, a sign, not for believers but for unbelievers, and prophecy for believers, not for unbelievers?' He proceeds to refute this view in the examples that follow.

23. Paul imagines *the whole church* assembled, with *everyone* speaking *in tongues* (the complete fulfilment of the wildest dreams of those who saw 'tongues' as the most desirable of the gifts). If now there come in some 'inquirers' (*idiōtai*, see on v. 16) *or some unbelievers*, the result will be disastrous. The effect of a massive display of 'tongues' on non-Christians, whether inquirers or rank unbelievers, will be to convince them that Christians are crazy.

24–25. The effect of prophecy is different. This time Paul uses the singular for *unbeliever* and for 'inquirer' (he employed the plural in v. 23), but the change is not significant, unless he is suggesting that conversion is always an individual matter. The effect of a display of prophecy on an outsider is given in striking terms. Prophecy conveys a divine message (see on 12:10), and this will have powerful effects. *Convinced* (*elenchetai*) means 'convicted'; it is used of the Holy Spirit's work of convicting the world of sin (Jn. 16:8). The divine word comes to the non-Christian with convicting power. For *judged* (*anakrinetai*) see on 2:14. The effect of the prophetic word is to reveal to the man his state. His whole inner being is searched out. Those things he fondly imagined to be hidden in *his heart* he finds reproved and judged, and he can ascribe this only to the activity of God. The result of prophecy is that he comes to *worship God*, recognizing that God is present in his church. Prophecy leads him to God.

5. *The practical outcome* (14:26–33)

This little paragraph is very important as giving us the most intimate glimpse we have of the early church at worship. It is not complete and, for example, it does not say whether passages of Scripture were read or not. But it is our earliest account of a service and it enables us to see something of what the first Christians actually did when they assembled to worship God. Clearly their services were more spontaneous and less structured than was normally the case in later days. We have no way of knowing how typical of the whole church worship at Corinth was, but it cannot have been very far from the norm, else Paul would have said so.

26. *Come together* means come together for worship. We need not press *everyone* (or 'each', *hekastos*), as though it meant that every member of the congregation always had something to contribute. But it does mean that any of them might be expected to take part in the service. It is curious that Paul does not speak of anyone having 'a prophecy', but perhaps *a revelation* means much the same. A *hymn* or 'psalm' (AV, JB; *psalmos*) properly denotes a song sung to the accompaniment of an instrument, but then more generally, a song. It was used especially of the psalms in the Old Testament, and some think that a Corinthian would come with one of these and perhaps a meditation on it. But singing was common among the early Christians (*cf.* v. 15; Mt. 26:30; Eph. 5:19; Col. 3:16), and the New Testament has a number of Christian songs (*e.g.* Lk. 1:46–55, 68–79, and the songs in Revelation). The more likely meaning is that a worshipper would bring a song of his own composition for the service. *A word of instruction* (*didachē*) is a piece of Christian teaching. *A revelation* will be some specific matter that God has revealed to the believer, perhaps a 'prophecy' or something akin to it. *An interpretation* will be the interpretation of *a tongue*.

There was thus a variety of ingredients in the service. But the guiding rule is 'Let all things be done for edification' (NASB), as Paul has been insisting.

27–28. As 'tongues' presented the principal difficulty, Paul deals with that subject first. He limits the number of speakers to *two – or at the most three*. Enthusiasts tend to go on and on, but there is a limit to what a congregation can take! They are to speak *one at a time*, which seems to show that the Corinthians had had experience of a number of people exercising this gift simultaneously, which must have been very confusing. Paul forbids it. *Someone must interpret* carries on the position Paul has consistently taken up. Edification is the supreme consideration, so 'tongues' must not be used unless there is an *interpreter*. This shows that we are not to think of 'tongues' as the result of an irresistible impulse of the Spirit, driving the man willy-nilly into ecstatic speech. He could *keep quiet*, and that, Paul says, is what he must do unless there is an interpreter. This also implies that he knows beforehand that he intends to speak – otherwise he would not be checking whether there was an interpreter present.

29–31. Prophecy is also subject to regulation. Just as in the case of 'tongues', there should be no more than *two or three prophets* speaking at one service. It is not certain who are *the others* who are to *weigh carefully what is said*. This may refer to all the other prophets, but as there is a special gift of distinguishing between spirits (12:10), it is more likely to refer to people who have this gift. It is also possible that the whole church is meant (*cf.* 1 Jn. 4:1), as Grudem holds (p. 62; so Barrett). The utterance of one who claims to be a prophet is thus not to be accepted uncritically, but is to be tested in the appropriate way. It would seem that certain prophets would normally be selected to speak, but the possibility might arise of a direct revelation to *someone who is sitting down* (apparently the speaker would have been standing; *cf.* Acts 13:16; the usual posture for teaching in antiquity was sitting, *TDNT*, iii, p. 443, and for the synagogue, *cf.* Lk. 4:20). The designated speaker should in this case give way. In the course of time *all*, which might mean all the congregation (Barrett), but more likely all the prophets, will have the opportunity of engaging in prophecy. The purpose is that everyone may be instructed and encouraged.

32–33. Just as those speaking with 'tongues' had the ability to keep silent when they chose, so is it with prophecy. It is not an irresistible divine compulsion that comes upon the prophet. The early church sometimes thought of such compulsion, and, for example, when the officers came to arrest Polycarp he prayed for two hours and could not be silent (*mē dynasthai sigēsai*, this last word is the verb used in v. 28; *Martyrdom of Polycarp*, 7). All three nouns in v. 32 are without the article, which makes it read like a proverb, 'Spirits of prophets are subject to prophets.' Prophecy is a means of divine illumination, but 'It is for prophets to control prophetic inspiration' (NEB). This arises from the fact that *God is not a God of disorder but of peace*. If the *prophets* had no control over their *spirits*, any prospect of an orderly assembly would vanish. But Paul sees the character of God as a guarantee against such disorder. God, because he is the kind of God he is, will produce *peace*, not *disorder*.

We should probably place a full stop after *peace* and take what follows with the next verse (as NIV). It is true that some follow AV and take it with the preceding (Robertson and Plummer, Barrett). But it is difficult to think that such a far-reaching principle should be qualified as no more than the custom of the churches.

6. *Women in church* (14:34–36)

Paul was concerned with the status of women in 11:2ff. (where see notes). This is a further application of the principles he set out there. Christian women ought not to be 'forward', they should not needlessly flout the accepted ideas of the day. Barclay comments: 'In all likelihood what was uppermost in his mind was the lax moral state of Corinth and the feeling that nothing, absolutely nothing, must be done which would bring upon the infant Church the faintest suspicion of immodesty. It would certainly be very wrong to take these words of Paul out of the context for which they were written.' We must exercise due caution in applying his principle to our own very different situation. For example, in recent discussions this passage is often cited as deciding the question of the ordination of women. But it should be applied to that question only with reserve. Paul is not discussing whether and how qualified women may minister, but how women should learn (v. 35).

34–35. If *As in all the congregations of the saints* (*cf*. 4:17) goes with this verse, Paul is calling on the Corinthians to conform to accepted Christian practice. For women to take on themselves the role of instructors would have been to discredit Christianity in the eyes of most people. Indeed, among the Greeks women were discouraged from saying anything in public. Plutarch says that the virtuous woman 'ought to be modest and guarded about saying anything in the hearing of outsiders' (*Advice to Bride and Groom*, 31); again, 'a woman ought to do her talking either to her husband or through her husband' (*ibid*., 32). Paul calls on them to observe the customs. He does more. He refers to *the Law* to remind them that they are to be *in submission* (he does not add 'to their husbands'; it is a general status of which he speaks, *cf*. Eph. 5:21). Most think he has in mind Genesis 3:16 (though, as elsewhere, he may be thinking of Gn. 1:26ff.; 2:21ff.). The silence of women in the churches is something of a problem. As Paul has countenanced their praying or prophesying (11:5), the rule against their speaking is not absolute (*cf*. Acts 2:18f.; 21:9). Moffatt takes the view that Paul 'never vetoed a devout woman from exercising, even at public worship, the prophetic gift which so many women in the primitive Church enjoyed'. He understands this prohibition to refer to 'matrons taking part in the discussion or interpretation of what had been said by some prophet or teacher during the service' (Grudem, pp. 249–251, essentially agrees, as do Thrall and others). Héring finds 'a clear distinction between a preaching woman . . . and a woman who is merely present at worship as an ordinary member of the congregation'. G. Delling sees here 'the prevention of self-willed speaking' (*TDNT*, viii, p. 43). Calvin took Paul to mean that, while the necessity may arise for a woman to speak in public, she must not speak in a regular church service.

We must bear in mind that in the first century women were

uneducated. The Jews regarded it as a sin to teach a woman, and the position was not much better elsewhere. The Corinthian women should keep quiet in church if for no other reason than because they could have had little or nothing worth while to say. It is not noticed as frequently as it should be, that Christianity from the very first assumed that women would learn as freely as men (*cf.* Lk. 10:39–42). Paul is here concerned with the way women should learn. He does not argue for this; he takes it for granted. He simply says that they should ask their questions of their husbands at home and not disturb the assembly. That would outrage propriety; it would be *disgraceful* (the same word as in 11:6), which Bultmann understands as ' "that which is disgraceful" in the judgment of men' (*TDNT*, i, p. 190).

36. This seems to indicate that the practice had actually been taking place at Corinth. More than once Paul has had occasion to complain of the pride of the Corinthians. Clearly they felt free to strike out on new lines, justified only by their own understanding of things Christian. It is in the light of such a temper that Paul inquires ironically whether *the word of God* took its earthly origin from the Corinthians, or whether it was to them only that it came. They must not think that they alone know what is Christian. They must give due attention to the customs and the thinking of 'all the congregations of the saints' (v. 33).

7. Conclusion (14:37–40)

Paul sums up the discussion in words reminiscent of the 'Whether they will hear or whether they will forbear' of the prophets. He has given his judgment faithfully on the matters raised and he is in no doubt that God has guided him in what he has said.

37. Paul makes the high claim for what he is writing, that it is *the Lord's command* (there is emphasis on *Lord*). He could not possibly make a higher claim (which we should not overlook for its bearing on the question of the way the New Testament writers viewed their inspiration). Not only is this the Lord's command, but anyone who is *a prophet or spiritually gifted* will recognize the fact. Some of the Corinthians claimed to have spiritual discernment. Let them show it by recognizing inspiration when they saw it.

38. There is a very difficult textual problem with this verse. Many MSS support the text behind AV (and LB), 'if any man be ignorant, let him be ignorant' (*agnoeitō*), but probably most students now agree with Metzger that we should read *agnoeitai*. This can mean 'he is not recognized' (RSV, NASB). But not recognized by whom? JB reads 'you should not recognize him', while NEB has 'God does not acknowledge him'. It is also possible to take the verb as future, in which case the meaning is as Moffatt, 'Anyone who disregards this will be himself disregarded' (*i.e.* on judgment day). Any one of these is possible and we have no way of knowing for certain which should be accepted. Fortunately the main thrust is clear: any spiritual person will recognize the voice of God in what Paul says and will ignore this at his peril.

39. In keeping with his attitude all along, Paul enjoins his friends to seek prophecy rather than 'tongues'. But they should not despise 'tongues'. These, too, are a gift from the Lord, and their use should not be forbidden.

40. The chapter closes with a notable principle. Public worship is very important. Everything in it must be done in as seemly a manner as possible, and with due regard for order. Indecorousness and undue innovation are alike discouraged.

VII. THE RESURRECTION (15:1-58)

Paul comes to the last great subject of his letter.[1] Some of the Corinthians had denied that the dead will rise (v. 12). He sets

[1] W. Schmithals has argued that this chapter should be understood as the climax of Paul's polemic against the Gnostics (*Gnosticism in Corinth*, pp. 156-285). But, quite apart from the fact that Gnosticism cannot be shown to be as early as New Testament days, Elaine H. Pagels has shown that the Gnostics did not in fact see 1 Cor. 15 as opposing their position, but as supporting it, though with an exegesis the orthodox did not accept (*JBL*, 93, 1974, pp. 276-288).

out to show that such a denial cannot be countenanced for a moment, for the resurrection of the believer is integral to the faith. Unless Christians are to rise in due course they are pathetic; 'to be pitied more than all men' (v. 19). Paul starts from first principles. He shows that Christ's resurrection is fundamental to the gospel, then that the resurrection of Christ implies that of Christians. He goes on to deal with objections that were, or might be, raised, and shows how baseless they are. This is the classic Christian discussion of the subject.

A. THE RESURRECTION OF CHRIST (15:1–11)

1. Despite most recent translations, Paul does not speak of reminding his friends of *the gospel* he had preached, for his verb (*gnōrizō*) means 'make known' (*cf.* Moffatt, 'I would have you know'). The word is itself a gentle rebuke; some Corinthians were evidently far from appreciating what the gospel meant. Yet they had *received* it (the aorist points to a decisive act), and they took their *stand* on it (*cf.* 2 Cor. 1:24). Clearly they recognized that it is fundamental, even if they did not understand it fully.

2. *By this gospel* is rather 'through which' (*dia*), the preposition drawing attention to the gospel as the means Christ uses to bring about salvation. *You are saved* is present continuous, 'you are being saved'. There is a sense in which salvation is once for all (as in 'received', v. 1), and another sense in which it is progressive (*cf.* 1:18; 2 Cor. 2:15). We do not exhaust the meaning of salvation by our experience when we first believe. Salvation goes on from strength to strength and from glory to glory. The word order is unusual: 'by what word I preached the gospel to you if you hold fast', and this poses some problems. Two main solutions have been suggested. (*a*) The construction is conditional, with the 'if' clause coming late in order to give emphasis to what precedes. The meaning would then be: 'if you hold fast with what terms I preached the gospel to you'. This is not a very natural Greek construction (though far from impossible); also against it is the fact that it makes Paul demand that they hold fast, not only to the gospel, but to the actual words in which he presented it (*cf.* Moffatt, 'provided you adhere to my statement of it'). (*b*) We could connect 'by what word I preached to you' with 'I make known' (v. 1). This would give the sense, 'I make known to you . . . in what terms I preached. . . .' The difficulty with this is the following 'if you hold (it) fast', for Paul is not telling them something 'if they hold it fast'. He is telling them whatever their attitude. Perhaps 'if you hold fast' is a kind of parenthesis, or it may attach to 'you are being saved' (as Goodspeed, RSV, *etc.*). Or the conditional may be seen as fulfilled, 'if you hold fast (as you do)'. The construction is difficult, but the second solution is to be preferred. *Otherwise*, Paul goes on, *you have believed in vain*, where the last word, *eikē*, may be understood as 'without due consideration, in a haphazard manner' (BAGD). If people profess to believe the gospel, but have not given due consideration to what that implies and what it demands, they do not really trust Christ. Their belief is groundless and empty. They lack saving faith.

3. The derivative nature of the gospel is stressed. Paul did not originate the message he gave them. He simply *passed on* what he had *received* (for these verbs see notes on 11:23). This is the accepted language for the handing on of tradition. What follows is a very early summary of the church's traditional teaching. Paul is not giving us some views he has worked out for himself; he is passing on what had been told him. This is the *kērygma*, the proclamation, the gospel preached by the early church. Paul sees it as *of first importance*. Without this message we do not have the essential Christian position. The first point in it is that *Christ died for our sins*. That is to say, his death was an atoning death. The cross is at the heart of the gospel. *According to the Scriptures* shows that this was no afterthought. The saving death of Christ was foretold long before in sacred Scripture. It was not death as such, but Christ's death as a saving event that the Scripture foretold and the church proclaimed. Paul does not say what scriptural passages he has in mind, but they will be such as Isaiah 53.

4. In such a brief statement it is a little surprising to find this reference to Christ's burial (cf. the Apostles' Creed). The early church was in no doubt about the reality of the death of Jesus, and the fact of burial is evidence of this (it is mentioned in all four Gospels). While Paul does not explicitly mention the empty tomb, these words are the necessary prelude to it and seem to imply it. From the burial Paul moves to the resurrection on the third day and the burial has implications for this, too; 'if he was buried, the resurrection must have been the reanimation of a corpse' (Barrett). *He was raised* (*egēgertai*) is passive, which puts stress (as usually in the New Testament) on the activity of the Father in raising the Son (cf. v. 15). And it is perfect, which points to the permanent state; it 'sets forth with the utmost possible emphasis the abiding results of the event' (*Prolegomena*, p. 137). Christ continues in the character of the risen Lord. The perfect tense is used in this way six more times in this chapter (vv. 12,13,14,16,17,20), and once only in all the rest of the New Testament. It is likely that *according to the Scriptures* is to be taken with *was raised*, rather than with *on the third day* (so, for example, Metzger, *JTS*, n.s., viii, 1957, pp. 118–123). There is little Old Testament evidence for a rising on the third day (though some suggest Ho. 6:2, or Jon. 1:17), but Isaiah 53:10–12 may fairly be held to prophesy the resurrection (it speaks of activity after death; cf. the use of Ps. 16:10 in early preaching).

5–7. Paul gives a list of the resurrection appearances. It is not an exhaustive list, and we may speculate, for example, on the reason for the omission of all the appearances to the women. The apostle begins with an appearance to *Peter*. Actually he says 'Cephas', the Aramaic name, but NIV alters this to the Greek name (which Paul uses nowhere except in Gal. 2:7f.). This appearance is mentioned again only in Luke 24:34 (cf. Mk. 16:7). We may conjecture that the Lord, in his mercy, was concerned to give assurance of forgiveness to that servant of his who had three times denied him. *The Twelve* (here only in Paul) is clearly a general term, for Judas was not there, and, if the reference is to the appearance on the evening of Easter Day (Lk. 24:36ff.; Jn. 20:19ff.), Thomas was absent also.

The appearance to *more than five hundred of the brothers* is mentioned here only (unless, as is probable, it is that referred to in Mt. 28:16ff.). It is obviously important, for on no other occasion could such a large number of people testify to the fact of the resurrection. Paul's insistence that most of them were still alive shows the confidence with which he could appeal to their testimony. They could be interrogated and the facts elicited. Notice the beautiful way he refers to those who have died. Death, which is an antagonist no-one can withstand and which was viewed with horror by most people in the ancient world, has become for the Christian nothing more than sleep (see further, *TNTC* on 1 Thes. 4:13f., pp. 89–91).

The second name given in this list is *James* (linked with Cephas again in Gal. 1:18f.). It is not certain which James is meant, but most agree that it is James the Lord's brother. It is not unlikely that it was this appearance that led to his conversion and through him to that of the other brothers. They did not believe in Jesus during his ministry (Jn. 7:5), but as early as Acts 1:14 we find them among the believers. What else accounts for the sudden change? *All the apostles* puts emphasis on *all* (BDF 275(5)); not one was missing. This may refer to an appearance like that in John 20:26ff., but more probably points to the appearance at the time of the ascension (Acts 1:1ff.).

This muster of witnesses indicates the importance Paul attached to the resurrection of Jesus. He is about to show its consequences for Christian faith, and he lays the foundation by showing how well based is belief in it. He does not give a complete list of witnesses, but he gives enough to show that the fact is extremely well attested. So reliable is the evidence that it must be accepted, and Paul can go on from there.

8. The apostle puts his vision on the road to Damascus on the same level as the other resurrection appearances. He sees himself as the last in the line of those who have seen the Lord. He calls himself *one abnormally born* (*tō ektrōmati*, 'the abortion', 'the miscarriage'). This strong and unexpected term has been interpreted in more ways than one. Some point to the fact that the Twelve had been with Jesus for years, whereas Paul was born into the apostolic band suddenly, without the period of gestation that might have been expected. The emphasis then would be on the abnormality of the process. Others point out that the word is 'an offensive word' (Héring), and see it as a term of abuse (*cf.* BAGD). Paul was not a handsome man (2 Cor. 10:10), and critics may have combined an insult to his personal appearance with a criticism of his doctrine of free grace, by saying that, 'so far from being born again, Paul was an abortion' (Barclay). This is supported by the fact that Paul goes on to refer to his unworthiness. *To me also* comes last in the Greek with a certain emphasis. Even to Paul, the abortion, Christ appeared.

9. The emphatic personal pronoun *I* again draws attention to the greatness and the condescension of Christ. The risen Lord appeared even to Paul, *the least of the apostles*. This is not a reference to gradation within the apostolate, for elsewhere he can say, 'I do not think I am in the least inferior to those "super-apostles" ' (2 Cor. 11:5). In this spirit he could resist even Peter (Gal. 2:11). What Paul means is that his character as a persecutor had made him the least of them all; indeed, he was not worthy to be an apostle at all. Paul holds firmly to two things. The one is the high dignity attaching to his position as an apostle, as we see from several passages in his writings (*cf.* ch. 9). The apostolate is the highest office in the church, and Paul is an apostle in the fullest sense, because Christ called him to it. The other is his profound sense of personal unworthiness. He is the chief of sinners (1 Tim. 1:15). He is not worthy to be an apostle, for he has persecuted that church that is the church of God.

10. Paul freely ascribes all that he has done in Christian work to *the grace of God*. It was *grace* alone that transformed him from a persecutor into a zealous preacher. He would not appear before the Corinthians as an apostle were it not for that *grace*, and what it had done in him. Far from being *without effect* (*kenē*, 'empty', 'without content'), it had caused him to work *harder than all of them*. His word for *worked* (*kopiaō*) means 'labour to the point of weariness'. Deissmann holds that the expression 'came originally from the joyful pride of the skilled craftsman' (*LAE*, p. 313). Paul stresses that he had toiled hard in the discharge of his apostolate. He does not say that he has accomplished more, but that he has worked harder than others.

Than all of them could mean 'more than all of them put together', or 'more than any one of them'. As he is magnifying the grace of God it is perhaps more likely that the former is his meaning, and as far as our information goes this was indeed the case. Though his beginnings had been so unpromising, yet *the grace of God* had enabled him to accomplish a prodigious volume of work. This might be interpreted as reflecting credit on Paul, so he immediately adds, *yet not I*. It was not the man, but *the grace of God* that was effective. He speaks of this grace as *with* him, rather than 'in' him or the like. This way of putting it almost makes *grace* a fellow-labourer, working alongside him, and thus emphasizes that the credit does not belong to Paul.

11. The upshot of all this is that there is but one gospel, whoever might preach it. Paul has stressed that he received the gospel, he did not originate it (v. 3). He has listed some of the more important points in the apostolic message, in particular the strong evidence for the resurrection. Now he is able to say that this is the common message of the preachers (*cf.* Knox, 'That is our preaching, mine or theirs as you will'). *We preach* is the present continuous tense; this is the way both Paul and the other apostles habitually preach. This is the authentic gospel, that which all the apostles make it their habit to proclaim. *This is what you believed* reminds the Corinthians that this was the basis of their faith. It was this message and not another that they had believed when they became Christians. Anything else is an innovation.

B. THE DENIAL OF THE RESURRECTION (15:12–19)

The exact views of those who said 'there is no resurrection of the dead' (v. 12) are not clear. They may have held the typical Greek view of the immortality of the soul and rejected any idea that the body would rise. Death for such meant the liberation of the soul from its prison in the body, for the body (*sōma*), they held, was a tomb (*sēma*). They may have thought of the state of the departed as the life of the 'shades' in Hades. They may have rejected the thought of bodily resurrection as a reaction to some Jewish views that the body will be raised exactly as it was when it died. Or, starting from the fact that the Christian has risen with Christ (Rom. 6:5–8; Col. 3:1–4, *etc.*), they may have held that the resurrection life believers live now is all the resurrection there is. But Paul insists that the fact that God raised Jesus from the dead is of central importance. He shows the theological consequences of the position of the Corinthians. If dead men don't rise, then Christ did not rise. If Christ did not rise, the Christian faith is empty. The objectors are striking at the heart of the faith.

12. In the summary of Christian tradition in the foregoing verses it is the resurrection that is stressed: the resurrection of Christ is central to the gospel. Paul says, 'if Christ is preached, that he rose . . .' (not *if it is preached that Christ . . .*); to preach Christ is to preach the resurrection. He goes on to inquire how, in the light of that, it is possible to deny the resurrection. There is no article with *dead*, which makes it perfectly general, 'resurrection of dead men'. It is the concept of resurrection, rather than 'the collective dead', that is being discussed (BDF 254(2); in this chapter the article is used with *nekros* only in vv. 29,35,42,52).

13. Paul proceeds to show the consequences of holding that 'dead men don't rise'. If dead men in general are not raised, *then not even Christ has been raised*. *Oude* (translated *then not even*) here means 'neither' (BAGD). Paul is reasoning that, since Christ was genuinely human and died a human death, if men are not raised 'neither has Christ been raised'.

14. The logic is carried on remorselessly. If Christ was not raised, *our preaching is useless*. The inferential particle *ara* (which NIV omits; RSV, 'then') indicates that what follows is the necessary logical consequence of the preceding. *Useless (kenon)* comes first with emphasis. The word means 'empty'. If there is no resurrection of Christ, the preaching, which Paul has shown is not peculiar to himself but common to all the apostles (v. 11), has nothing in it, no substance. It is the resurrection that shows that God is active in Christ, and if the resurrection did not take place the gospel is a sham. *Preaching* (*kērygma*; see note on 1:21) means, not the act of preaching, but the content, the thing preached, the message. The word order in the latter part of the verse is 'empty also your faith', which again puts the stress on 'empty'. The faith of the Corinthians depended on the gospel that had elicited it. If the gospel was a sham, then so was the faith it produced.

15. There is a further consequence. If there is no resurrection, all the apostles are shown to be liars. *We are found* means 'we are caught out' (Moffatt, 'we are detected'). It cannot be said that they are honest men, who in sincerity have given advice they thought to be good, though it is now shown to be not as good as they had imagined. Christianity is not a system of good advice, and the preachers had not simply told people of a good way to live. They had said that something happened; God raised up Christ. Christianity is basically a gospel, the good news of what God has done. The function of preachers is to bear witness to God's saving acts. The apostles had done just that. They had testified that God raised Christ. But if 'dead men don't rise', then dead Jesus did not rise and it is a lie to say that God raised him. Paul is saying in effect, 'Christ rose or we all lied'. *Testified about God* is more literally 'testified against God'. They said he did something (almost they accused him of something) that he did not do. *If in fact* (*eiper ara*) is an unusual combination. There is an emphatic 'if' coupled with the implication that what follows is another's opinion: 'if, as they say' (BDF 454(2)).

16. Paul repeats his statement of v. 13, with the change from 'no resurrection' to *are not raised* (*i.e.* 'by God'). The repetition drives the point home. The Corinthians must be made to see the logical consequences of the position they have taken up.

17. As he had repeated the sense of v. 13, so Paul now repeats that of v. 14. Instead of 'useless' he has *futile* (*mataios*) and (as with 'useless') puts it in the emphatic position. Faith in Christ is a fruitless exercise if the result is *you are still in your sins*. To 'be in one's sins' is not a common expression, though Jesus spoke of dying in sin (Jn. 8:21,24) and Paul of being 'dead in sins' (Eph. 2:1,5; Col. 2:13). If people are still in their sins, what does 'Christ died for our sins' (v. 3) mean? In that case, Jesus' death has accomplished nothing. 'Christ dead without resurrection would be a condemned, not a justified, Christ. How could He justify others?' (Godet). Faith would then be futile. The words can be given a second meaning. If Christ was not raised, believers would still be living in their sins like any pagan. But they have a new power over sin, stemming from faith in the living Christ. Therefore Christ must have been raised.

18. A further consequence concerns the fate of the departed. Few things are more characteristic of early Christianity than the changed view of death it gave people. For pagans death was the end of everything. It was an adversary that would in the end defeat everybody. But for Christians it was no more than sleep (see further, *TNTC* on 1 Thes. 4:13f., pp. 89–91). Christ had drawn the sting from it (v. 55). Death is now 'gain' (Phil. 1:21), so that Paul can 'desire to depart and be with Christ' (Phil. 1:23). Thus when believers died they were not mourned as people irretrievably lost. They were with Christ. But only, Paul insists, if there is a resurrection. If Christ did not rise, then neither will they. In that event, they *are lost*, they 'have perished' (RSV). Edwards brings out the force of the aorist: ' "perished" in the act of falling asleep, as they thought, in Christ.'

19. The perfect *ēlpikotes* carries the idea 'we have set our hope and continue to hope'. *Only* comes at the end of the clause and is best understood as applying to the whole: 'if in this life we have set our hope on Christ, and that is all' (though some take it to mean 'if in this life we have no more than hope', 'we are only hopers'). In that case *we are to be pitied more than all men*. If there is no resurrection Christians are pitiably deluded people. They have set their hopes on a Lord who they think will bring them a richer, fuller life, and all that distinguishes them from others is a special form of hardship (*cf.* 2 Cor. 6:4ff.; 11:23ff.). While Paul never minimizes the compensations the believer has in this life in the way of peace within and the like, yet it is only common sense that, if this world is all there is, the believer is 'a martyr to an illusion' (Héring). Anybody is better off than he.

C. THE CONSEQUENCES OF CHRIST'S RESURRECTION
(15:20–28)

From the hypothetical statements of the previous paragraph (with its seven *ifs*) Paul turns to certainties: the certainty of Christ's resurrection and of its consequences. He shows that Christ's resurrection implies that of believers, and goes on to enumerate the due order of events at the last time. All things will be subdued to Christ; even death will be destroyed. With a few bold strokes he paints an unforgettable picture of God's final, complete supremacy. In the end, that is what matters.

20. 'But it is not so! Christ did rise from the dead' (Moffatt). *But* is adversative; far from Christians being the most to be pitied among men, the fact of the resurrection alters the whole situation. Paul states this fact with simplicity and assurance. Clearly he has no doubts at all. He uses the perfect tense *has been raised* (see on v. 4) with full meaning. Not only did Christ rise on a certain day in history, but he continues permanently in his character as the risen Lord. *The firstfruits* point us to the first sheaf of the harvest, which was brought to the temple and offered to God (Lv. 23:10f.); it consecrated the whole harvest. Moreover, *firstfruits* imply later fruits. Both thoughts are to the point here. Christ was not the first to rise from the dead. Indeed, he had himself raised some. But they would die in due course. His resurrection was to a life that knows no death, and in that sense he was the first and the forerunner of all those who were to be in him; 'the resurrection of Christ is a pledge and proof of the resurrection of his people' (Hodge). *Those who have fallen asleep* is a perfect participle denoting the continuing state of the faithful departed (for death as sleep see note on v. 18).

21. The thought that Christ is the second Adam, which

209

underlies this paragraph, is more fully developed in Romans 5. *Death came through a man* refers to the penalty pronounced on the first sin (Gn. 2:17). This meant more than physical death, but it included it. 'When man sinned he passed into a new state, one dominated by, and at the same time symbolized by death. It is likely that spiritual death and physical death are not being thought of as separate, so that the one involves the other' (Leon Morris, *The Wages of Sin* (Tyndale Press, 1955), p. 12). Adam's sin brought disaster not only on himself, but also on all his posterity. But if Adam's sin had far-reaching consequences, so had Christ's resurrection. It concerned not himself only, but those also who should believe in him. Just as death came into the world through Adam, so life came into the world through Christ. Paul's repeated *through a man* points to the reality of the incarnation. Christ was as truly a man as was Adam. It was fitting that, as it was *through a man* that the corruption entered the race, so it should be *through a man* that it was overcome.

22. The thought is further developed. *In Adam all die* points us to the mortality of the race because of our kinship with our first parents. But it points beyond that to the spiritual evil of which physical death is at once the symbol and the penalty. We are involved with Adam in a solidarity of guilt. There is a sense in which the race is one. But just as Adam's sin brought untold consequences of evil, so Christ's work brought untold consequences of good. But the *all* who are in Adam are not identical with the *all* who are in Christ. 'Each of the two Adams acts as the head of a humanity – the old and the new' (Héring), and not all people, of course, belong to the new. This verse gives no countenance to universalism. Paul is saying that in Adam all that are to die, die, while in Christ all who are to live, live. *Be made alive* refers to more than resurrection as such. It includes the thought of the abundant life that Christ brings to all who are 'in' him.

23. This giving of life does not take place all at once. *Tagma*, which NIV translates as *turn*, was originally a military term, referring to a detachment of soldiers, though it came to be used more generally. In the first *tagma* there is only *Christ, the* *firstfruits* (it is unusual to have only one in a *tagma* and Barrett suggests the meaning 'rank'). In the second are *those who belong to him*, or more exactly 'those who are Christ's'. *When he comes* ('at his coming') makes it plain that Paul is referring to the second advent. He uses the word *parousia*, which basically means 'coming' or 'presence' (as in 16:17), and which came to be used among Christians as the technical term for the Lord's return. The examples cited by Deissmann (*LAE*, pp. 368–373) make it clear that the word was in common use for a royal visit. Christians used it for the coming of the supremely royal One.

24. *Then* (*eita*) does not necessarily mean 'immediately after'. It indicates that what follows takes place at some unspecified time after the preceding. There are some (*e.g.* Deluz) who hold that *the end* points to a third *tagma* or 'order'. The first was Christ, the second ('at his coming') the redeemed, and now we have a third, the unbelievers. This is an unlikely meaning. The word for *end* is *telos*, which never means a group of people (as a third *tagma* would require). Héring is 'unable to find a single text, sacred or secular, in which *telos* has this sense'. It means the end or aim, and there is a sense of purpose about it. It points to the consummation of all things, the climax to which everything is destined to lead up. In any case, throughout this whole chapter the discussion is concerned with believers and Paul does not deal at all with the fate of the wicked. He speaks of two 'orders' only, Christ and believers; then he moves on to the final phase, and says nothing about the lot of unbelievers. *When* is the indefinite *hotan*; the time is not known. There is a dynamic meaning to the Greek *basileia* (*kingdom*); it is 'rule' rather than 'realm'. Paul's thought is that Christ will at the last exercise full and complete authority over all things and all people; he will reign in majesty (*cf.* 2 Thes. 1:7ff.). Then he will 'deliver up' this authority, this rule, to his Father. All that opposes God will be subdued. So Paul speaks of Christ as destroying *all dominion, authority and power*. These three words are probably not meant to define with precision different kinds of authority. Rather they together emphasize that in that day there will be no governing power of any kind that will not be completely subservient to Christ. *Destroyed* (*katargeō*; see note on 1:28) basically means 'render null and void', 'make inoperative', and this is much in point here. Paul does not speak of battles, or of rulers being dethroned. But he does speak of all rule, other than that of Christ, as being rendered completely inoperative. Although this is mentioned after the delivering up of the kingdom it takes place before it (as the change of tense in the Greek shows).

25. There is a compelling divine necessity about Paul's *must*. He is speaking about what God has determined and therefore there is no shadow of doubt about it. No matter how strong the powers of earth and hell may seem, no matter how much the Christian may fear that the wicked will triumph, at the climax of history it is Christ and none other who reigns and *must* reign. This reign is a career of conquest, as *all* the enemies are put *under his feet* (*cf.* Ps. 110:1). These *enemies* are not named, with the exception of 'death' in v. 26. But this exception perhaps indicates that the *enemies* Paul has in mind are evil forces rather than evil people.

26. Strictly it is *death* (which has the definite article) that is the subject and *last enemy* (which lacks it) the predicate: 'Death will be destroyed as last enemy.' There is some emphasis on death as our *enemy*, and *last* enemy at that. *Destroyed* is *katargeō* again, as in v. 24 (where see note). The tense is present, and the use of this tense for future action strikes a note of vividness and certainty. Death will be robbed of all its power. Lenski sees death as dependent on Satan, sin, *etc.*; when then all of these have been dealt with, death as the last enemy will also disappear. In v. 12 'some' said, 'There is no resurrection', but Paul replies, 'There will be no death' (*cf.* Findlay).

27. Some think that *he* means Christ, but there seems rather to be a clear reference to the Father (*cf.* RSV). The opening words are very similar to those of Psalm 8:6. There they refer to the dominion God has given to mankind, the summit of creation. Here they apply to Christ only, and they are more far-reaching, for, as the context shows, they include everything except the Father himself; 'all things' is emphatic. There is an interesting change of tense. He *has put* is aorist, pointing us to the single, once-for-all act of subjection. But *has been put under him* is perfect; it includes the thought of the permanent state of subjection. *Who put* is aorist again, pointing to the same action as that of the first verb. Paul's point, then, is that God the Father has given to the Son unlimited sovereignty over all creation. This, of course, does not involve any infringement on the Father's own sovereignty. For Paul this *is clear* (*dēlon*).

28. The connection of thought with the previous verse is somewhat obscured in NIV, for *When he has done this* and *will be made subject* both render the verb that was three times translated 'put under' in v. 27 (and is translated the same way later in this verse). Paul hammers home his point by using the same verb six times in two verses. The climax of this process of 'putting under' comes when *the Son* (the one occurrence of this designation of Jesus in Paul) is 'put under' the Father. This presents a difficulty, for it appears to some that one member of the Trinity is seen as inferior to another. But we must bear in mind that Paul is not speaking of the essential nature of either the Son or the Father. He is speaking of the work that Christ has accomplished and will accomplish. He has died for us and has risen. He will return and will subdue all the enemies of God. The climax of this whole work will come when he renders up the kingdom to him who is the source of all. In that he became man for the accomplishment of that work, he took upon him a certain subjection that is necessarily impressed on that work right up to and including its consummation. The purpose of this (*hina*) is that *God may be all in all* (he says 'God', not 'the Father'; it is all that 'God' means). This is a strong expression for the complete supremacy that will then so obviously be his. Calvin says, 'all things will be brought back to God, as their alone beginning and end, that they may be closely bound to him.'

D. ARGUMENTS FROM CHRISTIAN EXPERIENCE (15:29–34)

Now comes an abrupt change. Paul turns from Christ to the Christian and shows that certain practices, both among the Corinthians and in himself, logically imply the resurrection. Unless there is to be a resurrection in due course, the procedures of the Corinthians with regard to baptism and of Paul in his evangelism are inexplicable.

29. 'For otherwise, what will they do . . .?' is an unexpected opening, with its future tense and the verb *do*. Perhaps it means, 'What is the value . . . ?' This problem, however, pales into insignificance alongside that of the meaning we are to assign to being *baptised for the dead*. The most natural way to understand the words is to see a reference to vicarious baptism. Some of the Corinthian believers may have been baptized on behalf of friends who had died before baptism (we can scarcely believe that they would have done this for people who had not come to believe, or that Paul would have mentioned the practice so calmly if that were the case). Parry says: 'The plain and necessary sense of the words implies the existence of a practice of vicarious baptism at Corinth, presumably on behalf of believers who died before they were baptised.' He regards all other interpretations as 'evasions . . . wholly due to the unwillingness to admit such a practice, and still more to a reference to it by S. Paul without condemnation'. That Paul is quite capable of reasoning from a practice of which he disapproves is shown by the way he refers to sitting at a meal in an idol's temple without saying anything about this being wrong (8:10), though in a later passage he connects idol feasts with demons (10:21ff.). It is perhaps significant that, while Paul does not stop to condemn the practice of which he speaks here, he dissociates himself from it ('what will *those* do . . . ?'; contrast 'why do we endanger ourselves . . .?', v. 30). He simply mentions the practice as taking place, and asks what meaning it can possibly have if the dead do not rise. Vicarious baptism is attested in the second century among heretics (Chrysostom says the Marcionites practised it). If something like this was known at Corinth it would strongly support Paul's argument for the resurrection.

But the practice is not known from the first century, nor from the orthodox. Strange things happened at Corinth, but perhaps this is too strange even for Corinth. So the suggestion has been put forward that some believers had died, and certain of the living, as yet not church members, were themselves baptized in order to be united to the deceased in due course. Others think of the symbolism of baptism (Rom. 6:1ff.), though it is not easy to see the relevance of this to the resurrection of the body. Others again see a reference to the martyrs ('baptism in blood'), or to a practice 'with a view to (the resurrection of) the dead'. Many other suggestions have been made.[1] As Conzelmann says, 'the ingenuity of the exegetes has run riot.' There is little point in canvassing even the more plausible suggestions. The language points to vicarious baptism. If we reject this we are left to conjecture.

30. Paul turns from the practice of the Corinthians to the experience of Christians generally and of apostles in particular. They were in constant danger, even in the absence of official persecution. Why should people run the risks attendant on joining themselves to such a religion if death is the end of everything?

31. 'Daily I die' comes first in the Greek for emphasis. Paul's danger was very real and very constant; he was never out of peril. He uses the strong affirmative *nē* (often used in oaths; only here in the New Testament), and follows it with 'your boasting which I have'. This is not an easy expression. It may mean Paul's boasting about the Corinthians: 'the glory (or boasting) I have because of you', taking 'your' as objective (as in Rom. 11:31). Or it may mean the Corinthians' boasting about Paul: 'the glory (or renown) which I have among you because you are the fruit of my ministry'. NIV is probably right in choosing the former. Moffatt brings this out with 'Not a day but I am at death's door! I swear it by my pride in you, brothers'. It is interesting to see this expression of Paul's basic satisfaction

[1] Ernest Evans says there are more than 200 interpretations; see his edition of Tertullian's *Treatise on the Resurrection* (SPCK, 1960), p. 312. K. C. Thompson agrees with this estimate (*Studia Evangelica*, ii (Akademie-Verlag, 1964), p. 647, n. 2).

with his Corinthian converts, despite the many things for which he had to rebuke them.

32. Some hold that this verse is to be taken literally, and think that Paul had actually been put into the arena with wild animals, possibly at the time when he was in great danger in the province of Asia (2 Cor. 1:8ff.; Ephesus was in this province). It is objected that, since Paul was a Roman citizen, he could not be compelled to fight wild beasts. This, however, cannot be pressed, for even Roman aristocrats occasionally appeared in the arena. Acilius Glabrio, for example, an éminent Roman, was compelled by Domitian to fight wild beasts. However, if that had happened to Paul he would have lost his citizenship, and Acts is evidence that he still had it at a later time than this. Moreover he would surely not have omitted such a happening from his list of troubles (2 Cor. 11:23ff.). Further, had he been thrown to the wild beasts he is unlikely to have survived. But 'fighting with wild beasts' is often used metaphorically, as when Ignatius writes to the Romans, 'From Syria even unto Rome I fight with wild beasts, by land and sea, by night and by day', and proceeds to explain this as 'being bound amidst ten leopards, even a company of soldiers' (5:1; Lightfoot's translation). A. J. Malherbe has shown that language of this sort is freely used when sages describe the opposition they encounter (*JBL*, lxxxvii, 1968, pp. 71–80). Again, R. E. Osborne, arguing similarly for the metaphorical use, is able to cite a Qumran parallel (*JBL*, lxxxv, 1966, pp. 225–230). Paul is surely employing this metaphorical use. The aorist points to a specific occasion, but we have no way of knowing what it was. The Corinthians knew and could appreciate the reference. If there is no resurrection, Paul's whole life in general, and his conduct in the Ephesian incident in particular, are inexplicable. If there is no resurrection the logical course would be to follow the easy-going proverb Paul quotes (Is. 22:13; *cf.* Ec. 9:7–10). Deissmann cites 'the exhortation to drink in anticipation of approaching death' as 'one of the well-known formulae of ancient popular morals' (*LAE*, p. 295).

33. *Do not be misled* introduces a proverb found, for example, in Menander (*Thais*, 218; some think it is perhaps as early as Euripides). *Homiliai* is probably rightly translated *company* here, but the word is often used of the communications people make with each other, especially speeches (we get our word 'homily' from it). *Character* renders *ēthē*; the word is plural and would be better translated 'habits' (BAGD). Paul is saying that keeping the wrong kind of company (that of people who deny the resurrection) may well corrupt good Christian habits, and turn people away from the truth.

34. *Come back to your senses* is a free translation of *eknēpsate*. The verb originally meant 'become sober after drunkenness' (*cf.* Weymouth, 'Wake from this drunken fit'). It is very appropriate to an appeal to 'come to your senses'. Robertson and Plummer suggest that perhaps 'these sceptics claimed to be sober thinkers, and condemned the belief in a resurrection as a wild enthusiasm'. If so, Paul's verb is much to the point. *Stop sinning* reminds us that all of life is interwoven. On the face of it Paul is discussing a doctrinal question, not a moral issue; indeed, throughout his correspondence, the apostle insists on right doctrine. For doctrine leads to conduct, and unsound doctrine in the end must lead to sinful behaviour. *For* shows that Paul is linking failure to live rightly with failure to think rightly. *Who are ignorant* is 'have *agnōsian*' (*i.e.* 'hold on to ignorance'); the noun points not so much to intellectual ignorance as to ignorance in religious things. It is used in the mystery religions of a 'lack of religious experience or *lack of spiritual discernment*' (BAGD). The error with which Paul is concerned arises basically (as do so many others) from a lack of real knowledge of God. The seriousness with which Paul regarded it is seen in his avowed intention of writing to shame his friends (contrast 4:14). 'I say to you, "For shame!"' ' (Orr and Walther).

E. THE RESURRECTION BODY (15:35–49)

Paul turns his attention to the nature of the resurrection body. Some had evidently ridiculed the idea of a resurrection by asking questions about the nature of the body with which people would rise. 'How can people possibly rise when their bodies have completely rotted away?' seems to have been the kind of objection raised, an objection not unfamiliar in modern times. Paul counters by pointing to the miracle of harvest. The seed is buried, but it is raised up with a new and more glorious body. From this he goes on to consider that there are different kinds of body, and different kinds of glory. This leads to the triumphant climax that, though our bodies are 'sown' in corruption and dishonour and weakness, they will be raised in incorruption and glory and power. As God has willed that we should have bodies fitted for our life on earth, so he has willed that we shall have bodies fitted for our heavenly existence. Paul's insistence on bodily life should not be overlooked. Those who held to the immortality of the soul, but denied the resurrection of the body, usually looked for nothing more than a shadowy, insipid existence in Hades. It is fundamental to Paul's thought that the after-life will be infinitely more glorious than this one. This necessitates a suitable 'body' with which the life is to be lived, for without a 'body' of some kind there seems no way of allowing for individuality and self-expression. But Paul does not view this 'body' crudely. He describes it with the adjective 'spiritual' (v. 44), and he expressly differentiates it from 'flesh and blood' (v. 50). His thought is in marked contrast to that of Judaism. There we find that the body to be raised will be identical with the body that died. The writer of the *Apocalypse of Baruch* asks whether there will be any change when men rise, and the answer is that 'the earth shall then assuredly restore the dead. . . . It shall make no change in their form, but as it has received, so shall it restore them' (50:2; the writer thinks that later on they will be 'glorified'). Paul will have nothing to do with this view (see vv. 42ff., 52, *etc.*). While there will be identity there will also be difference.

35. Some hold that in the lively style of the diatribe Paul has posed his own question, others that he is dealing with a question raised at Corinth. We have no way of knowing. *But* is the strong adversative *alla*. Far from conforming to the kind of conduct Paul has just outlined, someone (the word is indefinite) will offer an objection. Paul either quotes the person, or uses the words he would imagine an objector would use. *How are the dead raised?* queries the mechanics of the process. *With what kind of body will they come?* inquires as to the form they will have. It was clear to these Greek sceptics that a body quickly decomposes, and they thought to laugh the idea of resurrection out of court with their query about the body. What kind of body would arise from a heap of decomposed rubbish?

36. Paul deals sharply with such objections; he begins with 'Fool!'. Modern translations usually soften this, as RSV 'You foolish man!', while NIV makes it an impersonal exclamation, *How foolish!* and JB shifts the derogatory word from the questioner to the question: 'They are stupid questions.' But Paul is being blunt. He is making it clear that he finds such arguments worthless. His *you* is strongly emphatic. He uses the personal pronoun, which is emphatic by itself, and he adopts the unusual course of putting it before the relative pronoun: 'Fool! You, what you sow. . . .' The effect is to make it clear that what Paul has been saying about the resurrection is not without its parallels in activities familiar to, and even engaged in by, the objectors. If they only thought about what they were doing, they had the answer to their objection in their own habitual practices. They sowed seed, which was destroyed, at least in the form in which it was sown. The act of sowing (a 'burial'!) was so similar to what follows death among mankind that Paul can speak of the grain as dying (*cf.* Jn. 12:24). Carrying on this metaphor, the growth that follows is a giving of new life and that new life does not come unless the grain first 'dies'. The seed must be destroyed if the new life is to appear. Familiarity with the marvel of harvest has dulled our sense of wonder. But if we did not know, how would we ever guess that casting a seed into the ground and burying it is the way to produce a living plant? Why, in the light of this, should we regard as incredible the transformation of a dead body? AV correctly translates *zōopoieitai* as 'is quickened'; the verb is passive, not middle. The seed does not come to life of itself, but God gives it life. NIV's *does not come to life* misses this. Paul is preparing the way for his further statement of what God does in giving new life (v. 38).

37. It is important that what dies is nothing like what appears. A dead-looking, bare, dry seed is put into the ground, but what comes up is a green plant, vigorous and beautiful. It is not *the body that will be* that is sown. Paul will presently develop the thought that the body that is raised is incomparably more glorious than the body that is buried. Here he leaves it to be implied. Far from the decomposition of the body presenting an obstacle to the resurrection, it merely prepares us for the truth that the body that is raised is much more wonderful than the body that is buried. Plant life is always on hand to teach us. We sow nothing more than *just a seed*, whether it be *corn* or anything else; this is common to all seeds. At sowing there is no indication of the plant with its stem and leaves and flowers. But they come. There is a combination of identity and difference. The difference between seed and plant is obvious. But there is identity, too, for the seed produces that particular plant and no other.

38. Paul explicitly mentions the divine oversight of the whole process only here, but this must be held to be determinative of his thought throughout. Plants do not rise (and people do not rise) of their own volition. Nor do they do it by chance. They do it because that is the way God has determined it shall be. There is a change of tense here. God *gives* is present; it indicates the habitual practice. God is always giving seeds bodies in this way. *As he has determined* is the aorist, signifying a decisive action. Once and for all God planned what should be and all things continue to follow his plan (the present has continuous force). There is regularity as this plan unfolds, but no uniformity, for God gives *its own body* to every seed.

39. From grain and plants Paul turns to *flesh*. *All flesh* is not of the same kind. The flesh of *men*, *animals* (the word strictly means 'bought', and thus domestic animals, beasts of burden, cattle, but the point is not important), *birds* and *fish* are all different. Paul is preparing the way for the thought that there can be a difference between the kind of body we have before the resurrection and the kind we shall have after it.

40. Similarly there is a difference between *heavenly bodies* and *earthly bodies*. We use the term 'heavenly bodies' of the stars, and some see this as Paul's meaning, though usually with the rider that the stars were seen as living beings. But this is probably not Paul's thought. He comes to the stars in the next verse, and further, the counterpart of 'heavenly bodies' in that sense of the term is 'the earth', not *earthly bodies*. It was an accepted idea that heavenly beings, or at least some of them, had bodies. Paul's point is that their bodies are bodies proper to heavenly beings, while those on earth have different bodies, bodies proper to earthly beings. Proper both may be, but they are not the same. The *splendour* of earthly beings is of a different order from that of heavenly beings. The beings are different and their *splendour* is different, too.

41. This leads to a consideration of the heavenly bodies in our sense of the term. The sun, the moon and the stars are all glorious, each in its own way, and each in a way differing from anything on earth. Even the stars differ *in splendour*; one is more glorious than another. Wherever he looks Paul sees evidence of this principle of differentiation. It is a marvellous universe, and in it God has set so many things, so many glorious things, which yet differ markedly from each other.

42. It is along this line of differing bodies and differing splendours that the resurrection is to be understood. There is a definite article with *the dead* (*i.e.* 'the collective dead'; see on v. 12). Paul does not insert a subject for the following verbs, but he is clearly referring to *the body* (which NIV inserts; it is not in the Greek). He has pointed to a wide variety of phenomena in his examples, with his different kinds of flesh, heavenly bodies, *etc.*, but *is sown* shows that what is primarily in mind is the sowing of seed, with the resultant new and vigorous life (vv. 36f.). He points to a number of differences between the body now and the body raised, and begins with perishability. The words NIV translates by *perishable* and *imperishable* are more strictly 'corruption' and 'incorruption'. While 'corruption' refers primarily to the body's liability to decay, the analogy between physical and moral corruption may not be out of mind. 'Incorruption' was in common use to indicate the quality of life in the hereafter, and it is particularly telling at this point. The chief objection the typical Greek had to any doctrine of resurrection was that the body is essentially corruptible. By its very nature it is subject to decay. He looked for an existence when the soul would no longer be handicapped by this corruptible body, when the soul would exist 'in incorruption'. Paul associates this very state with the resurrection body. He agrees that liability to decay is a property of our earthly body, the body that is to be put into the grave. But he insists that the body that will be taken from the grave at the resurrection will be a transformed body (*cf*. Rom. 8:21). It will be 'raised in incorruption'. That very feature that the average Greek regarded as incompatible with the body, because he thought only of the present body of flesh and blood, Paul sees as characteristic of the resurrection body.

43. Paul continues to pick out those features of bodily life that seemed to the Greek to demonstrate the folly of the idea of the resurrection, and to show that they have no relevance to the resurrection body. *Dishonour* translates *atimia*, a word that applies in various ways. It is sometimes used of loss of the rights of citizenship; a corpse has no rights. Again, there are 'less honourable' parts of this body (12:23), and when dead the whole body lacks honour. Further, the Jews held that a dead body conveys uncleanness (Nu. 19:11). Look at it how you will, there is nothing honourable about a decaying body as it is put into a grave. But that has no relevance to the way the body is when it is raised. The resurrection body is a glorious body, just as far surpassing the present body as the beautiful plant surpasses the seed from which it sprang. The Greek's doubts arising from the dishonourable nature of the body that now is are groundless. The body that is to be raised will be a body *in glory*.

Again, the present body is characterized by *weakness*. Cultivate it as he would (and the Greek did cultivate bodily prowess), it still remains a weak instrument, far outspanned by the mind that is in it. And when it dies (the primary reference is to the dead body), it is the very symbol of powerlessness. But the resurrection body will not be limited as this body is. Just as surely as this body is characterized by weakness, so the body that is to be raised will be characterized by *power*.

44. *Natural* translates *psychikon*, 'pertaining to the soul or life' (*psychē*); Conzelmann has 'psychical', NEB 'animal'; Thrall explains, 'the human being considered as part of the natural world.' It has to do with the present life in all its aspects, especially as contrasted with the supernatural life (*cf.* its use in 2:14 of the merely 'natural' man). There is nothing necessarily sinful or blameworthy about it (unless someone deliberately chooses to live on a lower plane when he could live on a higher). Here it means that the body we now have is a body suited to the present life. It is adapted to the *psychē*, the rational principle of life. But such a body is ill-adapted to life in the world to come. For that a body is needed that is attuned to the spirit, in fact *a spiritual body*. This does not mean a body 'composed of spirit', but rather 'which expresses spirit', 'which answers to the needs of spirit'. At the end of the verse the apostle argues that, just as there is a body related to the *psychē*, so there must also be a body related to the spirit. The *spiritual body* then is the organ that is intimately related to the spirit of man, just as the present body is intimately related to this earthly life.

45. Characteristically Paul appeals to Scripture to clinch his argument. This is not something he has thought up for himself. Yet we should notice that he does not employ his usual formula of quotation *kathōs gegraptai*, 'as it is written', but *houtōs kai gegraptai*, 'in this manner also it is written'. This may indicate something other than exact quotation. Paul refers to Genesis 2:7 (inserting *first* before *man* and *Adam* after it). His point appears to be that the characteristic of man from the very beginning is *psychē*, 'soul' (NIV *living being*). That was true of Adam and it is true of all his descendants. The first Adam passed on his nature to those who came after. The Scripture passage cited does not include Paul's second point. He may have intended to prove only the first one from Scripture, the second being his own addition. Or he may mean that Scripture as a whole witnesses to Christ as *a life-giving spirit*. Or he may mean that this is implicit in Scripture. That is to say, Adam was the progenitor of the race, and his characteristics are stamped on the race. In the same way, Christ is *the last Adam*, the progenitor of the race of spiritual people. In modern times we often read of 'the second Adam', but Paul never uses this term (though *cf.* 'the second man', v. 47). There is a finality about 'the last Adam': 'There will be no other Head of the human race' (Robertson and Plummer). By virtue of his office as *the last Adam* he stamps his characteristics on those who are his. The first Adam implies the last Adam, and the first Adam's work implies the last Adam's work. In this office Christ's characteristic is that he is *a life-giving spirit*. Not only is he the pattern of those who are in him, but he is the source of that spiritual life that will result in the bodies of which Paul speaks. We should understand *became* with this expression. Paul sees Christ as having become a life-giving spirit in his work of saving sinners. Some narrow this down to the incarnation, or the resurrection (about which this chapter says so much), or the second advent. But Paul is not specific.

46. Paul insists on the right order of things. He begins with the strong adversative *alla*. This is puzzling, for what follows is not in strong contrast with the preceding (which may be why NIV omits it). Perhaps it contrasts the following 'broad statement' with the preceding details (Ellicott). Or Paul may mean that, though the 'life-giving spirit' is before all time and before all men, yet in the order of creation we now see not what is particularly related to him, *the spiritual*, but what has particular relevance to life in the here and now, *the natural*. We enter *natural* life first; it is only after that that we may enter into *the spiritual*. It is perhaps worth noticing that Philo held that God created a 'heavenly man' after his own image (Gn. 1:27), and only later an 'earthly one' (Gn. 2:7; *De Opif. Mund.* 134; *Leg. Alleg.* i, 31f.). Paul may be contradicting Jewish teaching of this sort.

47. *The first man* is, of course, Adam. He is *ek gēs*, 'of the earth' (*ek* indicates origin), and he is *choikos*, 'made of dust' (Gn. 2:7). *The second man* is Christ, set over against Adam once more, this time not in terms of work accomplished or natural constitution, but of origin. Though he appeared on earth, and lived and died and rose again on earth, he is not to be thought of as originating from the earth, as did Adam. He is *from heaven*. Some see here a backward glance to the incarnation and some a forward look to the second advent. But Paul is surely not looking specifically at either. He is contrasting Christ's heavenly origin with Adam's earthly one.

48. *As was the earthly man* points us to Adam once more. He is the pattern for all his descendants. As is his nature, so is theirs; all mankind are, in this sense, 'earthy' (*choikos*). Over against this is set 'the heavenly' (which, in accordance with v. 47, means *the man from heaven*). The use of the adjective ('the heavenly') rather than 'from heaven' points to his nature as a heavenly being, rather than his origin. But the really important point is the conclusion, *so also are those who are of heaven* (Greek, 'the heavenly'). There is no question in the minds of either Paul or the Corinthians (or of the Greeks at large) that all people are 'earthy'. Our bodies are earthy bodies and they share in the corruption that is part and parcel of earthy things. But Christians are not only earthy; they are also 'heavenly' because of their relationship to Christ. This means that Christ's people will be like him (*cf.* 1 Jn. 3:2). The resurrection body of Christ shows us something of what life will be like for believers in that new world that their resurrection will usher in. Then he will change their 'lowly bodies' so that they will be 'like his glorious body' (Phil. 3:21).

49. *We have borne* translates the verb *phoreō*, which is more intensive than the more usual *pherō*. Whereas the latter means simply 'to bear', the former conveys the idea of bearing continually or habitually (it is often used of wearing clothes; *cf.* v. 53). It is thus a natural word to use here, where Paul conveys the thought of our habitual state. The use of the aorist may, as Parry thinks, be inceptive, 'began to wear, put on'. Or, from the standpoint of the resurrection, it may look back on earthly life as a completed whole. The bearing in question is seen in the whole of life, not simply in some parts. The *likeness* (*eikōn*), better 'image', is used of man being 'the image of God' (11:7). It can denote simply representation (as in the *eikōn* of the Emperor on a coin), or it can denote something more exact. Here it will be the image that corresponds to and reproduces the original. The majority of the more ancient MSS read 'let us bear' instead of *we shall bear* in the second part of the verse. If this reading be accepted (as it is by Findlay, Williams and others), then Paul is exhorting the Corinthians to put on their heavenly state, progressively to make it their own ('let us also try to be like the man from heaven', Goodspeed). This sounds as though it were something people can do by their own efforts. But this is so far from Paul's usual approach that we are justified in regarding 'let us bear' as a primitive corruption of the text by scribes interested in ethical exhortation, and not quite certain what the apostle meant. The context seems to make it clear that *we shall bear* is the right reading, and this is supported by some good authorities for the text, including Codex Vaticanus. Paul is saying, then, that just as throughout this life we have habitually borne the form of Adam, so in the life to come we shall bear that of our Lord. Just as surely as we have done the one, so surely shall we do the other. This is not a matter for doubt. For Paul the considerations adduced are decisive.

F. VICTORY OVER DEATH (15:50–58)

The chapter comes to a magnificent climax. Paul makes it clear that those who rise will not be creatures of flesh and blood. They will be 'changed', as will those who are alive when that day comes. They will no longer have bodies liable to death and decay. In a lyrical passage the apostle exults in the triumph Christ has won over death itself. This calls forth a thanksgiving to God, the source of victory, and an exhortation to steadfastness.

50. *I declare to you* heightens the significance of what follows, and emphasizes that it is important. *Flesh and blood* is not an uncommon way of referring to life here and now (*e.g.* Gal. 1:16;

Heb. 2:14). It directs attention to two of the most important constituents of the physical body, and two which are peculiarly liable to decay. The expression is thus an apt reminder of our mortality and of the weakness of our mortal frame. It does not signify moral frailty, as *flesh* by itself often does (Chrysostom found here a reference to 'evil deeds'). The combination *flesh and blood*, however, seems always in the New Testament to have a physical meaning. The blunt statement that flesh and blood *cannot* participate in the kingdom plainly excludes all crude ideas of resurrection. It is not this body that will enter the life of the world to come. J. Jeremias insists that the expression does not refer to the resurrection of the dead, but to those alive when Christ comes (*NTS*, 2, 1955–56, pp. 151–159). Incidentally, *cannot* is singular; *flesh and blood* are taken as a unity. *Inherit* must not be pressed. Strictly the word means 'receive by inheritance', but in the New Testament it includes secure possession, whether brought about by inheritance or in some other way. For *perishable* and *imperishable* see notes on v. 42. The combination of *flesh and blood* and *the perishable* means that neither the living nor the dead at the coming of Christ will go into the kingdom as they are. Both must be changed.

51. Paul continues in an emphatic style. *Listen* (actually, 'Look', *idou*) has the effect of focusing attention on what follows. For *mystery* see the note on 2:7. People could never have worked out for themselves what will happen at the second coming, but God has revealed it. For *sleep*, see on v. 18. Some think that Paul means that the second coming will take place in his own lifetime, but this is to press his words illegitimately. The same process applied to other passages (*e.g.* 6:14; 2 Cor. 4:14; 5:8; Phil. 3:11) would show that he would then be dead! But Paul often classes himself with those he is describing, without any implication that he is one of them (*cf.* 6:15; 10:22). The plain fact is that Paul did not know when these events would take place, and nowhere does he claim to know. When he says *we* he means 'we believers', 'Christians alive at that day'. Some will not die, but whether we are among that number, or whether we die before that day, *we will all be changed*. This obviously means difference, but we should not miss the fact that it also means identity. This body will not be destroyed or abandoned; it will be *changed*. Notice that the difficulty is the opposite of that facing the Thessalonians (1 Thes. 4:13ff.). There Paul assured his readers that those who die before the parousia will be at no disadvantage. They will rise first. Here the problem is one for the living, for Paul has just said 'flesh and blood cannot inherit the kingdom of God'. How then can the living enter the kingdom? The answer is, *we will all be changed*. Early scribes found great difficulty with the text of this verse and there are several variant readings. One is important, for it found its way into the Vulgate, and thus represents the way Roman Catholics have usually understood the words. In Knox's rendering it runs, 'we shall all rise again, but not all of us will undergo the change I speak of.' The second clause has been understood to mean that the unsaved will be raised, but not undergo the change of which Paul speaks. However, the text behind NIV is to be preferred, as Knox concedes in a footnote (so also, more recently, JB).

52. The change will not be a long-drawn-out affair. The resurrection of the dead might be likened to the slow growth of a seed, but the change in the living will take place with startling suddenness. *Flash* translates *atomos*, 'that which cannot be divided', *i.e.* the smallest possible (we get our word 'atom' from it). It signifies the shortest possible time. *Twinkling* (*rhipē*) is connected with the idea of throwing. *The twinkling of an eye* is the time it takes to cast a glance, or perhaps to flutter an eyelid. The *trumpet* is linked in the Old Testament, in the teaching of Jesus and in contemporary Judaism with the events in the end time (*cf.* 1 Thes. 4:16 and the note in *TNTC*, p. 93). Trumpets were frequently used at times of festivity and triumph, ideas which are both in place here. The sounding of the trumpet seems to be the signal for the dead to rise. *Last* refers not to the last in a series of trumpet blasts (as in Rabbinic speculation), but last among events on earth. It marks the end of things as we know them. The dead will be raised *imperishable*, which prepares the way for Paul to repeat his statement that *we will be changed*. He makes it abundantly clear that he does not envisage a return to the sort of life we live now.

53. Paul brings out something of the nature of the change, singling out the cessation of 'corruption' (liability to bodily decay) and mortality. These things are totally incompatible with life in the hereafter. Paul stresses the continuity between our present and our future states with a fourfold use (in this verse and the next) of the word 'this': 'this' perishable, 'this' mortal (NIV omits all four). Paul is emphasizing that it is *this* perishable and *this* mortal that will be clothed with imperishability and immortality. *Clothe itself* is a metaphor pointing us to the truth that the body is not the real person; it is only its clothing. In the life to come the real person will put on another suit, so to speak. *Immortality* (*athanasia*) is found but rarely in the New Testament (only in v. 54; 1 Tim. 6:16).

54. It is characteristic of Paul to see in all this a fulfilment of Scripture (Is. 25:8). What God has planned long since, and has revealed to his servant the prophet, he will certainly fulfil. *Swallowed up in victory* points to the complete defeat and destruction of death.

55. In language reminiscent of Scripture (Ho. 13:14), Paul sings of the triumph to come. He is not basing an argument on Scripture, but using scriptural language for his exultation over the total defeat of *death*. The word *kentron* (*sting*) may refer to a goad (as in Acts 26:14), but it is also used of the sting of bees, scorpions and the like (*cf.* Rev. 9:10). Death is a malignant adversary, torturing people. But Christ has drawn its sting, and it is harmless to those who are in him.

56. Moral issues are the serious ones. It is not *death* in itself that is harmful; it is that death that is 'the wages of sin' (Rom. 6:23) that matters. Death, considered simply as the passing out of this life into the immediate presence of the Lord, is a gain, not a loss (Phil. 1:21,23). Where sin is pardoned, death has no sting. It is quite another matter where sin has not been dealt with. There death is a virulent antagonist. The *sting* is not in death; it is in *sin*. And sin has an unexpected ally and source of power, *the law*. The law is divine in origin, and Paul can speak of the commandment as 'holy, righteous and good' (Rom. 7:12).

But it is quite unable to bring people to salvation (*cf.* Rom. 5:12ff.; 7:7ff.; 10:4). Indeed, by setting before us the standard we ought to reach and never do, it becomes sin's stronghold. It makes sinners of us all. It condemns us all.

57. *But*, says Paul (Barrett speaks of 'this great *but*'), introducing as it does the very opposite, the victory that defeats death and sin and law. Christ is victorious over death (Rom. 6:9); indeed he has abolished it (2 Tim. 1:10). He has satisfied the law's claims, for he 'redeemed us from the curse of the law by becoming a curse for us' (Gal. 3:13). He has replaced the 'reign' of sin with that of grace (Rom. 5:20f.); he has drawn its sting. So Paul can say, *thanks be to God!* (*cf.* Rom. 7:25). The use of the present participle (NIV *gives*) may convey the thought that it is God's characteristic to give victory. There is also the implication that we participate in that victory now, and that we participate in it daily. Chrysostom asks, 'For whence, after all this, is death to prevail?' and answers, 'Through the law? Nay, it is done away. Through sin? Nay, it is clean destroyed.' The Christian life is characteristically a life of victory. The use of the full title *our Lord Jesus Christ* heightens the sense of the majesty of his Person. There is victory for the Christian, but it comes only through what Christ has done for him.

58. Arising out of all this comes an exhortation to Christian stability. *Hedraioi* (*firm*) was used in 7:37 of having 'settled the matter'; there is the thought of stable purpose, something that will not easily be disturbed, for the person's whole bent is behind it (*cf.* Col. 1:23). *Let nothing move you* underlines this thought. The Corinthians were prone to fickleness, shifting without reason from one position to another. Let them get a firm grip on the truth of the resurrection, on God's final plan for all people and all things, and they will not be so readily shaken. The imperative *ginesthe*, 'be' (NIV *stand*), might be translated 'become'. Paul sets before his readers a state from which they were as yet all too far, and urges them to continue in it. They should be 'always abounding in the work of the Lord' (AV, RSV). The Christian life is an abundant life. There is nothing cramped or narrow in the genuine Christian experience. Edwards speaks of faith in the resurrection as producing 'a consciousness of boundless and endless power for work', and adds, 'In the case of a believer, youth's large dreams never contract into commonplace achievement.' *Because you know* is probably not the right way to translate the participle 'knowing'; it introduces the accompaniment of the foregoing, not the reason for it (the reason is surely the resurrection truth that Paul has been expounding). Because of the resurrection with all that it means of God's final triumph, and of the survival of the believer through death, Christian *labour* (*kopos*, labour to the point of weariness) is *not in vain* (*kenos*, 'empty'; Moffatt, 'never thrown away'). Deissmann sees in these words 'a trembling echo of the discouragement resulting from a piece of work being rejected for alleged bad finish and therefore not paid for' (*LAE*, p. 314). The Christian faces no such discouragement. His labour is *in the Lord*. And what is done in the Lord is never done *in vain*.

VIII. CONCLUSION (16:1–24)

The great themes of the epistle have been dealt with. But there are still some matters requiring attention, and Paul turns to them. In a little 'chatty' section he gives direction for the collection for the poor, outlines his projected movements, speaks briefly about mutual friends, and brings his letter to a close.

A. THE COLLECTION (16:1–4)

1. *Now about* (*peri de*) is the formula that introduces topics mentioned in the letter from Corinth (see on 7:1). *The collection* (a word in common use, more especially for a collection for religious purposes) meant much to Paul. This is the first time he mentions it in his extant writings (but *cf.* Acts 24:17; Rom. 15:26; 2 Cor. 8:1ff.; 9:1ff.). Here he says it is 'for the saints' (NIV *God's people*), but other references (*e.g.* v. 3) show that it was intended specifically for poor Christians in Jerusalem. Some see this as the Christian equivalent of the half shekel that male Jews throughout the world sent annually to Jerusalem for the temple. But there are significant differences. Paul's collection was a once-for-all effort, not an annual one, and there was no obligation. Nor was it aimed at supporting a Christian equivalent of the temple; it was for the poor. Paul was very anxious for it to be a success. We do not know why the Jerusalem church was so poor, evidently poorer than other churches. But Jerusalem as a whole was not rich; it was largely dependent on the generosity of Jews from outside Palestine. Christians would be excluded from such bounty; indeed, they were the objects of special hostility and persecution (1 Thes. 2:14f.), and might well be in dire straits. There were famines from time to time (e.g. Acts 11:28–30). They may well have suffered also from the after-effects of the community of goods practised in the first days (Acts 4:34f.). Another motive for Paul would arise from the fact that, just as the Jews helped their poorer brothers, so did the Greek religious brotherhoods (the *eranoi*). It would never do for the Christians to lag behind the Jewish and pagan world in their care for their poorer members. We should also remember that Paul himself and the whole Gentile mission were held in suspicion by some of the more conservative elements in the Jerusalem church. Paul doubtless felt that a generous response to the need of the poor in that church would strikingly demonstrate the solidarity of the Gentile churches with the mother church, and do much to promote unity. In any case, the Gentile Christians owed so much to the Jews that common gratitude demanded some such response (Rom. 15:27). The collection was being made throughout the Gentile churches of Paul's foundation, as we see from the references to *the Galatian churches* (and those of Macedonia, 2 Cor. 8:1ff.; 9:1ff.). The reference to other churches evokes from Bengel the comment, 'There is great force in examples.'

2. The collection was to be made *on the first day of every week*. This is the first piece of evidence to show that Christians observed that day, though there is no reason to doubt that it was their custom from the first (*cf.* Jn. 20:19,26; Acts 20:7; Rev. 1:10). Paul does not mention worship, but it is probably in mind. As distinct from the Jewish sabbath, the first day was a weekly commemoration of the resurrection of the Lord, which indicates the importance the Christians attached to that event. *Each one of you* indicates that every believer, no matter how poor, would make a contribution. The most natural meaning of *should set aside* is, as many commentators from Chrysostom down have maintained, that each is to keep the money in store at home. But as Paul expressly deprecates the collecting of the money when he arrived (which would be necessary if they all had it at home), it is perhaps better to think of it as stored in the church treasury. Certainly in the second century money was collected at worship on the first day of the week (Justin, *Apol.* I.67.6). Paul does not indicate a definite amount or definite proportion of one's income that is to be contributed; he leaves it to the conscience of each. Each should give 'whatever he (or it) has been prospered'. The subject of the verb is not expressed. AV supplies the word 'God'; others 'he' or 'his business' (so NIV with *in keeping with his income*). W. Michaelis argues for 'gathering "all that he can (as much as possible)"' (*TDNT*, v, p. 113). The verb may be either present or perfect; either gives a good sense, and both point to a continuing state. The meaning is then that one's giving should be in direct proportion to the way one prospers; it should be determined as a matter of principle, not something done on impulse. Paul wants *no collections* when he comes; he is not looking for a last-minute effort with emotional pressure. *When*, incidentally, is the indefinite *hotan*, 'whenever'. The time of the visit is uncertain.

3. Letters of commendation were not uncommon in the world of that time (Deissmann cites one dated 12th September, AD 50; *LAE*, pp. 170f.). It is not surprising that Paul should want such letters to go with the bearers of the collection. But it is not clear who would write them. NIV opts for Paul with *I will give letters* (so NEB and others), while RSV indicates the local church, 'those whom you accredit by letter' (so JB, *etc.*). Since Paul says 'I will send' the bearers, it is perhaps more likely that the former suggestion is correct. *Letters* is plural, pointing to a number of commendations for the individual delegates. These men are to be those approved (the word is almost a technical term for 'passing as fit for a public office', MM) by the Corinthians. Paul is scrupulously careful. He did not plan to touch the money at any time. The Corinthians would raise it, keep it till he came, and send it by their own approved messengers to its destination.

4. Paul's plans were uncertain. He did not know whether he would be going to Jerusalem or not. If it was fitting (*axion*) he would accompany them. He may mean 'if his schedule is *suitable*' (Orr and Walther), but more probably if the collection amounted to a worthy sum (it would not be seemly for an apostle to supervise in person the delivery of a niggardly amount). Moffatt translates, 'if the sum makes it worth my while to go too, they shall accompany me.'

B. PAUL'S PLANS (16:5–9)

Paul's movements are tentative. But he wants his friends to know that he plans to stay with them, perhaps even to spend a whole winter with them. But he cannot let his projected visit take him away from Ephesus until his work there is finished.

5. Paul has foreshadowed a visit to Corinth (4:19), and has intimated that there were some there who thought that he would not come (see note on 4:18). Now he says firmly, *I will come to you*, and places the time of his visit as *After I go through Macedonia*. *After* is the indefinite *hotan* ('whenever') once more. He does not know when this will be. *Go through* looks like a systematic tour of the various Macedonian churches. The addition, *for I will be going through Macedonia*, seems to show that this part of the plan was new to the Corinthians. They evidently knew that he was planning to visit them (even if some of them said that he would never make it). But they had not known of Paul's plan for Macedonia. Now he tells them what he hopes to do, and they can see just where his visit to their own city fits in. His use of the present tense for future action is not uncommon; it lends an air of greater definiteness to the plan.

6. *Perhaps* (*tychon*) shows the uncertainty of the rest of the apostle's movements. Paul is not committing himself. But he would like his visit to Corinth to be more than the passing visit that is all that the Macedonian churches can expect (that is the force of his verb 'go through'). *You* is emphatic; it contrasts the Corinthians with the Macedonians. At Corinth Paul may well *stay* (*katamenō*), and even pass the whole of winter (when travelling was normally suspended in the ancient world). This would give the Corinthians the opportunity of 'bringing him on his journey', *i.e.* providing such things as he had need of for the way. Once again *you* is emphatic: 'that *you* may be the ones to bring me. . . .' *Wherever I go* reflects Paul's uncertainty about his destination. He was clear about his plan to visit Macedonia, then go to Corinth; but from that point on he had no such firm intentions. It is worth noticing that, while Paul evidently had to change his plans more than once, and was accused of fickleness accordingly (2 Cor. 1:15ff.), the plan outlined here was the plan eventually adopted: he went from Ephesus to Macedonia, then to Greece, where he stayed three months (Acts 20:1–3).

7. Paul reiterates that he did not want to make only *a passing visit* to Corinth. For the third time his *you* is emphatic. He wants to spend time with these friends. He adds the qualification *if the Lord permits* (*cf.* 4:19; Acts 18:21; Heb. 6:3; Jas. 4:13–15). He is the Lord's servant. He must go where the Lord wills. All his plans must therefore be subject to the proviso (expressed or not) that the Lord may intervene and direct him elsewhere.

8–9. But his hopes of seeing the Grecian churches must be deferred. Paul's immediate task is at Ephesus, and it will not be finished before *Pentecost*. He speaks of 'a great and effectual door', as being open to him, where 'effectual' is an unusual adjective to qualify a noun like *door*; NIV gives the sense of it, *a great door for effective work. Has opened* is the perfect tense; the door 'stands open'. There is the thought of a continuing opportunity. We do not expect to find a reference to *many who oppose me* in such a connection. Paul's abrupt reference to them reminds us that the Christian is not usually left to pursue his work unhindered. It is part of the conditions under which we serve God that when we have great opportunities of service we have also serious difficulties. Overcoming opposition is part of the opportunity. Acts 19 shows how great were Paul's adversaries at Ephesus.

C. TIMOTHY AND APOLLOS (16:10–12)

10. Paul spoke earlier of sending Timothy to Corinth (4:17). It seems that Timothy was accompanied by Erastus, and that they went to Macedonia first (Acts 19:22). It is possible that Paul doubted whether Timothy would reach Corinth, but his *if* need not imply uncertainty (it may be like 'If winter comes, can spring be far behind?'); Moffatt and RSV both translate 'when'. Paul's instruction, that they see that *he has nothing to fear* among them, points to Timothy's rather timid disposition and to his youth (he was still young years later, 1 Tim. 4:12). From this very letter we may fairly infer that there were some among the Corinthian believers who were confident and self-willed. Paul evidently feared that Timothy might not be adequate for a confrontation with such people, a fear that subsequent events were to show was well founded. But Paul puts in a word for his young assistant. He calls on the Corinthians to do nothing to frighten him, and he reminds them that he and Timothy are engaged on the same work, *the work of the Lord*.

11. The work Timothy does is a reason that he should not be despised (*cf.* 1 Thes. 5:13). *Refuse to accept* (*exoutheneō*; see on 1:28) is a strong term, meaning 'make absolutely nothing of'. It shows what Paul feared for Timothy. *Send him on his way* employs the same verb as that used in v. 6 of helping Paul on his journey. He asks that they do for Timothy what they do for him. The fact that he looks for Timothy to return shows that Paul had sent him on specific tasks, not with a roving commission. The reference to *the brothers* is not clear. Acts 19:22 mentions only Erastus as being with him, though, of course, there may have been others. Paul may mean that he expects Timothy to come back with some brothers from Corinth. It is also possible that the brothers are with Paul, and that together they await Timothy's return (*cf.* JB, 'the brothers and I are waiting for him').

12. This is the last occurrence of the formula *peri de*, which introduces topics from the Corinthians' letter (see on 7:1). Clearly Apollos was held in high esteem at Corinth, and in their letter the Corinthians had evidently expressed the desire that he should pay them another visit. Paul now tells them that he himself had *strongly urged* him to go to Corinth *with the brothers*. This last phrase was used in v. 11 in connection with Timothy and it may mean that Timothy had travelled with some other Christians and that Paul had wanted Apollos to join the party. Or perhaps Paul means that when Timothy returned some of the brothers would be going to Corinth and that he had tried to persuade Apollos to be of their number. Whichever way we understand it, Paul had urged Apollos to go to Corinth, but had been unsuccessful. It was not altogether 'the will' that Apollos *go now*, which raises the question, 'Whose will?' Many scholars point out that an unqualified 'will' may well mean God's will (*cf. TDNT*, iii, p. 59, n. 24; see Rom. 2:18, and perhaps Mt. 18:14). Others think that Apollos himself was not willing (so NIV). Whichever way we understand it, Paul had done his best. The past tense of the verb *was* and the absence of any greeting from Apollos seem to indicate that he was not with Paul at the time the letter was written. Paul's warmth (*our brother Apollos*) shows that there was no unfriendliness between him and the Alexandrian, whatever the state of the parties in Corinth. Paul had not tried to keep Apollos away, nor had Apollos jumped at any chance of getting to Corinth. That did not mean that Apollos was unwilling. He will come, Paul says, *when he has the opportunity*. This may mean that he was currently too busy and would come when he had more leisure, or that he did not think the time was yet ripe for him to pay the visit in question.

D. EXHORTATION (16:13–14)

Paul interjects a short, sharp exhortation. The Corinthians had shown a distressing immaturity in some things, and the apostle in a series of compelling imperatives points them to a better way.

13. *Be on your guard* (*grēgoreite*), like all the verbs in these two verses, is a present imperative. Paul is not speaking of momentary attitudes, but of continuing states. The word denotes more than the mere absence of sleep. It implies a determined effort at wakefulness: 'Be on the alert' (Barclay). It is often used of watching for the second coming (Mt. 24:42f.; 25:13; Mk. 13:34ff.), and this may well be in mind here. *Stand firm in the faith* (or perhaps 'in faith', Barrett) points to the stability of the Christian firmly grounded in Christ, a stability distressingly absent from the Corinthians. *Andrizesthe*, 'act as men (*andres*)' may refer to courage (as NIV, *be men of courage*), but more probably it is meant to counter the immaturity so manifest in some of the Corinthians. Paul wants them to act like responsible adults. Moreover, they are engaged in a desperate strife with the forces of evil, and it is imperative that they play the part of men. *Be strong* (*cf.* Ps. 31:24) may be passive, 'be made strong'. The strength of Christians is not something native and inherent in them; they derive it from God.

14. It is significant that *Do everything in love* follows the exhortations to manliness and strength. In manliness Paul is not looking for aggressiveness or self-assertion, but the strength that shows itself in love. As in ch. 13, he is concerned with the all-pervading nature of Christian love. Nothing we do is outside its scope. We should not overlook the significance of *in*. Love is more than an accompaniment of Christian actions. It is the very atmosphere in which the Christian lives and moves and has his being.

E. MEN LIKE STEPHANAS (16:15–18)

15. It is always helpful to have a good example to follow. Paul has had much to say by way of blame, but he now finds some among the Corinthians he can hold up for admiration, namely *the household of Stephanas*. Paul has already mentioned that he baptized this household (1:16). Now we have the additional information that they were the 'firstfruits' (*aparchē*) of the province of Achaia. As this province included Athens, where Paul had some converts before he preached in Corinth (Acts 17:34), this raises a minor problem. It may be that the household of Stephanas was converted in some way before Paul preached at Athens (which would justify NIV's *the first converts*). It may be that, while there were earlier conversions of individuals, this was the first household to be won. Or it may be that 'firstfruits' means those fruits that gave promise of the harvest to come. 'To the Apostle's mind the pledge of a future Church came not in Athens, but in Corinth' (Edwards). They were shining examples of what Christians should be for they *have devoted themselves* to Christian service. Chrysostom comments, not ' "they minister," but, "have set themselves:" this kind of life they have chosen altogether, this is their business in which they are always busy' (Moffatt speaks of the verb as 'a trade metaphor' and points to its use by Plato of tradesmen who 'set themselves to the business of serving the public' by retailing farm produce). Stephanas and his family have taken as their particular responsibility, their piece of Christian service, the task of *the service of the saints* (the same as 'God's people' in v. 1). They did not assume a place of leadership or prominence, but one of lowly service.

16. That is the Christian way, and Paul commends this example to the church at large. Christians should *submit* to such people. Paul speaks a good deal about Christians submitting themselves to one another (*cf.* Eph. 5:21), which he probably finds necessary because it is a natural human tendency, and specifically that of the Corinthians, to do the reverse. It may not be an accident that his verb (*hypotassō*) is a compound of the verb he has just used of the household of Stephanas setting

239

themselves (*tassō*) to lowly service. And not only should they submit to Stephanas, but also to others who help and labour, and in fact to all helpful Christian souls. On the word *labours* (*kopiaō*, 'labour to the point of weariness') Edwards has the succinct comment, 'Many work, a few toil.'

17. Stephanas and two other people otherwise quite unknown, Fortunatus and Achaicus, had recently reached Paul, and he lets us see something of his pleasure at the meeting (though it is uncertain whether we should understand *parousia* to mean 'arrival' or 'presence'). He does not spell out the meaning of *what was lacking from you*, but it seems that Paul was feeling his separation from the Corinthians; 'my lack of you' is the sense of it. He had missed his Corinthian friends and this trio had 'filled the gap of your absence' (Héring). In their persons they had brought him 'a little bit of Corinth'. *Supplied* (*aneplērōsan*) has the meaning 'filled up'. The three had left no lack.

18. They had *refreshed* Paul's spirit, where the verb is that used of our Lord's giving rest to those who 'labour and are heavy laden' (Mt. 11:28). It seems to show that Paul had been restless without news from Corinth. But the coming of the three had been a real refreshment to his spirit. *And yours* is an interesting addition. Not only was it good for Paul to receive news from Corinth, but it was good for the Corinthians to have sent their messages to Paul. People like these three *deserve recognition*. Believers should know them for what they are and ascribe to them their true worth.

F. FINAL GREETINGS (16:19–24)

19. *Asia* is, of course, the Roman province of that name, roughly the western third of what we now call Asia Minor. Paul sends *greetings* from the churches of this region. *Aquila and Priscilla* (the lady's name is always 'Prisca' in Paul's letters, but for some reason NIV always uses the form Luke prefers) were a devoted couple. Aquila was a Jew, originally from Pontus (on the southern shores of the Black Sea), but he had evidently settled in Rome. When the Emperor Claudius expelled all Jews from Rome, he and his wife Prisca went to Corinth. When Paul first came to that city he lodged and worked with them (Acts 18:1–3). They evidently had the habit of using their home in the service of the Lord, for they had a church in their house when they were in Rome (Rom. 16:5), just as they did at Corinth. Such a church would be small. R. Banks says 'The entertaining room in a moderately well-to-do household could hold around thirty people comfortably' (*Paul's Idea of Community* (Anzea, 1979), pp. 49f.; *cf.* also *SPC*, pp. 153–158; see Fig. 3, p. 242, for the plan of a house in Corinth). Aquila and Prisca were courageous, for they risked their lives for Paul, though we know no details (Rom. 16:4). They were able, for they instructed no less a personage than Apollos in the correct understanding of the faith (Acts 18:26). An interesting point is that, in four of the six places where this couple is mentioned, Prisca's name comes first. Evidently she was an oustanding person in her own right. *Greet you warmly in the Lord* goes beyond a normal polite greeting. It expresses a depth of Christian affection.

20. It is not clear who *all the brothers* were, but the expression is comprehensive. The custom of kissing was rather more widespread in the ancient world than in the modern West. Several times Paul suggests *a holy kiss* as a proper mode of greeting for Christians (Rom. 16:16; 2 Cor. 13:12; 1 Thes. 5:26; *cf.* 'kiss of love', 1 Pet. 5:14).[1] Such a warm greeting at Corinth would itself be a rebuke to all cliquishness. The New Testament passages refer to a greeting, not to the liturgical 'kiss of peace' (a kiss exchanged during Holy Communion). Doubtless passages like this led in time to the liturgical practice.

21. It was Paul's custom to dictate his letters to an amanuensis, who wrote them down. But as a letter drew to its close the apostle would take the pen and write a few words himself. His handwriting, he says, 'is the distinguishing mark in all my

---

[1] See further the discussion in *TNTC* on 1 Thes. 5:26, pp. 112f. *Cf.* J. Denney, on the significance of the kiss in Thessalonians, 'Show your Christian love to one another, frankly and heartily' (*The Epistle to the Thessalonians* (Hodder & Stoughton, n.d.), p. 261).

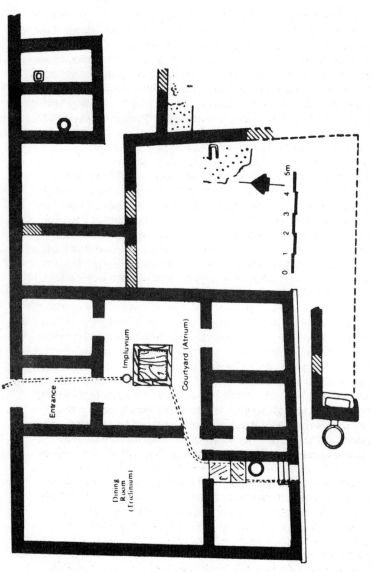

Fig. 3. A TYPICAL VILLA AT ANAPLOGA, IN CORINTH

If a house church met in a villa like this, it would use the triclinium and the atrium. Murphy-O'Connor argues from the dimensions that fifty people 'would have meant extremely uncomfortable overcrowding' in this villa (SPC, p. 158). Thus a house church would necessarily be small. We are left wondering where 'the whole church' (14:23) would meet. If there were several house churches in Corinth it might have made it easier for cliques to develop.

letters' (2 Thes. 3:17; see note in *TNTC*, pp. 151f.), *i.e.* it is his custom to authenticate his letters in this way. Sometimes he draws attention to this (Gal. 6:11; Col. 4:18; 2 Thes. 3:17; Phm. 19), sometimes he does not. But, as he says it was his custom, we should understand that he did it in the other letters also. Deissmann cites a letter dated 12th September, AD 50 in which the writing is in one hand, and the final greeting and date in another, clearly that of the author, though there is no mention of his taking the pen (*LAE*, pp. 170ff.). This is interesting contemporary evidence of Paul's practice.

22. Paul calls down a solemn curse on *anyone* who *does not love* (*phileō*; again in Paul only in Tit. 3:15) *the Lord*. He does not speak of the absence of some special degree of love, but of the lack of love for Christ at all. Love is of central importance for all Christians. For *curse* (*anathema*) see note on 'cursed' in 12:3. The strong expression (immediately following Paul's taking up the pen himself) shows the depth of the apostle's feelings on the importance of a right attitude to the Lord. If anyone's heart is not aflame with love for the Lord, the root of the matter is not in him. He is a traitor to the cause of right. Paul cannot contemplate such a person calmly.

He follows with the Aramaic *Maranatha* (which NIV translates *Come, O Lord!*). Being Aramaic, the expression cannot have originated among the Greeks, but must go back to the early days of the church in Palestine. Moreover it must have expressed a sentiment that the early church regarded as very important, else the foreign word would never have been taken over in this way by Greek-speaking Christians (we still use words like Hallelujah and Amen). It is not certain how we should understand the expression. The first part is the word *Mar* which means 'Lord', and we should not overlook the importance of the ascription of this title to Jesus in the early days of the Palestinian church. 'Our' is conveyed in Aramaic by the addition of *an* or *ana*. The latter part of the expression is from the verb *'atha*, 'to come'. If we read *atha* it might mean 'has come', in which case there is a reference to the incarnation as Chrysostom held. Or it could mean 'comes' (*cf.* Mt. 18:20). It might even be future, 'Our Lord will come' (so Edwards;

Conzelmann says this is impossible; Caird refers to Phil. 4:5). Probably the best way of taking it is to divide the expression as *Marana tha* and take the verb as imperative, 'Our Lord, come' (a prayer like that in Rev. 22:20, 'Come, Lord Jesus'). It would then express the eager longing felt by the church in those early days for the speedy return of the Lord. Others have suggested that the words mean 'the Lord art thou', or 'Our Lord is a sign', but both seem improbable.

23. Paul's invariable conclusion to a letter is a prayer for *grace* for his readers. He can expand this (as in the well-known formula in 2 Cor. 13:14), while the shortest form is 'Grace be with you' (Col. 4:18). But he always has a prayer for grace.

24. This time Paul closes on an especially tender note; he sends his *love* to them all, an ending he has only here. Despite everything, there is not the slightest doubt that Paul regarded the Corinthians with tender affection. So he finishes his letter by sending his love to all the members of the church (*cf.* 2 Cor. 11:11: 'God knows' that he loves them). Notice the *all*. He had some doughty opponents at Corinth, and there were some whom he had had to rebuke sharply. But he bears no malice. He sends his love to all of them, a love *in Christ Jesus*. Paul's last word to the Corinthians is *Jesus*.